# A RIGHT TO READ

# A RIGHT TO READ

Segregation and Civil Rights in Alabama's
Public Libraries, 1900–1965

PATTERSON TOBY GRAHAM

THE UNIVERSITY OF ALABAMA PRESS
*Tuscaloosa and London*

Typeface: Janson Text

∞
The paper on which this book is printed meets the minimum requirements of American
National Standard for Information Science–Permanence of Paper for Printed Library
Materials, ANSI Z39.48–1984.

Library of Congress Cataloging-in-Publication Data

Graham, Patterson Toby, 1969–
    A right to read : segregation and civil rights in Alabama's public libraries, 1900–1965 /
Patterson Toby Graham.
        p.   cm.
Includes bibliographical references and index.
    ISBN 0-8173-1144-0
    1. Public libraries—Services to African Americans—Alabama—History—20th century.
2. African Americans—Civil rights—Alabama—History—20th century. 3. Civil rights
movements—Alabama—History—20th century. I. Title.
    Z711.9 .G73 2002
    027.4761—dc21
                                                              2001005918

British Library Cataloguing-in-Publication Data available

A shorter condensed version of this research was first published as a
journal article entitled "Public Librarians and the Civil Rights
Movement: Alabama, 1955–1965," in *The Library Quarterly* 71 (January
2001): 1–27. *The Library Quarterly* is a publication of the
University of Chicago Press.

For Suzanne,
My favorite librarian

# Contents

List of Illustrations ix

Acknowledgments xi

Introduction 1

1. Black Libraries and White Attitudes, The Early Years:
   Birmingham and Mobile, 1918–1931 6

   Birmingham and the Booker T. Washington
   Branch Library 9

   Mobile and the Davis Avenue Branch Library 17

2. Black Libraries and White Attitudes II:
   The Depression Years 26

   Black Libraries and Philanthropy during the
   Depression: Walker County 27

   The Works Progress Administration and
   Black Libraries 32

   The Tennessee Valley Authority: Black Libraries and
   Regional Development 36

   Welfare Capitalism and the National Youth
   Administration: The Slossfield Negro Branch Library 43

3. African-American Communities and the Black Public
   Library Movement, 1941–1954 49

   The Dulcina DeBerry Branch Library, Huntsville 49

The Union Street Branch Library, Montgomery 56

Birmingham Negro Advisory Committee 62

4. The Read-In Movement: Desegregating Alabama's
Public Libraries, 1960–1963 69

Mobile, 1961 71

Montgomery, 1962 75

Huntsville, 1962 81

Birmingham, 1963 82

Anniston, 1963 91

5. Librarians and the Civil Rights Movement, 1955–1965 99

Juliette Hampton Morgan and the Montgomery
Bus Boycott 100

Emily Wheelock Reed and *The Rabbits' Wedding*
Controversy 102

Patricia Blalock and the Selma Public Library 112

The American Library Association 120

The Alabama Library Association 126

Conclusion 131

Notes 139

Bibliographic Essay 163

Contemporary Literature on Segregated Libraries, 1913–1953 163

Contemporary Literature on Segregated Libraries, 1954–1972 166

Atlanta University Theses 168

American Library Association 169

Library History Secondary Works 171

Segregated Libraries and Progressivism 174

The Civil Rights Movement in Alabama 176

Other Historical Works on Race 181

Unpublished Sources 182

# Illustrations

Booker T. Washington Branch in Birmingham, 1919      13

Davis Avenue Branch, Mobile, 1931      23

Mobile Public Library, 1926      23

Elizabeth Parks Beamgaurd visits the Dulcina
     DeBerry Branch, 1951      55

Bertha Pleasant Williams and the Montgomery "Friends
     of the Library," 1960      62

Montgomery City-County Library, 1961      80

Montgomery's Cleveland Avenue Branch, 1961      81

Sit-in at the Birmingham Public Library, 1963      88

Miles College student speaks to librarians, 1963      89

Anniston's Carnegie Library, circa 1938      92

Cover of *The Rabbits' Wedding*, 1958      105

# Acknowledgments

The present study lies at the confluence of my abiding curiosity about southern race relations and my commitment to librarianship. I embarked upon the project—originally my doctoral dissertation—as yet another in what had become a series of self-indulgent educational enterprises. It has become more than this, I hope, and the book contains a number of stories that needed to be told. The fact remains, however, that its writing has been richly rewarding in a personal sense. I am deeply indebted to those who aided me and lent their support along the way.

Dr. Margaret Stieg Dalton spent many hours on the various revisions of the work at the dissertation stage. Almost as important as her guidance was her own scholarly example, which prompted me to be a better student than I otherwise would have been. Dr. Annabel Stephens was attentive, encouraging, and generous with her own research. Dr. J. Gordon Coleman, Jr., was a consistent source of assistance and support during my time at The University of Alabama. Dr. Ellen Garrison contributed her formidable historical knowledge and editorial ability to the manuscript. As a teacher and a reader, Dr. E. Culpepper Clark lent his expertise in civil rights history. Dr. Louise Robbins shared a significant piece of evidence that she had discovered in her own research.

Several individuals generously shared their time and their memories. Patricia Blalock, Judge U. W. Clemon, Dr. Jack Dalton, Addene Drew, Emily Wheelock Reed, Shelly Millender, Teresa Temple, and Bertha Pleasant Williams patiently explained their life stories, and the information they provided significantly enhanced my understanding of the relationship between race relations and libraries during the era of segregation.

Two of these individuals passed on during the preparation of the book. Jack Dalton, former dean of the Columbia University library school, truly was a leader in his profession. Though I had only a brief association with Dr. Dalton toward the end of his life, he was a man whom I held in great esteem.

Emily Wheelock Reed—whose 1959 stand against censorship in Alabama went unrecognized by her profession for forty years—was chosen for the Freedom to Read Foundation Roll of Honor Award in 2000. In addition, the American Library Association Council passed a resolution in recognition of her contribution to the cause of intellectual freedom. Ms. Reed died only weeks before she was to travel to the ALA annual convention in Chicago to receive the belated acknowledgement.

I am grateful to the many librarians and archivists who assisted me in my research. Among these are Becky Cothran-Nichols at the Selma-Dallas County Public Library; Juanita McClain-Owes at the Montgomery City-County Library; George Ewart and Holley Roland at the Mobile Public Library; Don Veasey, Jim Bagget, and Renee Blalock at the Birmingham Public Library; Rene Pruitt and Judy Purinton at the Huntsville-Madison County Public Library; Sandra Underwood at the Carl Elliot Regional Library; and Thomas Mullins at the Anniston-Calhoun County Public Library. I also received assistance from staff members at the Alabama Department of Archives and History, National Archives and Records Administration (Washington, D.C. and Southeastern Branch at Eastpoint, Georgia), and the Municipal Archives of Mobile, Alabama.

During the course of my research, I visited each of the public libraries covered in the manuscript, poring through their records. It should be said to their credit that these institutions that once barred their doors to African Americans now exemplify the changes that have come to public library service in the South since the 1960s. In 1962, Montgomery's public library desegregated under a federal court order. Today, it has an African-American director, Juanita McClain-Owes, and the noise of the after school crowds of black and white children arriving at the library is heard in the afternoons.

I would also like to respond in advance to a perception that some may develop in reading the manuscript that the book is an indictment of librarians in the South or of their profession's national association. It is not my intention to question the professionalism or the contribution of any individual or group. Rather the study is intended to describe an important chapter in what Louise Robbins calls librarianship's "odyssey of self-definition." Librarians adopted a Library Bill of Rights in 1939, but the development of the American library profession into a vocal advocate for intellectual freedom and access to information was a long and sometimes painful process. Addressing civil rights was a crucial part of this evolution. The journey bears resemblance to that of the nation at large. Americans expressed a commitment to freedom and equality long before the country truly reflected these values in its actions. American history can be seen as a conflict among values, during which ideals were tested against other impulses. This also was true for librarianship, and the internal struggle left it with a louder and more effective voice for its ideals.

I am thankful for the aid of The University of Alabama's National Alumni Association, which provided a fellowship to fund a year of my research and writing. The Council of Presidents at The University of Alabama provided a grant to defray research expenses. The University of Southern Mississippi through the office of the Vice President for Research assumed the cost of use fees for several images that appear in the book. I am also proud and grateful for the opportunity to have studied at The University of Alabama's School of Library and Information Studies. Its faculty, staff, and students were at all times an encouragement to my work.

My parents, Patterson Tony Graham and Marie Harrington Graham, have been an unwavering source of support and guidance throughout the preparation of this manuscript, as they have been during each learning experience of my life. Their commitment to education has been an inspiration and the standard toward which I continue to strive.

My sister, Dana Graham Mozingo, has been a treasured source of moral support. I am also grateful for the company of friends who contributed to the quality of my life through the course of my research.

# A Right to Read

# Introduction

At approximately 3:30 P.M. on September 15, 1963, W. B. McClain and Quintus Reynolds, both African-American ministers, arrived at the Carnegie Library in Anniston, Alabama, to apply for membership at the recently integrated facility. What happened next was one of the most disturbing events in the history of American public libraries. Before they finally escaped from the waiting mob, the ministers would be knifed, chain-whipped, and savagely beaten on the steps of that public institution of culture and education. Racial fear had turned to violence as angry whites played out a worst-case scenario of library discrimination in the United States. The events in Anniston represented an extreme expression of the racial order that excluded African Americans from public libraries, and from full citizenship, in the segregation era.

The tradition of American public libraries is closely tied to the perception that individuals, regardless of their social backgrounds, may freely access information in those institutions in the interest of self-improvement, social awareness, and entertainment. Born of a democratic impulse, or at least a reform-minded one, this right to read is associated with national issues of intellectual freedom and freedom of expression. There have been, however, vast exceptions to this ideal. Quantitatively, the most significant of these exceptions was the exclusion of millions of African Americans from the public libraries of the American South during the years before the civil rights movement. Like the nation's other contradictions of democratic ideal and actual practice, public library segregation was part of the conflict of values that characterizes the whole of American history, particularly in regard to race relations.

Southern public libraries, including those in Alabama, developed in a pattern dictated by a segregated society. In the course of the 1890s, the states of the American South created a new law of the land that sought to separate the races in every aspect of public life. The Supreme Court ratified the states' actions in *Plessy v. Ferguson* (1896), asserting that separate facilities could be considered equal ones. Equality was, however, rare, and libraries were no more equal than other segregated institutions. Imbued with a distinctly southern style of progressivism, whites established free public library service for themselves. Black libraries were created as afterthoughts, pale attempts to satisfy black demands and white conscience.

Alabama's first commitments to public support for white public librarianship came in 1904. The first public libraries for African Americans arrived fourteen years later. By the mid-1930s, a system of segregated libraries existed in a few Alabama cities and in Walker County. "Negro branches" were scarce, small, understaffed, and poorly funded institutions supported by a combination of black civic and religious organizations, city governments, and occasionally the federal government or philanthropists. Despite the disadvantages imposed by segregation and a legacy of poor education, black Alabamians proved enthusiastic library patrons, raising money, making personal donations, and contributing their own physical labor. The efforts of blacks and their persistent demands for better service moved some library boards to action. These white boards may have been motivated by paternalism or a sense of ethical responsibility, but they did act, often in the face of opposition from other whites who argued that blacks had little need or desire for libraries.

By 1960, African Americans had turned their attention from building segregated branches to integrating the "white" libraries through legal action and protest. The "read-in" movement in Alabama's public libraries touched each of the state's largest cities, and over the course of three tumultuous years (1960–1963), it effectively ended public library segregation in urban Alabama. The Mobile Public Library was the first to integrate, after a series of sit-ins in 1961. United States District Judge Frank Johnson ordered the Montgomery Library Board to desegregate its facilities after a 1962 sit-in at the city library led by youth activist Robert L. Cobb. After being named in a civil rights case in 1963, Huntsville's director called for integration in that city. In the spring of 1963, during the Birmingham demonstrations, students from Miles College staged a read-in at the Birmingham Public Library. Selma integrated its library in 1963, largely as a result of demands by the city's strong-willed and liberal-minded librarian. The following September, Anniston's Carnegie Library desegregated after the white mob's attack on McClain and Reynolds. Despite the changes taking place in the state's libraries, the Alabama Library Association continued to exclude blacks from its membership until 1965, when it changed its policy because of the persistence of Tuskegee librarians and a sympathetic association president.

White response to desegregation efforts in public libraries varied. In Mobile, Selma, and Huntsville the library boards chose to integrate the white libraries quietly and voluntarily to avoid judicial action and further demonstrations, and the unfavorable publicity these would bring. Each of these cities enjoyed a relatively smooth transition into integrated service. Some of the other cities were not as fortunate. In Montgomery, the library board conformed to the letter of Judge Johnson's desegregation order but not the spirit. It ordered "stand-up integration," removing all of the tables and chairs from the building to minimize the interaction of the races in reading areas. Klansmen demonstrated at the library and police harassed whites who used the former "Negro branch."

Librarians in the South became deeply embroiled in questions of race. Circumstances presented them with a choice between regional values and professional ones. The years of the 1950s and 1960s were difficult for those who chose to question the racial status quo. Juliette Morgan, a public librarian in Montgomery, endured years of persecution for her support of civil rights. Alabama legislators publicly assailed state librarian Emily Reed for her opposition to censorship of books they considered to espouse integration. African-American librarians were pioneers in their communities, but at the same time they often dealt with overt discrimination from their white superiors and were excluded from the state library association by their white peers.

Discrimination in library service was not peculiar to Alabama or to the South. It was a national problem. But in Alabama, the practice of de jure segregation in public libraries presents an example of discrimination that is particularly vivid. The state's central role in the civil rights movement makes it a powerful model for examining racial integration of public libraries, as well. As the nation searched for a solution to its racial dilemma, Alabama became a focal point of the movement for civil rights. The Montgomery Bus Boycott in 1955 and 1956, the violence surrounding the freedom rider campaign in 1961, the Birmingham demonstrations in 1963, George Wallace's "stand in the schoolhouse door" in 1963, and the Selma voting rights march in 1965 made Alabama a center of national attention and the country's most important battleground over civil rights. The desegregation of the state's public libraries was part of the larger effort to integrate society. It occurred in dramatic ways that resembled and sometimes coincided with the direct action campaigns at large.

The result of Alabama's segregationist practices at its public libraries was a massive, albeit indirect, form of censorship. For library scholars this leads to important questions related to the development of professional values. What is the role of a library and of a librarian in an intolerant and fearful society? Have librarians been active agents or just passive observers in the ebb and flow of social change and social conscience? The civil rights movement of the 1950s and 1960s proved to be a time of crisis for librarianship, a time when its perceived professional values were dramatically challenged and examined, and its priorities reordered. Notions of activism, social responsibility, and information equity, which helped to transform librarianship on the national level, had their origins in that era of protest. Thus, addressing these questions is a beginning toward refocusing the historical understanding of the profession by describing social change in the context of southern public libraries.

One of the most heated debates among library history scholars has been over the question of whether public libraries have been designed as instruments of social control. The development of segregated public libraries in the South, which provided tacit support for a culture of white supremacy, provides perhaps the ultimate example of this phenomenon in American libraries. It also demonstrates, however, the complex and contradictory nature of southern librarians and library boosters as they lent their support to the efforts of a beleaguered but determined people creating a black public library movement.

In addition to its relevance to the profession of library service, library segregation was part of a larger social issue. As a somewhat typical feature of the Jim Crow South, segregated public libraries serve as a microcosm of broader human interaction and as a metaphor for social change. Libraries are, after all, a product of the society within which they exist. Librarians themselves are members of the society, as are library board members, philanthropists, administrators, and patrons. The public library is a place of social interaction that reflects social priorities. For this reason, the history of public library segregation reflects the nature of racism and changing racial mores.

Thus, the civil rights movement in public libraries provides more than a professional or an institutional history, and it suggests a number of questions about American society. What, for example, does the experience in the provision of library service to blacks during the segregation era reveal about the nature of racism? What does the effort by blacks to establish library service for their race reveal about the nature of African-American communities under segregation? What types of library-related activism did African Americans undertake, and what does this reveal about the struggle of southern blacks for social and political equality? How did whites respond to the civil rights movement in libraries, and how important to segregationists was maintaining racial separation in public libraries as compared to other institutions and facilities?

America's social conscience in regard to race changed between 1900 and 1965, and with it, librarianship changed. The two, society and public libraries, were inextricably linked, and the transition in neither came easily. Events, such as the savaging of the Reverends McClain and Reynolds in Anniston, demonstrated that access to public libraries was closely tied to issues of racial equality, freedom of expression, and intellectual freedom in the United States. The question of whether black citizens would have the right to read in southern public libraries became a test of American democracy, one that resulted in conflict and occasionally in violence.

# I

# Black Libraries and White Attitudes, The Early Years

## *Birmingham and Mobile, 1918–1931*

Public libraries developed later in the South than in other regions. Unlike that of the Northeast, whose tax-supported free library service came into its own during the second half of the nineteenth century, the South's public library movement was for the most part a twentieth-century phenomenon. Examining New England between 1629 and 1855, Jesse H. Shera identified the causal factors he believed led to the growth of Northern libraries. These were economic ability, a demand for scholarship, awareness of a need for publicly supported educational services, a faith in self-education, a demand for vocational education, and "other causal factors," including a belief that reading was a "good" thing in itself. As a region, the South exhibited none of these characteristics until the last years of the nineteenth century.[1]

In her 1958 book on the development of southern public libraries, Mary Edna Anders contends that its defeat in the Civil War left the South without the financial wherewithal to match the North in library development. The war left the South impoverished and largely subject to economic interests outside the region. In the immediate postwar years, the South lacked a well-heeled indigenous class of men and women with the leisure time, finances, and inclination to work toward the establishment of institutions of culture. It should also be noted, however, that even before the war, the South had an individualistic, provincial, and sometimes anti-intellectual nature that did not lend itself to public library development. In the antebellum South, a widespread conviction that governments should provide agencies of education for the masses had yet to emerge.[2]

By the 1890s, however, the South had changed. It was in the midst of an economic transition that made the region more industrial and more

urban. Modernization brought the rise of a new middle class of professionals and businessmen in southern cities. Anders asserts that the improved southern economy provided a "more favorable climate" for the
establishment of public libraries than had previously existed. Out of the
new professional and business class came a demand for educational facilities and services, including libraries. By 1900, the southern public
library movement was underway.[3]

The public library movement in the South was distinguished from
its northern counterpart in several respects, including its ties to southern progressive reform and the presence of racial segregation of library
facilities. With the transition of the old agrarian South into the "New
South" that was trying to be both industrial and urban came an awareness within the new bourgeoisie of a need for social improvement. In
Alabama this progressive impulse translated into tax reform, a work-
man's compensation law, a child welfare department, and governmental
support for public health, roads, and education. In a state that had traditionally lagged in literacy and general education, the progressives recognized that the need for agencies for learning was particularly acute.
The public library movement in Alabama and in the urban South came
out of this spirit of reform.[4]

Anders points out that clubwomen were the first to adopt libraries as
a cause, but businessmen, educators, clergy, and librarians followed.
These individuals worked to found libraries in the interest of education for children, self-help for adults, local culture, and civic pride. Municipal leaders believed that presence of a public library provided evidence that a community was progressive in its thinking. According to
Marilyn J. Martin, library development was also a beginning point for
other social improvements, "a first step toward activist reforms typical
of the Progressive Era."[5]

With the arrival of new libraries in Alabama, librarianship emerged
as a profession at the turn of the twentieth century, during the region's
period of modernization. Partly as a result of the generosity of Andrew
Carnegie, the state had nine public libraries for whites by 1904. Representatives of these institutions, along with others from college, religious, and women's club libraries gathered in Montgomery that year for
the first meeting of the Alabama Library Association. The organization's goal was to promote the library movement in the state by creating
an esprit de corps among Alabama's fledgling library community and to
press for public funding for library service. "Let us demonstrate by
what we do," association president Thomas M. Owen urged the group,

"that we are alive to an appreciation of the library as one of the great, if not the greatest, educational forces of the time." With the universality characteristic of early library movement rhetoric, Owen called on Alabama librarians not to rest until "every community in the state is properly supplied with good books free to the use of all the people."[6]

Along with the progressive desire for social improvement expressed in the first library association meeting, however, came an impulse toward social control. In his 1967 book, *Search for Order*, Robert H. Wiebe contends that American progressivism was about establishing a social order in times that were decidedly "out of joint." For southern progressives, this search for order was seen most vividly in the emergence of racial segregation and the disfranchisement of blacks. In the aftermath of Civil War and Reconstruction, white southern reformers believed that segregation was necessary for social stability and peaceful race relations. Historian Dewey Grantham calls segregation a "fundamental component" of southern progressivism. For Jack Temple Kirby, it was the South's "seminal reform." Freed from the dangers and complications of building new institutions in a heterogeneous society, white reformers could establish a public system of schools and libraries. Thus, both segregation and the public library movement emerged from progressive reform at the turn of the twentieth century.[7]

As a result, the southern library movement was characterized by a complex and often contradictory set of priorities. Though seemingly at odds, a desire for both social uplift and social control drove library supporters to act as they did. Their racism was a paternalistic sort. White library boards evidenced a belief in the inherent intellectual inferiority of African Americans, but also in a responsibility to do something to help them. Libraries, they felt, served to improve their users socially and culturally. This was true for blacks as well as whites. Library boards considered it worthwhile to provide library service for blacks, so long as that service was inexpensive and did not suggest in any way a social equality among the races.

Birmingham and Mobile, the state's two largest cities, were the first to offer library service to urban African Americans. Both cities' support for black library development was well within the accepted parameters set by the segregated society. Both excluded blacks from the main libraries; Birmingham even forbade the sharing of books among the races. Birmingham and Mobile contributed money to the operation of separate black libraries, but not much. The two cities hired black librarians, but only to serve black patrons and only at a fraction of a white librarian's salary. Much of the resources and labor of the black library movement came from the black community itself rather than from the white boards. Nonetheless, the boards were proud of their "Negro libraries." Birmingham's library board boasted that its black branch was the largest one south of Louisville. Mobile's believed theirs was "an experiment in interracial cooperation" that placed it within the foremost among southern cities in the area of race relations. The existence of segregated public libraries for blacks soothed the conscience of southern moderates and provided evidence of their "progressive" behavior.[8]

## BIRMINGHAM AND THE BOOKER T. WASHINGTON BRANCH LIBRARY

Birmingham was a New South industrial town exhibiting a complex progressivism that carried over into library development. Many of its iron barons and other industrial capitalists believed that they stood to gain from the existence of a large uneducated black labor pool. But a moderate white contingent saw social benefits in extending library service and other educational resources to blacks. Combining their efforts with those of the black community, they opened the state's first public library for African Americans in 1918. The library grew in popularity, physical space, and holdings and by the 1930s Birmingham's African-American branch had become one of the largest and most important in the region. Library service for African Americans in Birmingham developed within well-defined limits, however. Inherent in the reform-minded attitudes of the white board members was a social and legal obligation to sustain racial segregation. It was an obligation they took seriously and that they fulfilled with unwavering consistency.

Birmingham was still a new city at the turn of the century. It was founded in 1871, at the intersection of two railroad lines located at the southwest end of the Appalachian Mountains. Birmingham and its suburbs emerged throughout a series of parallel ridges and valleys ranging from 300 to 1,200 feet above sea level. The rocky and barren soil of the region was ill-suited for cotton production. But the ridges and mountains of Jefferson County did offer one of the Southeast's largest deposits of iron ore: three major seams of red hematite. In addition, the site was centrally located in relation to the state's largest coalfields, and it offered limestone in abundance. These three resources, ore, coal, and lime, were the essential ingredients for iron production, and their proximity to Birmingham made the new community uniquely qualified among the cities of the New South to become a leader in iron production. Henry DeBardeleben and T. T. Hillman built the area's first blast furnace in 1880 and by the middle of the decade Birmingham was experiencing an astonishing rate of growth both in industrial development and population. By 1900, Alabama ranked fourth among the states in pig iron production with 8.6% of the national total. The city's population increased by 245% in the first decade of the twentieth century.[9]

The industrial boomtown that boosters had begun to call "The Magic City" was more modern and more progressive than any city in Alabama, but this spirit of reform had its limits. The public library movement exhibited a progressive zeal. Birmingham opened its first free library in 1909. Located in City Hall, it held 20,000 volumes. By 1918, the library board had secured an annual appropriation from the city of over $25,000 and had opened three branches. In support of this movement, a booster wrote that "Every additional agency that will make us esteem human life, irrespective of the strain of blood or color of skin, may well be encouraged and worked for by every man and woman." Such rhetoric conveys the progressive tone of the movement, also its contradictions. For while the library supporters spoke in universals, they had to admit that the 80,000 blacks in the city received nothing but sympathy in regard to library service.[10]

The neglect of the intellectual needs of blacks was consistent with their perceived place in Birmingham's economy and its society. In a black worker, employers valued a strong back, not intelligence. Most jobs in Birmingham's furnaces and mines were low-paying, unskilled positions that required physical strength and endurance but little else. Work for blacks was the dirtiest, hottest, and most dangerous in the city. Pay was often barely above subsistence level. Most blacks that moved to Birmingham did so in the hope of improving the quality of their lives. They migrated from rural areas in Alabama and surrounding states to escape the cycle of debt and poverty that was all life as a sharecropper or tenant farmer offered. They hoped for a brighter economic future, one in which they held some control over their own destinies. But a rigid system of "industrial segregation" limited opportunities for African Americans. Management and white-dominated unions created a system of advancement that allowed upward mobility for whites and insured that blacks were restricted to what they referred to as "nigger jobs."[11]

Maintaining a high illiteracy rate within the black population suited the interests of capitalism, or so some industrialists believed. It helped to preserve a large supply of inexpensive, unskilled industrial laborers. White leaders often thought that workers who could read would only cause trouble; they were more likely to unionize. In 1912 Birmingham industrialist Colonel John C. Maben complained that there were simply not "enough illiterate niggers to go around." Maben believed that attempts to provide educational facilities for black iron workers were merely "coddling" the laborers. Other whites simply assumed that blacks had little need or desire for public library service. Under such circumstances, adequate access to libraries for the African-American community would have been entirely inconsistent with contemporary racial attitudes.[12]

Despite the reluctance of city leaders to provide public funding for black libraries before 1918, the African-American community in Birmingham had been working to extend access to their race since the late nineteenth century. Black educators and students played the most active part, raising money to open a facility for their own community. This was accomplished largely through entertainments held in the African-American schools. When the fund reached $350, school superintendent John H. Phillips authorized the opening of a library in the black Slater School. The facility opened in 1898 with an initial collection of 1,100 volumes. It was free for teachers, but the general public was charged a two-dollar fee.[13]

This effort by black educators and students to provide library service to African Americans in Birmingham foreshadowed black library development in the state for the next fifty years. The Slater School Library added only a hundred volumes in the eight years following its opening. It was, however, a pioneering effort considering that the first free public library for African Americans, located in Memphis, was opened as late as 1903. According to black library scholar Eliza Atkins Gleason, there was no service for southern blacks before 1900. Birmingham's diminutive facility began a trend that would carry through the decades before the civil rights movement. The experience of the Slater School Library demonstrated that service for blacks would, where it existed at all, be separate from that of the white population. It demonstrated that separate would be unequal. It also showed that whites would be reluctant to allow significant public expenditure to promote access to educational information by African Americans. Success would depend on the efforts of black communities and sometimes on intervention by outside agents as much as it would on public funding and the good will of white library boards.[14]

White library boards eventually played an important part in black library development, however, and their actions reflected the complex and contradictory nature of southern reform. Board members tended to be more moderate in their racial biases and placed a higher priority on educational and cultural resources for African Americans than did the general white population. Blacks brought pressure upon white library supporters who responded by lending support to indigenous black efforts, sometimes in the face of opposition by other whites who argued that blacks neither wanted nor needed library service. But the actions of the boards, while contributing to library development, served to affirm rather than challenge the racial order of the region.

In 1918, the Birmingham Library Board created a special committee to investigate the possibility of opening a branch for African Americans. It had been prodded into action by the black school principals who had continued their efforts to drum up support and money for library service. Booker T. Washington, president of Tuskegee Institute and the country's leading figure in Negro education, lent his endorsement to the effort after a visit to Birmingham in 1913. By 1917, school entertainments built a library trust fund of more than four thousand dollars. The group of principals turned the money over to the library board, but stipulated that funds be spent only after the board managed to secure an adequate appropriation from the city to keep a library open and pay its librarian. After delaying its work for several months because of draft disturbances brought on by the First World War, the board's special committee appealed to the city for a small appropriation to begin service for African Americans. In August, the board arranged to rent a vacant store in a black business district to house the branch.[15]

Alabama's first public library branch for African Americans opened on October 9, 1918. Though it was originally to be called the "Lincoln Branch," the library board ultimately decided to name the facility after Booker T. Washington. There was no grand opening for the Washington Branch. Spanish flu had swept the city and the municipal government prohibited public gatherings. The library was located at 1715 Third Avenue. The space was long and narrow, sixteen by one hundred feet. Though it had a rather awkward shape, the space was "otherwise favorable." The board visited the location and reported that it "is well ventilated, has a large sky light, is in good condition and rents for

The Booker T. Washington Branch Library in Birmingham, Alabama was the state's first public library for African Americans. This photograph from 1919 pictures librarian Reginald Gaines at the desk in the foreground. Courtesy Birmingham Public Library Archives.

55 dollars." The board appropriated five hundred dollars from the special fund raised by the black schools for furnishings. These consisted of shelving for three or four thousand books, also eight tables and forty chairs. The board appropriated $1,500 from the fund to pay for new books. In addition to the books, the Washington Library offered magazines and newspapers published "by and for the colored people."[16]

The board adopted a policy of almost complete separation, even prohibiting the interchange of books between the white libraries and the black branch. "Books for the colored branch are to be held entirely separate and distinct." Nor would the city contribute to acquisition of new resources. The "special fund" raised in the black schools paid for the branch's materials. To meet situations when patrons needed the more abundant resources of the Central Library, the board members created a rather unusual remedy. They prescribed that when "the need of a loan is urgent the copy from the Central Library may be *given* to the Branch and a new one bought from the colored library book fund to replace it." The arrangement was hardly equitable, and it illustrates the lengths to which southern library boards went to separate the races.[17]

The board hired Mattie Herd to be the state's first African-American public librarian. Herd, the daughter of a railroad switchman, was hand-picked by the foresightful black principals years earlier when she was a high school student. Booker T. Washington and library director Carl Milam also ratified the selection. As the board and the black leaders laid the plans for Birmingham's Negro branch, Miss Herd began acquiring library experience working after school at Birmingham's main library.[18]

Upon graduating from high school, Herd commenced formal library training under Reverend Thomas F. Blue in Louisville, Kentucky. Blue directed the city's "Colored Department," comprised of two branches. Under Blue, Louisville's African-American community read more books per capita than any in the South, black or white. Black students from all over the South came to Louisville to attend his training program. They had little choice; it was the only organized course of study in librarianship for African Americans until Hampton Institute opened its library school in 1925. Herd spent a year studying at Louisville's Western Colored Branch before returning to Birmingham by the summer of 1918.[19]

The board interviewed Mattie Herd in July in order to "question her knowledge in regard to the work." Following the interview, the members voted to hire Herd, but only at thirty-five dollars a month, approximately a third of other branch heads' salaries. Despite the fact that she was responsible for service to all eighty thousand of Birmingham's black citizens, Herd was given the title "library assistant" and was excluded from all staff meetings.[20]

Mattie Herd had been at her post for scarcely four months when the board decided the Washington Branch could use a masculine influence. "It was the belief of the Board that a man" with connections to "the business, club, fraternal, and church work of the negroes of Birmingham would accomplish wonders in stirring its membership and the use of books." The vice-director wrote to Thomas Blue in search of such a person, but with no success. On a trip to Washington, DC, however, library director Carl Milam met Reginald Gaines and hired him almost immediately. Milam instructed Gaines, who had no previous library experience, to visit Louisville's "Colored Branches" for a week "to observe methods there in force."[21]

Apparently, Gaines's weeklong introduction into library work was not adequate preparation for his new job as branch head, because his library career was brief and troubled. Milam hired Gaines at seventy-five dollars a month, more than twice as much as his predecessor's starting salary. Milam wrote to Gaines, "I am sure you will agree with me that for the first few months you will be handicapped by a lack of knowledge of library methods." But he assured Gaines that this could "be rapidly overcome . . . by study and observation." Milam suggested that Gaines learn a little about "how a catalogue is made and what questions you can answer from the World's Almanac." Milam's expectations regarding the quality of library service for Birmingham's black population could not have been high.[22]

By June, Reginald Gaines was close to losing his position. L. W. Josselyn, the vice-director wrote that in his six months of employment Gaines had "developed but poorly." The vice-director criticized Gaines for a lack of vision and an inability to perform the practical matters associated with librarianship. He wrote to Gaines, "you are not satisfactory to us," and gave the unfortunate man a choice between resignation and termination. The short-lived librarian's story demonstrates the haphazard manner in which the library administration handled the hiring of the city's black public librarian.[23]

The administration's reaction to bi-racial use of the Booker T. Washington Library reflected its stringency in sustaining segregation. Beyond his lack of aptitude for librarianship, the administration reprimanded Gaines for his practice of welcoming both black and white to the Washington Branch. Upon learning of a specific instance of a white using the branch, the vice-director scolded Gaines: "Do not permit a white person in the future to register at the Washington Branch." For the practice of segregation to endure, exclusion would have to be mutual. "Colored members are not enrolled (in the Central Library)," Josselyn argued, "nor should white ones join the Washington Branch." This issue would re-emerge forty years later, as the era of segregated libraries was coming to an end. Whites who attempted to use the formerly black libraries found that segregationists resented their use of those institutions almost as much as they resented black use of the central libraries.[24]

For the first two years of its life, the Washington Branch grew in popularity and in its holdings. Appropriations from the "special fund" were low, but steady. By 1920, the branch had circulated twenty thousand books in a six-month period, making it second among the city's branches. By the end of that year, however, the library was suffering. The Negro book fund had been depleted and no alternative sources replaced it. Birmingham administrators recognized the problem but asserted that there was little that they could do; the Washington Branch was not alone in its fiscal difficulties. "Not one of the branches has enough books to take care of demand," the board complained. Still, African Americans were worse off than the rest. The book budget given to the board in November 1922 reported that the system spent $8,934 on materials for white libraries and only $720 for black library. Though blacks comprised more than 40 percent of the county population, they received only 8 percent of the book budget. By 1924 that figure had dropped to 6 percent.[25]

Still, the library continued to make progress into the 1930s. In the years between 1920 and 1935 circulation at the Booker T. Washington Branch almost quadrupled. Earline C. Driver, a college graduate with some library school training, had replaced the unfortunate Reginald Gaines in 1921. In 1923 the library board lost its lease on the Third Avenue location, and obtained space in the new Colored Masonic Temple on Seventeenth Street. These quarters in the center of the black business district were rented as the original space had been. In 1927, the board also began renting the store next to the Masonic building for seventy-five dollars a month to expand the space available to the library. The African-American Masons volunteered to do the painting and to build an archway to connect the new space with the old. The library obtained the space on the opposite side of the Masonic building in 1933, giving the branch a total of 2,786 square feet.[26]

The board boasted that the Washington Branch had become the largest segregated public library for African Americans south of Louisville. It was responsible for providing service to a black population of more than 99,000 by 1930. Thirteen percent of those were registered borrowers in the middle of the decade as opposed to about 45 percent of the white population. The number of borrowers was heavily influenced, according to the library board, by the high illiteracy rate among African Americans. The board asserted that in the 1920s and 1930s the branch was most heavily used by teachers, ministers, students, and "the better element of the colored population." The reading that the patrons of the Washington Library chose was most often non-fiction, especially in the fields of religion, education, and "useful arts." Poetry, essays, and books on science were also popular.[27]

Though it was the black community itself that had been the driving force behind the creation of the Washington Branch, the board was proud of the library's accomplishments. It viewed the branch as an example of its own progressive behavior. The Birmingham *Age-Herald* related an alternative history of the Washington Branch in which a young black boy came to Lila May Chapman, the vice director of the central library, asking for a book called *A Boy Mechanic*. "If I had that book," the boy explained, "I could build a lot of things." The librarian was so moved by his choice of self-educative reading that she went to the board the very next day. She related the story "with the result that the Booker T. Washington Branch of the Birmingham Public Library was then and there determined on." This account excludes entirely the years of dedicated effort by the black citizens of Birmingham and illustrates the way many whites viewed their own role as one of promoting uplift among African Americans.[28]

There were numerous contradictions in the association of the white library establishment with black library service. The library board secured some funding for the Negro library; it rented the building and hired the librarian. The board handled the administrative aspects of black service, provided expertise, and put an official stamp on the Washington Library's activities. Though the black community provided the stimulus for the creation of the branch, whites took most of the credit. Their reports applauded their own enlightened behavior. At the same time, the white library administration maintained its faith in the policy of segregation unwaveringly. It separated patrons according to race, even excluding whites from the Washington Branch. It barred black librarians from attending staff meetings and even segregated the branch's collection from those of the main library and the white branches. The spirit of reform that animated board members and administrators presumed a belief in white supremacy and an obligation to uphold southern mores.

## MOBILE AND THE DAVIS AVENUE BRANCH LIBRARY

In Mobile, the central question related to the location of the segregated library facility for African Americans. White Mobilians generally believed that race relations were better in their city than in most of the state. It was a city based on commerce, not on agriculture like the rural South, nor on industry that bred labor-related difficulties. When black leaders asked that the city support public library service for their race in the 1920s, the city commission agreed with little debate. Heartened, interested blacks asked for a separate reading room within the main library. After a lengthy negotiation between the races and a legal challenge by racially conservative whites, the library board instead built a branch library physically removed from white patrons. The debate lasted four years and it reflected the nature of the racial attitudes of those involved. Especially interesting were those of the white moderates in Mobile, who wanted to provide service for blacks and were sympathetic to the black position on the location of the Negro facility. This was particularly true since the black bourgeoisie couched their arguments in the rhetoric of racial deference. White moderates earnestly wanted to do something to cement the relations between the races that they already felt were particularly good. Ultimately, however, maintaining the racial status quo emerged as the overriding concern.

While Birmingham was Alabama's newest urban center, Mobile was its oldest. Situated on a large bay opening into the Gulf of Mexico, Mobile was older than St. Augustine, Florida. The Spanish established a settlement there in 1559 and although their colony failed, the French followed in 1702. Under French rule Mobile served as the capital of Louisiana until 1722. Commerce was always the city's principal activity, but the cotton trade gave Mobile international economic importance during the antebellum period. It served as the outlet for the product of Alabama's fertile Black Belt, a region of dark, loamy soil and plantation agriculture.[29]

Alabama's port city had a population of 68,202 by 1930, roughly 40 percent of which was African American. Before emancipation, most blacks worked as domestic servants and laborers. In this, the situation for most blacks, whose largest single category of employment in Mobile was the black female domestic worker, had not changed by 1930. For black men, unskilled laborer was the most common occupation. Still, a small black bourgeoisie had developed in the city, and it led the movement to obtain library service for African Americans. There were 443 black professionals, doctors, lawyers, and educators. Business owners and managers numbered an additional 225. This small group, about 4 percent of African-American workers, became the black elite.[30]

Though the black bourgeoisie was proactive, it was not radical. Successful blacks desired an improved social environment for their race, but they also had a vested interest in the economic status quo. Of more immediate importance were the close relationships that they cultivated with prominent whites. They depended on leading whites for credit and other favors. Many of the black bourgeoisie were descended from the city's old Creole population; some were even related to the leading white families of Mobile. Their diminished "blackness" was an asset in dealing with whites, and they learned how to influence white allies by appealing to their racial pride and knowing which lines were not to be crossed. Thus, when blacks petitioned for library service, they couched their demands in the ingratiating rhetoric they believed would receive a positive response. They asserted that blacks should have service, not because it was wrong to act otherwise, but because the project would "place Mobile before the world as the most liberal and fair-minded Southern City in America."[31]

Library service was introduced to white Mobile in 1835. This early library was created by the Franklin Society, an organization intended to "foster greater knowledge and improve taste" among the educated white men of the city. In 1856 the YMCA started a library and in 1901 a larger subscription library opened to serve the white population. The Carnegie Corporation offered to build a free public library for Mobile in 1918, but the city declined in the face of opposition from the city's trade unions. The unions argued that such a library would be a monument to Carnegie, whom they believed to be one of the nation's "most infamous oppressors of labor." In the 1920s, however, a group of civic-minded white women took up the issue of public library development again. In 1925 they succeeded in convincing the city commissioners to approve a bond issue to fund the establishment of a free library. Voters ratified the bond issue at the polls, despite vocal opposition by the city's Finance Commissioner. As a result, Mobile found itself in 1926 with $250,000 with which to begin free public library service among its citizens.[32]

Blacks in Mobile saw the bond issue as an opportunity to obtain service for the first time. Soon after the election, African-American civic leaders began pressing the city government for a promise that the black community would get its share of the newly acquired resources. The city was cooperative. Commissioner Harry T. Hartwell assured them that he had taken up the matter with the commission; the needs of blacks would "be taken care of." With this determined, the two sides turned their attention to the question of location.[33]

Most concerned African Americans in Mobile desired a separate reading room within the new central library. This was a marked deviation from the standard Jim Crow–branch method of library segregation, but there was precedent. Such an arrangement would allow black patrons to take advantage of the holdings and professional service available at the main library. This was not integration, but it was the closest alternative conceivable in 1926 Alabama.

With calculated deference, black leaders appealed to the paternalism and racial pride of whites. Dr. E. T. Belsaw, a leading black citizen and chair of the city's Inter-racial Committee, wrote eloquent letters to commissioners and library board members urging them to accept the reading room plan. Suggesting that the proximity to whites would be a positive influence on blacks, he argued that visiting the main library would "increase the self-respect and deportment of my group." Blacks would be "inspired to live up to the highest ideals of citizenship." They would not be offensive to white patrons, but would always "strive diligently to be neat and decorous." Belsaw suggested that the shared library would make Mobile a model of successful southern race relations. There certainly would be, he asserted in placating tones, "no thought of 'social equality.'" The library board was not so sure.[34]

The discussion continued over the next two years. Belsaw wrote in June of 1928 asserting that the sentiment among the city's African Americans was 90 percent in favor of the reading room plan. During the same month a committee of black citizens met with the library board. The group consisted of representatives from several of the black civic and religious organizations. At the meeting the committee members presented a united front in favor of constructing a wing to the main library that would be dedicated to providing service for Mobile's black citizens. Blacks and whites in the city patronized a single segregated railway station, they argued. They shared movie houses and stores, so why not a library?[35]

There was some sympathy for the black position among moderate whites. A controversy surrounding the principal of a local black high school brought a prominent Mobile lawyer into the debate. In 1929, L. F. Morse, principal of Emerson High School was researching Mobile's history. He visited attorney Frederick G. Bromberg seeking information for his study. Bromberg referred him to the public library. The lawyer was apparently unaware of the library's strict policy excluding Negroes. When Morse advised him of the fact, Bromberg became so concerned that he contacted the library board on behalf of his friend and the other educated African Americans in Mobile. His suggestion was almost identical to Belsaw's reading room plan; Bromberg advised the board to build an annex for blacks. In the meantime, the lawyer hoped the board would allow educators to use the main library freely. "All the teachers of the public schools of Mobile are educated, and are ladies and gentlemen," and Bromberg saw no reason to exclude them from the public library. He added that "it never implies social equality to intermingle in places like the reading rooms of a public library."[36]

Bromberg believed that allowing blacks to use the facilities of the main library was the only acceptable solution. He asserted that a separate facility would suffice for people who wanted to read story books and novels, but that the "real student" required access to "a *genuine* public library." Bromberg differentiated among the educated Negroes and the less so, writing that "anyone can see that there will be a class of colored citizens of culture," whose presence would not be offensive to educated whites. Displaying a social, rather than racial, brand of elitism, the lawyer urged the board to follow his own inclinations. "In my plans for people," he wrote, "I never consider what is popular with the common, uneducated crowd, no matter what their color is."[37]

The library board was in a bind. Rationalizing a branch system for the provision of black service was easy for other cities, even northern ones. The realities of residential segregation made separate branches more convenient for the communities they served. Mobile was different. The site upon which the new main library was being built was central to both black and white residential areas. Accommodating both groups in a single facility also had obvious economic advantages over building and maintaining two institutions. Still, the board had its responsibility to white Mobile to consider. It would not accept an arrangement that advanced race mixing.[38]

Uncertain of how to handle the dilemma, library board president George Fearn, Jr., sought outside advice. He wrote to a paid consultant, Arthur E. Bostwick of the St. Louis Public Library, and to Carl Milam, ALA Secretary and former library director in Birmingham. "The question of the negro library is becoming acute," Fearn complained. "The negroes themselves are very anxious to have it on . . . the rear of the main library and as nearly a part thereof as possible."[39]

Fearn leaned toward supporting the position of Belsaw and the other black leaders, but the advice he received changed his mind. Fearn stressed to his correspondents the geographical and economic advantages of the reading room plan. The proximity of the main library to the greater part of the black population was unusual and might call for a decision that would be considered unusual in ordinary cases. He suggested that since blacks would have their own entrance there would be little interaction, and thus, little "friction" between white and black patrons. Milam and Bostwick disagreed. They believed that a shared but segregated building would not adequately separate the races "in their going and coming." The proximity of the races would make contact between whites and blacks inevitable. Perhaps worse, Bostwick added, African Americans would see more vividly the disparity in quality between library service for whites and their own. The comparison might result in a "dissatisfaction with the whole arrangement" that could be avoided by keeping the black patrons in another part of the city. Fearn and the library board were convinced. On May 2, 1929, the board decided to purchase a lot on Davis Avenue, the main black thoroughfare, for the purpose of building a Negro branch.[40]

To proceed with the branch, the board had to overcome the racially conservative element that opposed extension of library service to African Americans. In 1929, the city attorney issued a legal challenge to the library board's plans. Vincent F. Kilborn wrote to the Board of Commissioners in June, asserting that the bond funds could not legally be used to establish a library for African Americans. His position was that the white people of Mobile would have been "dumbfounded" had they known before the election that part of the money could be spent on a library for blacks. The result was a test case to determine the fate of Davis Avenue Branch. Ironically, the opposing attorney, Robert H. Smith, used a pro-segregation argument to save black library service in Mobile. He asserted that Alabama had wisely committed itself to the separation of the races, but that Mobile could only legally exclude blacks from the white library if it provided parallel service for them. The alternative to the Davis Avenue Branch, he argued, was desegregating the main library. Having convinced the court of the branch's importance in preserving the racial status quo, Smith won the case. Again, southern library supporters demonstrated that service would be extended to blacks only where it seemed to affirm southern racial mores.[41]

The structure Mobile created for African Americans was a conspicuous representation of the board's desire to provide a facility that was outwardly "separate but equal." Completed in 1931, the Davis Avenue Branch was an almost exact replica of the main library in miniature. George Rodgers, a prominent Mobile architect, designed the main library in the "Gulf Coast Style." The library board asserted that it wanted to reproduce a smaller version of this stately edifice for blacks as a "gesture of inter-racial good will and cooperation." Its decision had been unanimous. Unfortunately, the board did not have the money to complete the project, since most of the original $250,000 from the bond was already spent on the white library. A fund raised among con-

In an effort to provide a "Negro branch" that was outwardly "separate but equal," Mobile completed the Davis Avenue Branch in 1931 (top) (courtesy University of South Alabama Archives). It was an almost exact replica of the main library (bottom) in miniature (courtesy University of South Alabama Archives, Erik Overbey Collection).

cerned blacks combined with some of the proceeds from the sale of the old subscription library made up the difference. Work began in April of 1930. The result was a structure that occupied 1,892 square feet and had a maximum capacity of five thousand volumes.[42]

The board appealed to the Julius Rosenwald Fund for assistance in filling and staffing the library. Originally, the board asked for help in building the Negro branch. The Fund was interested in promoting library service for blacks in Mobile, but it normally did not involve itself in the construction of libraries. The Rosenwald agent agreed to help in other ways. The organization paid a declining percentage of the librarian's salary, which was a hundred dollars a month, over three years. It contributed a third of the original $36,000 spent on books.[43]

Expectations were high as the branch neared completion. The board envisioned a facility that was "far in advance of the ordinary negro branch." The library on Davis Avenue would set a standard of excellence for the African-American community. It would be a positive influence to blacks in Mobile and an "incentive to them to do better things." To lead this tiny agency of education and uplift, the board hired Elizabeth Jordan as librarian. She was a Huntsville native and a college graduate who had served briefly as a librarian in Walker County, Alabama. Dr. Belsaw also provided leadership, chairing a committee charged with book selection.[44]

The Davis Avenue Branch opened on July 14, 1931, but lost its funding after only three months. The library started with two thousand volumes and was open to the public mostly in the afternoons and evenings. The branch scarcely had time to make a beginning, however, before the commissioners voted to end appropriations for *both* of Mobile's libraries. Though the Depression fell more lightly on Mobile than on industrial cities like Birmingham, municipal leaders believed that public libraries were luxuries the city could not afford.[45]

The Davis Avenue Library survived the Depression by relying on gifts and user fees. Elizabeth Jordan turned to the black community for help, and it responded through fund-raising entertainments and personal donations. The library also charged patrons a dollar each year. Though these measures allowed the city to keep the doors of the library open, there was little money left to replenish the supply of books. Jordan reacted to this problem by appealing to benevolent individuals outside the South. In a 1932 letter to the *New York Times*, she described the library's predicament and asked readers to donate books. There was a need, Jordan wrote, for children's books, religious works, adult fiction, and books of the "cultural and instructional type." After the Depression, the city reinstated the funding of the Davis Avenue Branch. The branch continued to serve as Mobile's only public library facility open to African Americans until the main library desegregated in 1961.[46]

In Mobile, the maintenance of the prevailing racial order at the public library eventually superseded all other concerns. The perpetuation of segregation was more important than the wishes of the black patrons. It even outweighed economic concerns. Clearly, creating the black reading room would have been the frugal decision. In one sense, the events in Mobile are remarkable in that library leaders seriously considered serving both blacks and whites from a single facility, an advanced notion in the South of the 1920s and 1930s. In another, it is telling that the city ultimately went to the illogical extreme of building a replica-in-miniature of its main library to avoid admitting African Americans into the building whites used.

The actions of Birmingham and Mobile's library boards demonstrate the complex, often contradictory impulses that drove the public library movement in the South. In Alabama, white board members, administrators, and library boosters displayed an ambivalence with regard to race. Theirs was a paternalistic racism. They felt responsible for promoting the welfare of African Americans and wanted to improve the social environments in which blacks lived. They wanted libraries to uplift their users, but these institutions also had to conform to the racial order. It was acceptable, white moderates felt, to provide for black library service so long as it was inexpensive and did not challenge white supremacy. Scholars have vigorously debated whether American public library development was driven by progressive impulses or by a desire for social control. In Birmingham and Mobile, at least, white library supporters were characterized by a desire for social improvement that resulted in social control.

# 2
# Black Libraries and White Attitudes II

## The Depression Years

The Depression era was a time of growth for public library service in the South. The federal government, led by President Franklin D. Roosevelt, responded to the economic hardships of the 1930s by initiating the New Deal, an unprecedented plan of public relief. It included an ambitious program of federal projects intended to generate jobs for the unemployed. In the area of library development, New Deal agencies created jobs by sponsoring library construction and by hiring library workers and extension agents. In the South, the federal library aid resulted in new public libraries, strengthened state library agencies, and created a precedent of service among rural readers who had never had access to libraries before the Depression. Library philanthropy was also important to the South during the 1930s, particularly that of the Julius Rosenwald Fund. The Fund provided financial assistance to southern counties to initiate models of biracial countywide public library service. As a result of this social action by the federal government and by philanthropists, southern states like Alabama made significant strides in library development during the Depression.

The benefits of this growth in public libraries were unevenly distributed, however. The Julius Rosenwald Fund made library development among African Americans a priority and it made provision of library service to blacks a condition for granting aid. The New Deal agencies that were the most involved in library development had no such policy. Theirs was a decentralized, "grass-roots" administrative philosophy; decisions regarding black library projects were made at the state and local levels and reflected local social customs. When leadership in the area of black library development came from outside the region, gains were made. But the experience of the Depression demonstrated that the political leadership outside the region acquiesced to and often abetted the white South in the fulfillment of its racial objectives. Considering the possibilities the New Deal held for black library development, the 1930s was largely a decade of missed opportunities.

## BLACK LIBRARIES AND PHILANTHROPY DURING THE DEPRESSION: WALKER COUNTY

Philanthropy was an important impetus to the American public library movement, particularly in the South. From the 1880s through the Depression, millions of dollars were spent as a result of donations by men like Andrew Carnegie, Enoch Pratt, and Julius Rosenwald. These were individuals who amassed vast fortunes during the Gilded Age and the years after. Their sponsorship of libraries was so important to the South because, according to library historian Donald G. Davis, Jr., the region probably never would have entered the public library movement but for philanthropic support. Though less so than other states in the region, Alabama gained from this brand of benefaction. Birmingham, Montgomery, and Selma, among others, built library structures with Carnegie money. These Carnegie libraries were for whites only, however. The African-American colleges in Talladega and Tuskegee built libraries with Carnegie money. Still, in the area of public library development, blacks in the state saw very little progress as a result of northern philanthropy until the Julius Rosenwald Fund committed itself to promoting a biracial county library movement in the South on the eve of the Great Depression. Walker County, Alabama, received aid from the Julius Rosenwald Fund from 1931 to 1936. With philanthropic support, the county acquired a branch and a network of library stations for African Americans. It was the state's first thorough and systematic attempt to provide library service to rural blacks.[1]

The work of the Julius Rosenwald Fund represented the most extensive attempt to raise the level of black education in the South between the end of Reconstruction and the 1954 *Brown* decision. Rosenwald, son of an impoverished German-Jewish immigrant, borrowed thirty-seven thousand dollars to invest in the fledgling Sears and Roebuck Company at the turn of the century. The initial investment yielded millions. Rosenwald had a philanthropic nature that predated his financial good fortune. It was the influence of Booker T. Washington, however, that inspired the tycoon to dedicate his resources to the improvement of black education. Rosenwald read Washington's book, *Up From Slavery,* and was profoundly impressed. The two men met in Chicago in 1911, and following this initial introduction, Rosenwald visited Washington in Tuskegee. He was so stirred by his visit to Alabama that Rosenwald made black education his chief philanthropy. In a program planned by Washington and paid for by Rosenwald, the Fund contributed to the construction of 5,300 school buildings for southern blacks by the 1930s.[2]

The Julius Rosenwald Fund began its program of County Library Demonstrations in 1929. These were model systems designed to raise library standards for southerners of both races by providing examples of biracial countywide service. Seventy-one percent of southerners were without library service in 1928. The situation was worse for blacks than whites. Some urban areas offered service to blacks, rather modest service for the most part, but there was almost no rural service for African Americans in the South. The Rosenwald Fund sponsored systems that would provide access to everyone, rural and urban, black and white, through central libraries supported by a network of branches and deposit stations scattered throughout each county. This plan was not an initiative toward racial mixing. Library facilities were segregated according to the mores of the region. It was, however, an important beginning and a forceful impetus for reading among blacks. In their 1949 study of the Rosenwald program, Embree and Waxman assert that the Demonstrations brought a 200 percent increase in black readership in the United States. Ultimately, the Fund gave nearly $500,000 to eleven counties in seven southern states.[3]

Walker County, which entered the Rosenwald program in 1931, comprises an area of 808 square miles in North-Central Alabama. It is part of the broken and hilly country that makes up the Cumberland Plateau of the Appalachian foothills. Like the Birmingham District, most of Walker County is not well suited to farming. Only the centermost portion of the county was heavily used for agriculture; most of that was related to livestock.[4]

Coal mining was the area's dominant economic activity. As much as 85 percent of the county's work force was employed in the mines in the 1920s. Every town and settlement of any size was in some sense a "coal town." Though the existence of the region's abundant mineral deposits was common knowledge as early as the Civil War, few mines opened until the arrival of the railroad in the 1880s made it possible to take advantage of these resources. Birmingham's iron and steel industry provided a steady demand for Walker County coal and the region experienced a boom period in the 1890s and continued economic growth up to the Depression. A population increase accompanied the expansion of mining. The number of inhabitants grew from approximately 16,000 in 1890 to 59,445 in 1930.[5]

The lure of jobs in mining brought a significant number of African Americans to Walker County. The region's black population was traditionally a small one, especially in comparison to the cotton-growing counties farther south. But to satisfy the need for labor, mining officials began actively recruiting blacks from other areas to fill lower paying jobs. Many came from rural Mississippi, drawn by the appeal of steady pay and inexpensive housing. By 1930, blacks comprised just over 13 percent of the county's total population. Most of the gainfully employed black males were miners.[6]

The origins of library service in Walker County lie in the efforts of the county school superintendent coupled with the club work of the area's middle-class women. Superintendent J. Alex Moore had been working to improve library facilities for the county's schools since about 1920. He initiated library service in the county by opening a teachers' professional library in his office. Taking advantage of state matching funds, Moore accumulated a collection of several thousand books for both teachers and pupils by 1930. The most active among the women's groups promoting library development was the Thursday Study Club in Jasper that opened a library facility in a furniture store in 1928. The collection was small and the hours of operation limited. In 1929, Moore and the Study Club combined their efforts; their objective was to create a "real public library."[7]

These library boosters placed their hopes in the possibility of persuading the Julius Rosenwald Fund to intervene in their favor, but they would have to meet the Fund's conditions first. According to the terms set by the philanthropic organization, it would match each dollar raised by local sources in the first year, paying a decreasing percentage of the operating budget over the following five years. To receive the aid, the total annual budget for service could be no less than fifty cents per capita of the population served. Walker County was also required to provide housing for the libraries; the Rosenwald Fund did not pay construction costs. Most importantly for black library development, the county would have to initiate a biracial library program.[8]

Superintendent Moore submitted a request to the Rosenwald Fund on January 31, 1930. In his application, Moore assured the Fund administrators that he had managed to secure funds from the county and the state totaling $12,500 for the first year. He asserted that this appropriation would be large enough to serve all the people of the county regardless of race. The county would even provide, "if obtainable, a trained Negro librarian." The county had obtained a large antebellum home, the former residence of Senator John H. Bankhead, which it would remodel as a library for whites. Walker County had also secured space in a vacant store building in the center of the predominantly black section of Jasper to house the central branch for service to African Americans.[9] Satisfied that Walker County had met all of the requirements, the Fund supervisors accepted Moore's application. With an annual budget of $25,000, the Walker County library system opened in January of 1931.[10]

The white main library and the "Negro branch" were the central distribution points for their respective races. Library access was extended throughout the county by opening deposit stations in the outlying towns and settlements. Community centers were often used to circulate books and P.T.A.s and Women's Clubs remodeled vacant storerooms for that purpose. People's homes sometimes served as stations. In the mining camps that dotted the county, doctors' offices and churches became makeshift libraries. Schools also provided space for deposit collections. These school stations addressed the educational needs of students, but in black schools the libraries were designed to serve the surrounding African-American adult population as well. By the end of the second year of operation, there were thirty-nine stations for whites and ten for African Americans.[11]

Elizabeth Jordan directed library service for Walker County's black population. She was a college graduate and "a trained and efficient librarian" according to the Jasper *Mountain Eagle*, but her job was a difficult one. Her clientele was scattered throughout the mining camps of the county and providing library access for them presented a logistical challenge. The main library distributed books to the outlying white deposit stations using a book truck and driver provided with Rosenwald aid. Jordan had no such resources at her disposal; she carried books to the Negro stations herself using her own automobile. Children helped to enhance library access among adults, bringing books home from the school stations for their parents.[12]

The development of the library system during the 1930s was a troubled one. The Depression ended the mineral boom and left the county's coal industry crippled. Strained relations between miners and their employers erupted into violence in 1933 and 1934. Conditions became so unsettled that the state militia was called in to restore order. Such an environment was a tumultuous one in which to begin a library movement. But even in the hard times, and partly because of them, Walker County residents often expressed their appreciation for free public library service. Unfortunately for the new library patrons, the county's Board of Education responded to the economic downturn in 1933 by sharply cutting its appropriation to the library. Soon after, a bitter election-year struggle among the county's political leaders resulted in a withdrawal of all funding for library service. The system closed for five months, after which it reopened with a new board and a renewed financial commitment from the county. In order to get the money, however, the library board was obliged to sue the chairperson of the County Commission, John Gray, who refused to turn over the funds to the library.[13]

Despite the economic, social, and political obstacles the Walker County library system faced during the 1930s, the progress made in African-American library service was unprecedented among Alabama's counties. The number of books per capita at the disposal of blacks was similar to that for whites between 1931 and 1936. Throughout the Depression, blacks consistently had more deposit stations for their population size than whites. The numbers represent what could be considered closer to a fair arrangement within the parameters of segregation than in any other system in the state.[14]

The quality of service and level of readership among blacks in Walker County improved steadily during the Depression. Per capita circulation grew each year between 1931 and 1935, moving from .62 to 2.9. In 1934, black readership overtook that of whites. During that year per capita circulation for African Americans was 17 percent greater than circulation by whites. Through the years of the Depression, black borrowers used their limited book supply more heavily than whites used theirs. The average white library volume circulated six times a year; the average volume from a Negro library circulated 9.3 times. Also, blacks were slightly more likely than whites to be library members.[15]

In 1936, Leyton Davis, principal of the black high school in Jasper, described the importance of library service for African Americans in Walker County. Among the youth, he asserted, enhanced access to educational information had improved classroom performance. It increased the amount of knowledge students retained and developed their "everyday intelligence." Access to quality reading material improved young people's chances of success in college. Davis revealed that 90 percent of his students who attended black colleges after graduation ranked in the "first and second divisions in their classes." Before the library was established only 46 percent had done so. Davis believed that former students who were not college bound also benefitted from access to a library; many of these retained an interest in reading and self- education that enhanced their performance in occupational endeavors after graduation.[16]

The experience in Walker County demonstrated that a proactive leadership from outside of the region could result in substantial improvements in the cultural and educational environments of southern blacks. The progressive behavior exhibited by northern philanthropists should not be confused with a commitment to social equality. Their actions were forward thinking within the context of the times, but the Rosenwald Fund still worked within the prevailing social order. Library facilities in the South, regardless of their origin, were segregated in adherence to local custom and law. This was the only way they could have realistically been expected to be maintained in Depression-era Alabama, and in some ways the practice resembled the de facto segregation in place in other parts of America. Still, the demonstration in Walker County, along with the ten other library systems in the South similarly involved in the Fund's efforts, represented substantial progress within the parameters of segregation. It was a significant accomplishment for rural blacks to acquire library service when it was not available to the preponderance of whites in rural Alabama. It was remarkable, considering their educational disadvantages, that the African Americans who inhabited the mining villages of Walker County proved, at times, more active library patrons than their white counterparts.

## The Works Progress Administration and Black Libraries

The library program of the Works Progress Administration (WPA) was not comprehensively biracial, as the Rosenwald Fund's had been. The WPA's contribution to library development in the South was significant, however. In Alabama, it sponsored a new state library agency and an ambitious program of library extension. But WPA projects were controlled at the local level, and their administration reflected local priorities and prejudices. As a result, WPA officers often excluded African Americans from library work and left most black communities without WPA book deposits. For white Alabamians, the WPA library program was a boon, but the library projects for African Americans were subject to the racial discrimination that characterized most New Deal relief efforts.

Congress and President Roosevelt created the Works Progress Administration in 1935 to coordinate the New Deal work relief efforts. The WPA resulted from a recognition that the nation's unemployed would need government assistance into the foreseeable future and that a comprehensive public works effort was required. It was an attempt to lessen the reliance of the impoverished upon direct relief, instead engaging them in projects of enduring social value. WPA planners believed that public library development was an area of activity that carried this social merit. Of more immediate importance, however, they saw library projects as appropriate ones in which to employ men from white-collar backgrounds and women who qualified for WPA relief.[17]

The WPA created its Library Services Section in 1938 to serve as a clearinghouse for all of the agency's library projects. E. A. Chapman led the section, assisted by Nellie Glass, who would later become librarian at Montgomery. Their focus was on initiating a program of "cultural democracy" by providing service to those without it, particularly people living in rural areas. Normally, state library agencies and the WPA sponsored a statewide library program with public libraries and school boards cosponsoring individual projects. The WPA offered technical supervision and it loaned books on a matching basis. The Administration also provided personnel from among those who qualified for WPA work relief. The local agencies provided housing, furnishings, power and water, and funds for new books.[18]

The WPA helped existing institutions and it also participated in the creation of deposit stations and travelling libraries in areas that had never had library service. This included library deposits in such unlikely places as tool sheds, houseboats, tents, and remodeled chicken coops. In their efforts to extend library service to remote users, some WPA librarians resorted to delivering books by canoe, by horseback, and by hitchhiking. As a result of the Library Section's program, the WPA and the sponsoring institutions built 2,300 libraries, 3,400 reading rooms, and 53 travelling libraries; at its peak the WPA employed more than 38,000 people in library work. There had been only 30,000 American library workers altogether in 1930. More importantly, the program created a public expectation of library service that lasted much longer than the temporary WPA programs.[19]

The WPA effort was particularly important for library development in Alabama. It initiated an ambitious extension program and prompted the creation of Alabama's first state library agency. The new agency, the Alabama Public Library Service Division, was cosponsored by the Alabama Department of Archives and History and the WPA. The state archives provided quarters for the extension program. The WPA paid the salaries of the librarians and matched the state's expenditure for books, $10,000 in 1939. The WPA librarians became library pioneers in Alabama. These women, who furnished their Montgomery office with desks made from book crates, worked to extend service in a state that traditionally lagged in the area of library development. Lois Rainer, an Alabama native known for her extension work in Arkansas, served simultaneously as the director of the Public Library Service Division and the WPA state library supervisor. In the first year, the WPA contributed $260,000 to extend library service to Alabamians. Library agent Mildred Harrison remembers that "any place that would furnish light, heat, and a place for a library, if they had some WPA people that needed assistance that could work there, they could have a library." Eventually there were hundreds of the WPA deposit stations in the state. Only a few of these, however, were open to blacks.[20]

Despite the achievements of the Administration in expanding service to whites, it failed to provide adequate leadership in black library development in Alabama. Though it used the Rosenwald Fund's concept of county library demonstrations, the WPA did not share the Fund's emphasis on black library service. When an officer of the agency's Negro Services group wrote to Edward A. Chapman, the WPA library chief, inquiring about service to African Americans in the South, Chapman was hard-pressed to provide an adequate reply. His letter leaves the impression that the WPA was doing little in this regard. Arkansas had only 613 registered library borrowers among the African-American population. There were "no records available" to evidence any WPA-sponsored service for blacks in Louisiana. Alabama was not even mentioned, though support for black libraries in the state did occur. The WPA loaned books to some black schools. It provided aid for the few existing black branches and, in Huntsville at least, participated in the founding of a black public library branch.[21]

Local priorities rather than national leadership determined whether service for African Americans would be a part of WPA library projects. The Rosenwald Fund was successful in promoting libraries for blacks because it made service to African Americans a condition for receiving aid. The WPA had no such national policy. Some New Dealers desired to help blacks more actively; Harold Ickes, the WPA's director, was a race liberal. But the WPA was ultimately unable or unwilling to provide comprehensive leadership in regard to racial equity in relief programs. The New Deal legislation enlarged the role of the national government in people's lives, but decentralization of power was still the order of the day.

Blacks could not secure work relief through the Library Section's programs, and as a result, there was a low level of WPA activity in black library development. Many eligible blacks in Alabama were unable to secure a place on the WPA rolls. Throughout the South, WPA officials left black applicants until after all eligible whites were registered. In Alabama, however, it was common for certification officers to reject black applicants altogether after intense questioning found them "undeserving." Obstacles remained for blacks who managed to obtain relief work. The Library Section used its projects as a means to provide relief for women, but black women found themselves particularly susceptible to discrimination by the WPA. The Authority employed white women in non-physical types of projects, like libraries. African-American women often found themselves employed in manual labor positions normally filled by men.[22]

Despite the discrimination they faced in receiving WPA library aid, African Americans continued to express an interest in library extension. If for nothing else, they sought library work for their own financial well being. "It was hard times," extension agent Mildred Harrison recalled, "and people wanted those WPA jobs." A black Alabamian complained in a 1941 letter to the WPA, "I am a poor Colored girl with a widowed mother not able to do much work." She asked for a library post as a remedy for the economic distress her family faced. Most requests of this type were unsuccessful, however. For example, an African-American woman named Margaret Butcher wrote to the state librarian, Marie Bankhead Owen, asking for assistance in initiating a "Colored Public Library" in Selma. Owen referred her to the Rosenwald Fund.[23]

The case of Dalzie M. Powell of Luverne, Alabama, exemplifies the difficulties faced by blacks applying for WPA library relief. She wrote directly to Florence Kerr, the WPA supervisor of women's and professional work, after her appeals for a Negro library in Luverne were ignored by local WPA officials. Both Kerr and Lois Rainer, director of the state library agency, replied to Powell, encouraging her to petition the Pike County library supervisor again. In Powell's second appeal, she presented a roll of 209 local African Americans who had registered as members should the local supervisor grant the request for a WPA deposit. She suggested that the local black school was an appropriate place to house the collection. The county library supervisor continued to pay scant attention to the appeal. Powell again contacted Kerr. She wrote that she had been "put off" by local leaders and complained: "It is hard for a Colored person to get on anything here." It seemed to Powell that if the WPA and the county could afford three public libraries for whites, it could certainly pay for one small deposit for the black community. Kerr, reflecting the decentralized nature of WPA administration, asserted that she could not directly interfere. She referred Powell back to the local WPA officials where the request apparently foundered.[24]

The Works Progress Administration library program had a dramatic effect on library extension in Alabama, but it failed to extend equal opportunities for blacks. The WPA sponsored hundreds of new library facilities and improved service at existing libraries. It provided work for trained librarians and drew new ones into the profession. The WPA effort created a more widespread expectation of library service and resulted in the emergence of a state library agency. For the most part, however, the benefits of the program reached only whites. New Dealers at the national level proved unable or unwilling to provide leadership in this area. Provision of service to African Americans was not a condition for receiving aid as in the Rosenwald program. Instead, local officials determined the extent to which black Alabamians could participate in library activities. Local priorities and prejudices often resulted in unfair distribution of work relief jobs. African Americans were interested in library work, even if they were only mildly interested in libraries. The hardships of the Depression fell disproportionately upon them and black Alabamians, particularly women, needed the WPA library posts for economic relief. The WPA library program in Alabama was not a comprehensively biracial one, however, so African Americans were excluded from this effort toward "cultural democracy" that might have otherwise been an important step in black library development.

## The Tennessee Valley Authority: Black Libraries and Regional Development

In May of 1933, President Roosevelt signed the Tennessee Valley Authority Act. Headquartered in Knoxville, Tennessee, the immediate aims of the Authority were to improve navigation and flood control, also to produce inexpensive nitrate fertilizers to help the economically battered southern farmers. In reality, however, the TVA's was a much more ambitious task. The TVA and its supporters sought a broad program of regional development, an unprecedented experiment in federal action, that would contribute substantially to the welfare of the people of the Tennessee Valley, part of which lay within the borders of Alabama. The South was generally believed to be the "number one economic problem of the nation" in an era rife with economic problems; the TVA was charged with the task of pulling the region out of the abyss. In many areas, including the development of regional library service, the TVA was a success. It is also clear, however, that administrators were more concerned about progress among white Americans than they were for African Americans during the Depression. The agency made advances; the TVA projects provided relief work and occupational training for hundreds of needy blacks. It provided many of them with some kind of library service. At least at the national level of TVA governance, there were efforts to improve race relations and to achieve fair treatment. During the Depression, however, the discrimination in TVA library service was characteristic of a general trend of adherence to the southern racial status quo. The TVA activities represented an unrealized opportunity for the federal government to create a precedent in regard to the place of African Americans in the economic, social, and cultural development of the region.[25]

More than three million people lived in the Tennessee River basin during the 1930s. The basin covers 42,000 square miles in parts of seven states. The inhabitants were predominantly rural and suffered from a low per capita income, about 45 percent of the national average in 1933. Alabama occupies a large part of the basin where the Tennessee River cuts across the northernmost part of the state forming a wide valley traditionally used for cotton agriculture. Twenty-three percent of the population in Alabama's Tennessee Valley region was African American in 1930.[26]

When the TVA began its work there it was welcomed as an "agent of Modernization," by progressive southerners who favored the intervention of government to improve people's lives. As part of its effort to enhance the socioeconomic welfare of the Valley, TVA provided schools, training facilities, recreation areas, and libraries for its employees and their families. TVA leaders and reform-minded southerners saw libraries, in particular, as instruments of self-help and social uplift. TVA libraries offered, a contemporary author wrote, "the means of knowing and the means for doing for one's self."[27]

One of the progressive southerners who believed in the potential of the TVA was Mary Utopia Rothrock, who in 1934 became the TVA's Supervisor of Library Service. Rothrock was a Tennessean with degrees from Vanderbilt and the New York State Library School. She had served as librarian at the Cossit Library in Memphis and Knoxville's Lawson McGhee Library. Rothrock was active in promoting library development in the Southeast before joining the TVA, through her association with the Southeastern Library Association and ALA's Library Extension Board. One of her first actions as Knoxville's librarian was to help the black community in Knoxville secure its own Carnegie Branch in 1918. She was hired as library consultant by the TVA in 1933 and her position became permanent the following year.[28]

Under Rothrock's supervision, the TVA began its library-related efforts at its construction sites. Authority planners envisioned a system of camp libraries holding only the technical information workers required to complete the TVA projects. It soon became apparent, however, that a more general effort would be required in support of the Authority's educational, job-training, and recreational programs. Library service became part of the TVA's plan to nurture employee morale and to boost their social and economic well-being. Besides the libraries the Authority opened in community buildings of workers camps, it created deposit stations to serve employees living in outlying areas. Most workers had very limited educational backgrounds, so the focus was on making these facilities places where laborers would feel comfortable. The Authority wanted to avoid a perception among workers that TVA libraries were in anyway "high-brow." Under Rothrock's guidance, libraries came to occupy "a central and vital place" within the TVA's personnel programs. Library facilities were among the first training opportunities to open at a new dam or reservoir clearance site and among the last to close after a project's completion.[29]

African Americans in the Tennessee Valley received a much smaller share of the benefits from library development, following the TVA's general practice of racial discrimination. The Authority could have done much to set a positive precedent where economic and educational opportunities for African Americans were concerned, but TVA's planners instead deferred to local racial mores. Studying the TVA's relationship with black Americans, Nancy L. Grant asserts that the Authority projected a subordinate role for blacks that carried through the Depression and into the years that followed; it was "planning for the status quo." Specific complaints by black employees were exclusion from employment, unwarranted termination, and lack of opportunities for advancement. Blacks believed that they were "the last to be hired and the first to be fired." The TVA had only one African-American supervisor in 1933, the head of Negro training. Blacks also complained of inadequate housing, training, health, educational, and recreational facilities. They expressed a general dissatisfaction with their treatment by white supervisors. After 1935, the TVA worked hard, with considerable pressure from the NAACP, to rectify some of the racial inequities. The Authority's "grass roots" philosophy of administration gave individual managers a large measure of autonomy, however, so the TVA's racial policies were implemented in an uneven and unenthusiastic fashion.[30]

Race relations at the North Alabama TVA sites were particularly poor, especially in the beginning. In the initial reservoir clearance portion of the Guntersville Dam project, the TVA chose to hire only whites. It had acted similarly in East Tennessee work projects, providing the rationale that there was an insufficient number of local blacks to form segregated work gangs. Twenty-three percent of the population living within seventy-five miles of Guntersville was black, however, and several hundred of these were eligible for positions in the clearance project. During the dam construction phase, the TVA adopted a quota system to insure that blacks were hired at Guntersville. The black employees were used only for unskilled labor, however, and had a considerably more difficult lot than white workers. As a result of residential segregation and poor planning African Americans suffered from a shortage of housing. The Negro dorms were overcrowded and many black workers were left to sleep in automobiles on the roadside for a time. The children of African-American TVA workers faced the same type of discrimination in schooling that existed throughout the rural South, but at times the TVA abetted the unequal distribution of resources. In its support of education for the children of TVA employees, the Authority paid the Sheffield, Alabama school board fifty-five dollars for each white child and only thirty dollars for each black child.[31]

It was within this context that the Tennessee Valley Authority executed its program of library service for African Americans in North Alabama. Twenty-six regional libraries opened in the Tennessee Valley states as a result of the TVA library project led by Rothrock. It was a remarkable accomplishment, especially during the Depression and in a region that was one of the nation's poorest. But in Alabama, at least, the benefits of TVA support were enjoyed mainly by whites. The first fully affiliated public library branch for African Americans in Alabama's Tennessee Valley did not emerge until 1941, after the Authority had ceased to support library development in the region.

The Wilson Dam Library was the primary facility for TVA library service in the Muscle Shoals area and it was, in a limited way, integrated. The Muscle Shoals region, associated with the Wilson Dam project, included the cities of Florence, Muscle Shoals, Sheffield, and Tuscumbia. There was no public library service for blacks in the area before the TVA arrived. Each of the cities had a subscription library for whites, but even for them service was "miserably poor." The TVA library held about nine thousand books. It served an employee population that fluctuated between two thousand and five thousand and it also provided books for their families. Among this group, there were about eighteen African-American borrowers in 1939 "who made frequent use" of the Wilson Dam Library. Though this contingent of black readers was small, it represented a marked divergence from the standard TVA practice of racial segregation in recreational and training programs.[32]

The Wilson Dam Library carried out extension activities among whites and blacks. The library provided deposits of books to surrounding communities that agreed to provide a librarian and housing. It rotated collections from station to station to keep a fresh supply of books in each one. In 1939, the Wilson Dam Library had 17 deposits. Ten were located on the TVA reservations. Seven were in surrounding communities. There were four available to African Americans.[33]

The Wilson Dam Library targeted schools rather than the general black population in its extension activities among African Americans. Florence had a TVA deposit housed in the black WPA Recreation Hall; school children and teachers were its most active patrons. The TVA provided a small deposit in Sheffield's school for blacks. The Wilson Dam Library focused most of its attention in Negro extension on the black school in Tuscumbia, however. It held the largest collection for African-American readers and served as the headquarters for disseminating books to the other black schools in the Muscle Shoals area. The only library service for black adults in the area, other than the extremely limited access to the Wilson Dam Library itself, was at the TVA Negro Village. The camp recreation hall housed this collection intended for both training and recreational purposes.[34]

After 1936, the TVA began supporting regional library development by contracting out its library services to existing library agencies, and the first regional agreement took place in North Alabama. It became apparent to Rothrock that the TVA could provide more comprehensive service to its employees, particularly those who lived in areas remote from the worker communities, if it cooperated with library agencies already providing service in the Valley states. The involvement of the TVA, and the infusion of federal money it brought, also presented the opportunity for an investment in regional library development that carried long-term benefits to the Valley.

In 1936, the Tennessee Valley Authority entered into a contract with the Huntsville Library Board along with three counties in North Alabama, Jackson, Madison, and Marshall, to provide library service to the employees engaged at the Guntersville Dam site. The Huntsville Public Library became the administrative center of the Regional Library Service and TVA librarian Hoyt R. Galvin became its director. According to the Authority's plan, the TVA would contribute as much to the new regional library as it would have cost to provide similar service itself. Including the camp library, the Authority disbursed approximately sixteen thousand dollars into library development in the Guntersville Dam area in 1938. The sum decreased to five thousand dollars by 1940, after which time the Regional Library Service continued as a self-sustaining organization. Prior to the involvement of the TVA, the region had only two public libraries, one in Huntsville and another in Scottsboro. By March of 1939, the Regional Library Service was operating thirty-six library stations, six public libraries, and a book truck.[35]

The Authority's library project for blacks in the Guntersville area was a minuscule part of the overall library effort and it depended heavily on the efforts of philanthropic groups, other governmental agencies, and the involvement of individual African Americans. It was underway by the summer of 1937, providing books for segregated black schools. Cooperating with the Regional Library Service, TVA provided a small deposit of books for one of Huntsville's schools for African-American children. The TVA extended minimal library service to other schools in Madison and Jackson Counties by cooperating with the Jeanes Foundation workers there. Endowed in 1907 by Anna T. Jeanes, a Philadelphia Quaker, this philanthropic organization worked to improve education among rural blacks in the South, in part by supplying school districts with trained African-American teachers to supervise Negro education. The TVA provided support to the Regional Library Service, which in turn provided books for the Jeanes supervisors to distribute to the black schools. The Jeanes teachers also circulated books purchased with TVA money to adults, but to a much lesser degree.[36]

At least two civic-minded African Americans emerged in 1937 to extend library service to blacks in the region with the support of the TVA Training Division. In Scottsboro, Horace Snodgrass, a young African-American minister employed on WPA relief, but also considered an agent of the TVA Training Division, directed a makeshift county-wide library program in Jackson County. The TVA and the Regional Library System provided Mr. Snodgrass with a deposit of books. The books served as the nucleus for a collection that grew to approximately a thousand volumes by the end of the decade through the support of several black civic organizations. The local Jeanes supervisor helped to secure and equip a rented building in Scottsboro to serve as the center for the county's black library activities. The industrious library worker provided library service to African Americans in Scottsboro and in the outlying rural communities in Jackson County using his own automobile, which the Regional Library called a TVA "travelling library unit," to transport the books. In the tiny Owens Crossroads community, an African-American TVA employee interested in bringing library service to rural North Alabama opened a small library for blacks with the help of the Authority.[37]

The largest share of the TVA funds spent on black service in the area went to the Guntersville Dam camp training library. In 1938 the TVA allotted a thousand dollars to maintain the "Basic negro deposit," located in the Negro Recreation Hall. It was a multi-purpose library meant to "serve the needs of the employees in the recreation, general adult education and job training programs."[38]

The Tennessee Valley Authority had an opportunity to bring important and far-reaching changes in southern society. How it dealt with African Americans in an industrial setting could have created a precedent of fair treatment as the South continued its economic development after the Depression. Providing integrated, or even less discriminatory, library service to TVA employees could have initiated a custom of library service for blacks. It stood to enhance the expectation of adequate service among African Americans in the region and to place a lingering sense of obligation upon white library leaders. The TVA made sincere attempts to improve race relations among workers during the 1930s, but for the most part it was a decade in which black workers remained second-class citizens, discriminated against in hiring, promotion, housing, education, and library service.

## WELFARE CAPITALISM AND THE NATIONAL YOUTH ADMINISTRATION: THE SLOSSFIELD NEGRO BRANCH LIBRARY

A convergence of corporate, governmental, and community support led to the creation of Birmingham's second public library for African Americans, the Slossfield Branch of the Birmingham Public Library. Driven by his "golden rule" theory of labor relations, the president of the American Cast Iron Pipe Company (Acipco) created a social welfare system for his employees that eventually included library service. Acipco employed a biracial work force, so it duplicated the services provided for the workers. Having sponsored a YMCA library for whites, Acipco took advantage of aid from the National Youth Administration in 1939 to sponsor parallel library service for African-American workers and their families. The Birmingham Public Library became involved, administering the new library as one of its branches. Direction and financial support also came from the leading black civic group in Slossfield, the Acipco "Negro Auxiliary." It acted as an advocate for the library and raised money for its support by soliciting donations within the local African-American community.

The Slossfield Branch has its origins in welfare capitalism, a philosophy of employee relations introduced in Birmingham at the beginning of the century. Led by George Gordon Crawford, the Tennessee Coal, Iron and Railway Company (TCI) implemented a plan after 1907 designed to improve working conditions and to prevent social problems in the grim, dilapidated, and often violent workers' camps that dotted the Birmingham District. While competitors saw this as "coddling" the men, Crawford believed that an actively benign treatment of workers was simply "good business." He reasoned that quality schools and libraries, company-sponsored medical care, decent housing, and hygienic conditions in the mill and mining villages would attract and hold a better sort of employee, dependable family men. Cross-town rival John C. Maben thought such measures were encouraging union activity in the district by "spoiling" the laborers. But TCI's welfare capitalism fostered a benevolent, philanthropic, even paternalistic, character in the company's relationship with its employees and their families that management hoped would prevent rather than induce labor organization. As a part of this plan, TCI sponsored community libraries in both its white and its black industrial villages.[39]

TCI's Welfare Capitalism set the precedent for the American Cast Iron Pipe Company's plan of social improvement for its workers that included library service. Preaching "fraternalism-not paternalism," Acipco's devoutly religious president Jacob Eagan, created his own social welfare program which Eagan called his "Golden Rule" philosophy of labor relations. In its corporate villages that comprised the Birmingham suburb of Slossfield, Acipco sponsored medical and sanitation facilities, schools, athletic leagues, picture shows, and bathhouses. It built model homes used in home economics instruction for workers' spouses. Eagan introduced paid vacations and pension plans for his employees. As a part of this program, Acipco provided reading rooms and eventually complete libraries for workers. Religious conviction motivated Eagan, and he sought to promote an attitude among the workers that they shared a "common purpose" with management. Toward this end, Eagan willed all of his Acipco stock to the company's Board of Management, the dividends to be a supplement to workers salaries and to provide for the welfare of workers' families.[40]

Promoting fraternalism among racially segregated workers presented a formidable challenge, however. The company's response was to duplicate the welfare-type services, including libraries. The central community building that housed the white library was divided into two "departments." Services for whites were provided on the first floor with a door in the front. Acipco provided black services on the second story with a door from the rear of the building. According to an Acipco publication, the arrangement "promoted a more harmonious relation than ever existed before, the white men feeling a certain responsibility for the conduct of the colored men, and the colored workers maintaining a respectful attitude toward the place and its surroundings."[41]

The purpose of the Slossfield library branch was to provide service that paralleled the white YMCA library housed in the service building. By the end of the 1930s, the Acipco white library held about 600 volumes and counted 106 members among the employees and their families. Having secured this modest library service for whites, the company was obliged to sponsor similar service for its African-American constituents. The result was a new public library branch that evolved from the combined efforts of the National Youth Administration, Acipco and its Negro Auxiliary, and the Birmingham Public Library.[42]

The first of these elements, the National Youth Administration

(NYA), became involved in the library project in 1939. The NYA was a New Deal agency charged with the task of providing impoverished youth with gainful employment and job training. The agency, created in 1935, engaged high school and college-aged youths in a variety of public service projects that included library work.[43]

Unlike other federal relief organizations, the NYA showed a particular interest in the welfare of African-American youngsters during the Depression, recognizing the special hardships they endured. Nearly 38 percent of blacks between the ages of fifteen and twenty-four were in need of work relief during the early part of the Depression. In providing aid for this group, the NYA reflected the convictions of its director, Alabama native Aubrey Williams, who used his position of relative power to challenge American racial traditions. Williams, one of the New Deal's "race liberals," required that NYA state directors include blacks in the decision-making process by appointing at least one African American to each of the Administration's state advisory councils and hiring a director of Negro affairs for each state. The NYA insisted on equal pay for all of its relief workers, regardless of race. It emphasized projects that not only provided work relief, but also resulted in the transfer of skills that would help black youth gain employment in the future. To see that all this was done, Williams hired Juanita Saddler and later Mary McLeod Bethune, both African Americans and leaders in black education, to oversee the NYA's work among black youth.[44]

In Alabama, the NYA employed nearly fourteen thousand youths. Blacks were well represented; they comprised 28 percent of the NYA recipients in the state. Under the supervision of John E. Bryan, Alabama's NYA director, and Venice T. Spraggs, State Director of Negro Affairs, the NYA established one of its most successful youth programs in Slossfield. The program began as a boys' club opened to provide black youngsters who played in the congested streets and alleys of Birmingham with a safer and more productive way to spend their time. A local citizen donated the building to house a NYA center and the black community raised a thousand dollars to remodel and equip it. A NYA supervisor and twenty-five part-time youth employees began a program of athletics, choral groups, art classes, and discussion groups; it offered training in woodworking and eventually held free classes in reading, writing, and mathematics. When the NYA obtained additional space for its work in Slossfield in 1939, the time seemed right to also extend library service to the five hundred African-American youths who were taking advantage of the program.[45]

Acipco was a major sponsor of the NYA project, and its directors believed that the NYA program represented an opportunity to improve library service to its workers and to the black community as a whole. A larger scale public library project may not have been in the NYA's original plans, but it was consistent with the agency's goals. Approximately 12 percent of all NYA relief workers were employed in library projects. The agency paid library assistants, but it also was directly involved in building and furnishing library facilities. During the New Deal years, the NYA constructed 43 libraries or additions and repaired about 350 existing libraries. As part of its Out-of-School Work Program, NYA workers built shelving, charging desks, and other library furniture for existing libraries and WPA projects.[46]

In October of 1939 the Birmingham Library Board received a letter from the president of the American Cast Iron Pipe Company, asking for help in establishing a library for Slossfield. His suggestion was that the library board take advantage of the resources provided by the New Deal relief agency and by Acipco to create a second public library branch to serve African Americans in the Birmingham area. It was a logical move for both Acipco and the library board. Acipco could assure black workers that it was providing parallel library service for black employees. The plan made financial sense, because the project would require minimal capital outlay by the company and almost none by the city of Birmingham.[47]

According to the Acipco plan, much of the responsibility for the branch would be born by its Negro Auxiliary. This group of twelve was elected annually by the African-American employees. The object of the group was to "promote improvements of living conditions among the colored employees" and to "promote the moral, spiritual, educational and recreational development" of black workers. This group would act as fund-raiser and advocate of the new library.[48]

The Birmingham Library Board agreed to the plan with the result that the Slossfield Branch of the Birmingham Public Library opened in 1940. With the assistance of the Auxiliary, Acipco provided the equipment and books necessary to initiate library service. The company also paid the librarian, Daisy Jones and later Ludie Brown. The NYA provided the space for the library. It furnished materials and labor to prepare the space for use and it hired students from its relief rolls to work in the library. The Birmingham Public Library and its library board administered the branch. In particular, Earline Driver Barron, the librarian at the Booker T. Washington Branch, provided guidance in the management of the new African-American library.[49]

In the beginning, the city contributed almost no monetary resources to the branch. The only source of funds to sustain the library's development after the opening was whatever contributions the Negro Auxiliary could coax from the black community. In 1944, however, the board began an appropriation of fifty dollars a month to supplement the community's efforts. By 1948, it had assumed most of the financial responsibility for the branch. The library continued to provide service to Birmingham's African-American readers and to grow through the decades, until the city deemed it appropriate to build a modern structure for the Slossfield Branch in 1964.[50]

The founding of the Slossfield Branch of the Birmingham Public Library represented the culmination of governmental, philanthropic, and community action. It involved a library board interested in expanding its activities in the area of black librarianship, so long as the project was inexpensive and consistent with the racial status quo. It included philanthropy, of which welfare capitalism can be considered a type. In the case of the Slossfield Library, as in Walker County, corporate benefaction was an important sponsor of black library development. The African-American community helped to support the library and acted as its advocate. A New Deal agency played a part, but unlike the WPA and the TVA the National Youth Administration had a well-developed racial conscience that originated at the national level of leadership.

The Great Depression was a time of expansion for the public library movement in the South, particularly in Alabama, but the benefits often did not reach African Americans. The Rosenwald Fund was an important sponsor of black library development. By making the provision of service to African Americans a condition for receiving library aid, the Fund coaxed counties that otherwise would not have extended service to blacks into doing so. The Rosenwald agents did not advocate integration, but they did demonstrate that leadership in the area of race relations could result in a much more fair arrangement within the parameters of segregation. The New Deal agencies, except the National Youth Administration, failed to exercise this kind of leadership. Participants in the WPA library program were not required to include African Americans in their plans, and in Alabama they most often did not. The TVA included black workers and their families and it extended service to a considerable number of African Americans who had never before had access to libraries. Still, discrimination was an institutionalized part of the TVA library program. The projects of the WPA and the TVA had a decentralized, "grass-roots" policy of administration, so decisions regarding black library projects were made at the local level. These decisions reflected local customs; in Alabama this meant that discrimination was the result. The experiences of Walker County and of Slossfield demonstrated that black library development could have benefitted from the efforts of outside agents just as white libraries had. For the most part, however, the 1930s was a decade of missed opportunities for the growth of African-American library service in Alabama.

# 3
# African-American Communities and the Black Public Library Movement, 1941–1954

African Americans in southern cities responded to segregation by creating cohesive, but diverse, communities characterized by spirited civic action. Urban segregation bound together blacks of dissimilar social, educational, and economic backgrounds, facilitating the development of black institutions and a well-defined community identity. Since they had no representatives in municipal governments and few could vote, these individuals created strong, active civic organizations that served as the substitute for a political voice.[1]

As African Americans organized to improve their lives and social environments, they initiated and helped to sustain a public library movement to parallel the one whites had started at the beginning of the century. Blacks turned to white library boards and municipal governments for administration and financial support, and to lend legitimacy to their efforts. They solicited aid from federal agencies and the state public library service. But the initial efforts to secure black public libraries came from the communities they would serve. As events in Huntsville, Montgomery, and Birmingham during the 1940s and 1950s illustrate, the African-American public library movement in Alabama was, at its core, an indigenous enterprise driven by the work of black civic and religious organizations, educators, clergy, business leaders, and librarians.

## The Dulcina DeBerry Branch Library, Huntsville

The history of Huntsville's Dulcina DeBerry Branch exemplifies the importance of African-American communities in the development of library service for blacks living under segregation. Huntsville was 36 percent African American during the Depression, but this sizable portion of the city's population had no public library at its disposal until 1940. The Negro Library, that would become the "Dulcina DeBerry Branch" of the Huntsville Public Library, was one of the few black library projects of the WPA in Alabama. The Administration paid a librarian's salary and provided a few books. The WPA support was not sufficient to create an effective public library, however, and the city offered only a minimal financial commitment to library service for blacks. Under segregation, African Americans lacked the public funds for services whites enjoyed; often black communities had to erect their own civic infrastructure. Such was the case in Huntsville. It was the efforts of the city's black churches, educators, civic leaders, and its other concerned African-American citizens that started the library and sustained it through the 1940s.[2]

Huntsville has the longest history of white library service of any of Alabama's cities, but it had no library for blacks until 1940. The state's first public library opened in the frontier community in 1818, a year before statehood. It served the cultural needs of the "loghouse aristocrats," the educated men of political and professional distinction who settled the region in the early nineteenth century. The library was located in the county courthouse; women were barred from using it. In 1819, during the constitutional convention called to form the state of Alabama, James G. Birney asked the group to grant a charter for the Huntsville Library; the charter was given in 1823. In 1914, Huntsville secured a Carnegie grant to improve the library, which had persisted through several incarnations since the original 1818 facility. Using the $12,500 given by the Carnegie Corporation, the city opened a new library building on Madison Street in March of 1915. Though the institution received its support from the community as a whole, the Huntsville Library Board expressed clearly its intent to exclude African Americans from the new library. The board adopted a bylaw in December of 1915 stating, "The use of the library is hereby limited to residents of Madison County, of the white race." The arrival of the Tennessee Valley Authority in 1933 brought a needed infusion of funds and expertise to Huntsville's development of library service. The public library served as the administrative center for the TVA's Regional Library Service for the counties surrounding the Guntersville Dam site. But when the TVA library funding ended, the city still had no public library for its African-American population.[3]

The arrival in 1940 of a retired teacher and a minister's wife named

Dulcina DeBerry served as the catalyst for the opening of Huntsville's first branch for African Americans. DeBerry was born Dulcina Torrence in York, South Carolina, in 1878. Though poverty placed considerable strains on her family, Dulcina took her education seriously and was an interested reader from a young age. She managed to graduate from a black two-year normal school and worked as a schoolteacher at King's Mountain, North Carolina, for several years. She went to Talladega College in Alabama about 1903 to continue her education and there she met and married Perfect DeBerry, who was studying to be a minister. As an educator and minister's wife, she lived in North Carolina, Missouri, and Ohio for the next thirty-five years. In 1940, DeBerry settled in Huntsville to care for her aging parents.[4]

Dulcina DeBerry was well-educated and a devoted reader; it was natural that she was dismayed to learn that the Huntsville Public Library was closed to blacks and that no parallel service was offered. She discussed her concerns with Elizabeth Parks Beamguard, a librarian at the central library who eventually became director of the state library agency. Though it violated library rules, Beamguard covertly lent books to DeBerry. According to DeBerry's biographer, Missouri Torrence, Beamguard allowed her new patron to select books from the shelves of the Huntsville Public Library and invited her to return.[5]

The librarian was impressed with the retired teacher and she arranged a meeting between DeBerry and Hoyt Galvin, the library director, to discuss the future of library service to Huntsville's black community. The result of the meeting was a decision to begin modest service for the city's black population. Though the TVA library program had ended, the WPA was still active in the area of library development in 1940. Galvin believed that the WPA would support a library project for African-American readers, so long as he could secure accommodations for the library and find a qualified Negro to serve as librarian. Galvin offered the job of librarian to DeBerry. She accepted the challenge and a local black church, Lakeside Methodist, offered the use of its basement to house the facility soon thereafter.[6]

DeBerry had few resources with which to initiate library service. In May of 1940, Galvin took DeBerry to the Lakeside Methodist Church, unlocked the basement, gave her the key, and said, "make something of it if you can." The basement was dark and damp. The walls were water damaged and smoke stained. There was some library equipment; it was left over from a failed WPA reading project. This small collection contained sixty-five books for adults and thirty-seven for children. Shelving consisted of a large dry goods box adapted to the purpose. DeBerry was given two weeks to prepare for the opening.[7]

Support from the city's African-American community turned the mostly empty basement into a functioning library. Young men worked to clean the library and prepare it for the opening. The church and nearby neighbors lent tables and chairs to furnish the converted basement. The minister's wife donated a chair for the new librarian. Lakeside's girls' club, the "Busy Bees," donated growing flowers to decorate the windows. DeBerry's nephew lent art posters to cover the walls. Furniture received coats of paint and the ladies of the church provided refreshments for the opening, which took place in June of 1940.[8]

Circulation was slow at first, but interest increased as new resources became available. At the outset, the nascent branch had little to offer. Soon, however, the bookmobile began visiting the branch, exchanging new books for old ones. "Special requests" for books from the central library became an option for African-American readers whose interests lay beyond the narrow boundaries of the new branch's collection.[9]

DeBerry initiated a Vacation Reading Club and a Children's Story Hour during the library's first summer of operation to promote reading among the young. She believed in the importance of these programs to the development of Huntsville's black children. With few other alternatives for directed recreation, the reading programs provided a productive way for black youth to spend their summer vacations. "To the boys and girls surrounded by the best schools, libraries, playgrounds and swimming pools, a [reading] certificate means little," DeBerry wrote. "However, to the child who has none of these things, it is a treasure." The children received recognition for their accomplishments; besides being awarded certificates, they were named in the local newspaper. DeBerry's initiatives not only promoted reading, but also encouraged self-esteem among children whose educational resources were limited and whose sense of lack of worth was constantly reinforced by the racial customs of their society.[10]

The Reading Club's award ceremony held at the end of the summer served to publicize the library's activities and to appeal for additional support from the community. On August 31, 1940, the library held a public gathering to recognize the children who had completed the first Vacation Reading Club program. Twenty-nine received certificates. DeBerry invited parents, leading citizens, and representatives from churches and newspapers. One of the attendees suggested that a community library organization be formed to promote the development of the Negro Library. DeBerry responded, asking a few leading black citizens to serve on a library board, to become advocates for the Negro branch. It had become apparent to DeBerry that a relocation was necessary; the basement had insufficient heating and winter approached. The first assignment of the group would be to develop the ways and means to move the library.[11]

The unofficial black library board represented the leading African-American business and educational interests in the city. Dr. Joseph Drake, president of Alabama Agricultural and Mechanical College, served as the group's president. Myrtle Turner, principal of the Winston Street School and the city's first black principal, was secretary. The membership included Leroy Lowery, a prominent businessman and landlord, Edward Shelby Johnson, owner of a successful dry-cleaning operation, and Dr. R. S. Beard, a physician.[12]

The Negro Library Board decided to move the library to the Winston Street School. Turner had suggested her school as a likely location; after receiving approval from the superintendent and from the white library board, the Negro branch relocated there on November 30, 1940. There was adequate space in the school, but no furniture suitable for a library.[13]

The black board sponsored the Negro Book Week Musical to raise money for the library and to promote African-American literature and music. It held the event at Alabama A. & M. in February of 1941. The musical raised enough money to purchase the materials needed to construct the library furniture. African-American students built the furniture at the local NYA workshop. It consisted of a large book locker, tables, chairs, a bulletin board, a magazine rack, and display shelves. Circulation showed a marked increase after the move.[14]

The musical benefit became an annual event that sustained the Negro library's growth through the 1940s. Responsibility for directing the benefit rotated among the members of the Huntsville Teachers' Organization. It included soloists and musical groups from all age groups and served as an outlet for Huntsville's musical talent. Though the Negro library received no formal allocation from the city or county as was provided for white public libraries, the black library's board made the most of its fund-raising efforts to improve library service for Madison County's African-American population. It combined the proceeds of the second year's musical with a Rosenwald grant to add books to the library's collection. The following year it purchased additional shelving. The musical benefits continued until 1952, four years after the city began providing an annual allocation to its Negro branch.[15]

Unfortunately for the Huntsville Negro Library, Congress terminated the Works Progress Administration program in Alabama in 1943. At its peak, the WPA had employed 76,000 Alabamians and over five years had spent about $200 million on projects in the state. The Negro Library had been one of these projects; federal relief money paid DeBerry's salary. The library responded by closing for the summer of 1943. To resurrect the library, the City Board of Education voted to hire DeBerry as a "part-time library teacher" at the Winston Street School. Upon the Negro Library's reopening, the Huntsville Library Board officially recognized its status as a branch of the Huntsville Public Library.[16]

The Winston Street Branch was the primary unit for library service to Madison County's African-American population and as such it became responsible for provision of reading material for the county's black schools. Most schools for African Americans had no libraries and there was no bookmobile service to these schools as there was for white schools. DeBerry encouraged teachers to come to the Negro Library to borrow books for their classrooms. Thirty schools took advantage of the librarian's offer. Some set up "reading corners," small classroom libraries.[17]

The Negro Library also participated in the Huntsville Public Library's bookmobile program. In 1950, African Americans still lacked the bookmobile service that Madison County whites enjoyed. Elizabeth Parks Beamguard, who became Huntsville's library director in 1944, expressed her concern in this matter in her reports to the county government. "Negroes in Madison County have asked for books," she asserted. "We have found that they really want to read." Purchasing a bookmobile just for blacks was not an option, however, and state segregation laws forbade the Huntsville Public Library from providing integrated service. Beamguard suggested that the public library create a Negro section on the book truck it already operated. The Negro Library could select a collection from its holdings and place it on the bookmobile, she asserted, "thus giving [black readers] books, but books from their own collection." The county commissioners approved the suggestion; it offered expanded service and satisfied segregation requirements. Beamguard reported after a year that the system had been met with "enthusiasm and use."[18]

Huntsville's first black branch survived the desegregation of the

Huntsville librarian Elizabeth Parks Beamguard visits Huntsville's Dulcina DeBerry Branch, which opened in 1941 and was housed originally in a church basement. Courtesy Huntsville-Madison County Public Library Archives.

city's libraries and continued to operate as an integrated facility until 1968. In 1948, the library moved to a building on Pelham Street, a spot more centrally located to the city's African-American population. Beamguard believed that the branch needed its independence from the Winston Street School if it was to adequately serve all age groups. After the move, the white library board renamed the library the "Dulcina DeBerry Branch" of the Huntsville Public Library. DeBerry left for North Carolina in 1950 to care for an older sister. Fanny Jackson, DeBerry's assistant, took over operation of the branch. In 1951 the library moved to the Negro Community Center on Church Street where it remained into the 1960s. Horace Snodgrass, pastor of the city's largest black church and eventually a leader in local civil rights action, became DeBerry's librarian in 1955 and served in that capacity until the Huntsville Public Library replaced the branch with bookmobile service in 1968.[19]

In Huntsville, the involvement of the African-American community was responsible for the nurturing of a makeshift deposit station in a run-down church basement into a functioning public library. The branch adopted as its slogan George Washington Carver's words of advice, "Use what you have to get what you want." During the 1940s, Huntsville blacks exercised this advice. African Americans donated space, labor, money, and talent to sustain the Negro Library. In the absence of adequate public funding for black library service, they helped to create their own civic infrastructure and made the public library branch "an integral part of community life."[20]

## THE UNION STREET BRANCH LIBRARY, MONTGOMERY

Montgomery was the last of Alabama's major cities to provide library service for African Americans. The capital city was not a strong financial supporter of libraries in the first half of the twentieth century, even for whites, and it proved difficult to solicit the help needed to develop a credible library for blacks until after the Second World War. A black community library organization, called the "Friends of the Library Association," along with the city's women's clubs, initiated the first serious movement to establish African-American service in 1947. They offered space, labor, and financial assistance to begin library work among the black population. The need for the service was obvious and the group drew enough support from the city and the state library agency to open the Union Street Branch Library in 1948.

There were efforts to initiate library service for whites in Montgomery as early as 1860, but the city's first substantial public library opened above a Dexter Avenue drugstore in 1899. It was a product of the Montgomery Library Association, a group organized by the city's women's clubs in 1898. The Association managed to secure a Carnegie grant in 1901 and in 1904 the city opened a library on Perry Street. To meet the conditions set by Andrew Carnegie, the municipal government had agreed to allocate five thousand dollars a year to maintain the library. As the years passed, however, the city neglected to increase this sum. Though five thousand dollars sufficed in 1904, inflation and increased demand made it far from adequate in the 1940s. The president of the library association lamented that Montgomerians simply were not "library conscious." The city's librarian complained that she had to operate with less money per capita than any other similar library in the nation. Library service was poor for whites in Montgomery, but it was non-existent for African Americans. They were barred from the Carnegie Library and had no public library of their own until 1948.[21]

The black community had become increasingly vocal in its dissatisfaction with the prevailing public library situation by 1947. Testing the Carnegie Library's resolve to exclude African Americans, Dr. V. E. Daniel, Dean of Instruction at Montgomery's Alabama State Teachers College for Negroes entered the library and asked to be served. Daniel's complexion was "very fair"; the librarians were uncertain of his race. They began questioning him, and upon learning of his employment at Alabama State they determined that he was an African American and turned him away. Daniel was not alone in his discontent with the library system. Nellie Glass, the city librarian, reported in June 1947 that sixty or more African Americans had made requests for library service in the previous two weeks. She argued in her library report for the year: "There is NO public library service in Montgomery for Negroes. They pay taxes too—should they not have a branch at once?"[22]

Recognizing that no service would be forthcoming from the Carnegie Library, African-American community groups began to promote a library movement of their own. In June of 1947 the Montgomery Negro Ministerial Association held a meeting to discuss the organization of a library for blacks. The group invited Lois Rainer Green, the director of the Alabama Public Library Service Division, and Nellie Glass. Green offered her help. The state library agency could lend books to stock the library as soon as an institution could be established. Glass suggested that the Carnegie Library had some book stock it could contribute, "duplicate copies and similar material," but she was skeptical that the white library board would offer any of its already inadequate funds to support a black library project. The group of ministers resolved to initiate their own library association.[23]

Black civic leaders formed a committee, the "Friends of the Library Association," to pursue the creation of a public library for Montgomery's African-American population. Ralph A. Daley, one of the city's prominent black ministers, chaired the group. He had been working to remedy the lack of library service for Montgomery's African Americans since 1942 when he created a library in his church. Other members of the library committee were Zenovia Johnson, president of the City Federation of Colored Women's Clubs; Alice Martin, a Federation member; and M. L. Pace, Boy Scout Master. Professor Daniel also took part in the group's activities. The members decided to address the white library board at its July meeting. If this was unsuccessful, they agreed to appeal directly to the city government.[24]

The black library committee managed to secure the backing of the Carnegie Library board, based largely on the argument that the budget for a new library for blacks would be "extremely small." The city's only expense would be the salary of a librarian and a modest sum for book acquisition. The City Federation of Women's Clubs offered space for a library in its community house rent-free. The women's organization would also pay for electricity and water. The Friends of the Library Association assumed responsibility for renovating the space and providing furniture for the library. The state library agency would help with books. The board seemed open to the idea, but informed the black library committee that it would have to find a trained black librarian to operate the branch, one with an accredited library degree.[25]

Under the direction of the "Friends" group, black Montgomerians prepared the community house on Union Street. The women's clubs had recently acquired the building; it was in need of general renovation along with the provision of the specific accommodations required for a public library branch. Reverend Daley and his congregation purchased lumber and built the library's shelves. Over the course of a year, they painted, remodeled, and repaired until the community house was ready to serve its intended purpose.[26]

The problem of securing a trained librarian to operate the branch remained unsolved until August 1948, when a young Atlanta University graduate named Bertha Pleasant accepted the position. Pleasant was a native of Montgomery. In 1947, she was attending the library school at Atlanta University, one of the country's few black schools for professional library education. Pleasant first learned of the position at Montgomery from her school's dean, Virginia Lacey Jones. Zenovia Johnson had written to Jones on behalf of the city's women's clubs; she sought Jones's aid in recruiting a qualified librarian for Montgomery's planned Negro branch. Dr. Jones approached Pleasant with the letter and urged that she consider the possibility of returning to her hometown to initiate library service there. Pleasant had been offered more lucrative positions at Stillman College in Tuscaloosa, Alabama, and in Atlanta. She decided to accept Montgomery's offer, largely because of the wishes of her mother who was in failing health.[27]

Pleasant's first exposure to library work had been at a facility established by the Tennessee Coal, Iron and Railway Company for the use of its African-American employees and their families. After attending a black grammar school in Montgomery she went to high school in Birmingham where she lived with an older sister. During her teenage years in the Birmingham District, Pleasant befriended a white librarian who worked at the local TCI library for African Americans, "Mrs. Stratman." The librarian was from New England and Pleasant remembered her as more sympathetic toward African Americans than most whites she encountered in Birmingham. Pleasant began volunteering her time and she eventually began to operate the library by herself on the weekends when Stratman was out of town.[28]

Pleasant was a classroom teacher before turning to librarianship. She graduated from Alabama State in Montgomery with a degree in education and took a job teaching first grade at Snow Hill Academy in Wilcox County, Alabama. She stayed there for six years. After Snow Hill lost its accreditation because it lacked a trained librarian, Pleasant decided to begin her education in librarianship. In 1944, she applied for admission to the library science program at The University of Alabama in Tuscaloosa. Her application was unsuccessful; the university was segregated until 1963. The closest library school that admitted African Americans was Atlanta University. Pleasant studied in Atlanta for three summers before graduating in 1948.[29]

Upon accepting the position in Montgomery, Pleasant visited the small and inconspicuous building on Union Street that was to become the city's Negro library. Inside she found the many boxes of old books and magazines that the Carnegie Library had provided. Pleasant sorted through the boxes and found their contents to be "junk"; the books were discards of insufficient quality to circulate among her patrons. She informed the white library board of her refusal to accept the donation. Bertha Pleasant (Williams) remembers winning the respect of Nellie Glass, a headstrong librarian in her own right, by her stern reaction to the board. With the cooperation of Lois Rainer Green, the branch librarian selected the core of her initial collection from the holdings of the state library agency, the Alabama Public Library Service Division.[30]

The library opened on December 8, 1948, as the "Union Street Branch of the Carnegie Library." The branch began service with 1,700 volumes. Nellie Glass and the library board held the ultimate responsibility for administering the branch's activities. Bertha Pleasant Williams undertook the daily operation of the new library. Among her duties, she was charged with book selection, making community contacts, publicity, and "in general," representing "the library to the Negro population."[31]

The City Federation of Colored Women's Clubs and the Friends of the Library Association served as cosponsors of the black library. They worked to sustain the Union Street library by holding teas to raise funds and by soliciting contributions from the community. The groups contributed their time and labor, remaining a basic means of support for the under-funded institution through the 1950s and 1960s. According to Bertha Pleasant Williams, any basic needs the library board refused her, "my Friends" responded, "we'll get it."[32]

Circulation was slight at first, but the library became an important community institution as the awareness of the black population grew. Only forty books circulated during the first month of the branch's operation. "This let me know what I had to do," Bertha Pleasant Williams remembers. Montgomery blacks had never had access to a public library. She believed that a publicity effort was necessary to make them aware of the new community resource. Pleasant contributed columns in the local newspaper and became the first African American to speak on Montgomery's WSFA radio station.[33]

Apparently, Pleasant's public relations work had the desired effect. The branch became busier after the first months. In its first year, the Union Street Branch loaned 10,758 books. By the time the Carnegie Library issued the 1950–1951 annual report, circulation among blacks had more than doubled. It was responsible for about a quarter of the circulation from the city's two libraries, a strong start for an ill-equipped library serving a population unaccustomed to library service.[34]

During the 1950s, the Union Street library continued to expand its services. It opened a book station by 1952 to extend library service to one of Montgomery's black housing developments. The library initiated summer reading programs to promote reading among young blacks, as DeBerry had in Huntsville. The resourceful Union Street librarian obtained materials for the blind through a program directed by the Library of Congress. The branch began service to African-American schools that lacked library facilities. Bertha Pleasant Williams encouraged educators to set up reading corners in classrooms. She actively promoted reading in the schools by making principals aware of the branch's commitment to work with teachers and by holding reading programs in school auditoriums. To support this effort, the white board asked the city government for a bookmobile to serve the black population in 1953. The city denied the request. Lacking a book truck, the teachers charged materials at the library and transported the books themselves. Williams remembers teachers leaving the Union Street Branch carrying large boxes of books bound for the city's African-American schools.[35]

The branch experienced a decline during the mid-1950s. After the opening, the branch had quickly outgrown the resources provided for it. The space in the community house was already inadequate by 1952. There was no office space and shelving was in such short supply that Bertha Pleasant Williams resorted to storing old periodicals under the building. The collection was overtaxed, particularly the children's books. Nellie Glass wrote that "You can go to the Branch anytime at all and find almost no books on the shelves of the children's room." Circulation decreased each year from 1954 to 1957.[36]

The branch's move to a new building in 1960 reawakened the interest of the black community. In 1956, Montgomery floated a bond to improve the city's library facilities. The municipal government approved a plan to use ten thousand dollars from the bond issue to construct a Negro branch on Cleveland Avenue. It would be the black counterpart to a new main library. The decision was made in the aftermath of the bus boycott and the Montgomery *Advertiser* touted this new segregated institution as an example to the nation of white Montgomerians' benign treatment of African Americans. Regardless of the racial overtones, circulation among blacks increased after the move. Williams continued to serve as librarian at the Cleveland Avenue Branch through the civil rights movement. She was eventually replaced by her niece, Teresa Temple, who got her start as a page at the Union Street location when she was in high school. The branch, integrated in 1962, was still serving Montgomery in 1997.[37]

The origins of biracial library service in Montgomery lie in the civic action of black club women, educators, clergy and other concerned African Americans working toward the improvement of their social and cultural environment within the context of segregation. By providing a large measure of the resources required to commence and sustain a viable library, the community groups involved managed to acquire the backing of the city and the state library agency. Bertha Pleasant Williams, Alabama's first black public librarian with an accredited master's degree in library science, developed an agenda to promote reading that included summer reading programs, reading for the blind, and library service for schools. Despite the meager public resources at her dis-

Bertha Pleasant Williams and the Montgomery "Friends of the Library" at the
Cleveland Avenue Branch in 1960. Courtesy Mrs. Bertha Pleasant Williams with the
permission of the Montgomery City-County Library.

posal, Williams helped to establish the Union Street library as a central educational and cultural institution within Montgomery's African-American community.

## BIRMINGHAM NEGRO ADVISORY COMMITTEE

In 1953, African-American civic leaders in Birmingham created a Negro Advisory Committee to promote black library development. The committee mounted a publicity campaign on the library's behalf that brought a significant increase in the use of the Booker T. Washington and Slossfield Negro branches. The group also served a purpose the white library board had not intended. On the eve of the *Brown* decision, the Negro Advisory Committee vocalized black Birmingham's first salient demand for the desegregation of the city's library system.

Birmingham Library Board member Mervyn H. Sterne suggested in June of 1953 that the public library system solicit the aid of black civic leaders in bolstering the declining circulation at the Booker T. Washington Branch. The original group, which became the "Negro Advisory Committee," had three members. Director of Birmingham Negro Schools Dr. Carrol W. Hayes chaired the committee. Also serving were E. Paul Jones, the Jefferson County school director, and Mrs. M. L. Gaston, president of the Booker T. Washington Business College. Sterne became liaison officer between the Birmingham Library Board and the Advisory Committee. The board gave the advisory group two goals: to increase circulation at the city's two Negro libraries and to work toward expanding service for blacks in Birmingham and Jefferson County.[38]

The committee began with its first goal, raising the level of library use. The group decided that the inadequacy of resources made available for library service to African Americans explained the decline in book circulation. Birmingham blacks had "made use of the Booker T. Washington and Slossfield Branch libraries proportionate with the money spent on them." But it also understood that convincing the white library board and the city government to expend additional funds on black service would depend largely on the degree to which the community used the resources currently available.[39]

The advisory group began a publicity campaign on the library system's behalf. The committee's members believed that some African Americans hesitated to use library facilities because they felt that libraries were solely for the black elite. "We want to make it clear," the committee explained, "that the library is for the man in 'overalls' as well as for the one in 'tuxedo.'" To communicate its message, the Advisory Committee prepared articles for the local papers, both black and white. It also sent speakers to radio and television stations, churches, schools, industrial sites, and clubs.[40]

The group called on all sectors of the community for support. It asked parents to join the library and to encourage their children and neighbors to do the same. It urged them to discuss books that their children read. The committee asked educators to better integrate library resources into their teaching. It hoped that teachers would encourage students to join the library, bring classes for visits, assign work that required library use, and make their information needs known to the librarians. The committee appealed to the clergy, asking them to promote library use among their congregations and to permit visiting speakers to do the same. It asked employers to commend employees who joined the library and to provide space for deposit stations. Potential patrons were urged to communicate with their librarian regarding the types of books they would like to see in the library. The readings did not need to be of a scholarly nature, according to the committee. Patrons might consider instruction books like "how to make good biscuits" or "how to cultivate a beautiful flower garden." The Advisory Committee involved a host of community leaders to participate in its activities. It invited forty-three ministers, employers, educators, and media personnel to become "co-chairmen" for the Advisory Committee. The committee members were optimistic about their efforts: "We believe, as a result of this concerted community-wide effort, circulation in these two branches will increase overwhelmingly and convincingly."[41]

They were correct; circulation increased 20 percent over the preceding year. The number of enrollments was 60 percent greater. Attendance at the libraries increased by 33 percent. The Advisory Committee had achieved its initial goal. Still, black library service in the Birmingham area was limited to two small branches. The group looked next to expanding service.[42]

The white library board was interested in extending the service it provided to African Americans, but it was uncertain how to proceed. The white group was beginning to flirt with the idea of partial desegregation of the Central Library. In January 1954, Sterne asked for opinions from the board members regarding the future of library service for blacks. The library board was considering a plan to construct a central library for the African-American community using money from a 1953 bond issue. A board member, Mrs. L. S. Evins, objected to this plan. She believed it was redundancy of effort and resources. Evins suggested that the library board open the Central Library to blacks for the limited purposes of reference and research. The suggestion was not adopted. The board decided to delay any action of that sort until "such a time as a ruling is handed down by the Supreme Court on the matter of segregation." They were waiting for the outcome of the *Brown* case, which was currently under litigation.[43]

The Negro Advisory Committee was eager to address the related issues of library expansion and library desegregation. It argued that "Interest, use, need, population, taxation, economy, inequalities, and democracy," all pointed urgently toward an improvement in library facilities for African Americans. The committee invited twelve other black civic leaders to advise it on how money from the bond issue should be spent. These twelve included the PTA president, the president of the traditionally black Miles College, a pastor, two doctors, two principals, club women, a housing project manager, and a mental health worker. Civil-rights attorney Arthur Shores was among those invited. This group met with the white library board and the library director, Fant Thornley, on February 25, 1954, to discuss whether blacks should have a central library or new branches, and where such facilities might be located.[44]

The committee asserted unequivocally that racial integration was the logical solution to Birmingham's problems in the area of black library service. According to the committee's report, "without a single exception, every Negro who was at this meeting first expressed the hope" that Birmingham would integrate its library system. Rather than wasting resources to make special arrangements for the African-American community, the city should keep its money for the renovation of existing facilities. The black leaders believed that Birmingham should also build additional branch libraries where population growth indicated a need, but that each of the library facilities, starting with the Central Library, should be opened to all of Birmingham's citizens.[45]

Expecting a negative response to their call for desegregation, the Negro Advisory Committee provided a second proposal, but it was an expensive one. The group asserted that, if the city chose not to integrate, then Birmingham's African-American population should have its fair share of the bond money. "In as much as Negroes constitute more than 40% of the population of Birmingham," the Advisory Committee reasoned, "it is felt that 40% of the [bond issue] money should be spent" on the black community. Moreover, the attendees contended that "the very nature of the long-standing inequalities," suggested that blacks be given first priority on new spending.[46]

The Negro Advisory Committee argued that if the city would not integrate its libraries, then African Americans should have a conveniently located central library of their own, modern in construction and air conditioned. The building should have adequate space for adult and children's reading rooms, a conference room, a work room, a periodicals room, and an auditorium. The group asserted that the city should hire trained librarians to staff the black central library. In short, the black community leaders insisted that separate facilities be truly equal ones. Before *Brown*, this was a common strategy used by civil rights workers who knew that southern municipalities could not afford to reproduce exactly the public services they provided for whites.[47]

The white library board ultimately decided to construct two libraries for black Birmingham, one near each of the city's largest federal housing projects. Sterne had written a brief letter in response to the Advisory Committee's report. The subject of integration was broached at least twice by the Birmingham Library Board during 1954, but Sterne chose to ignore the committee's call for library desegregation in his letter. Sterne suggested that the Advisory Committee could expect 35 percent of the $500,000 library bond revenue at most, that $75,000 would be a generous sum. At the suggestion of the Advisory Committee, the city used the money to construct a library in the Smithfield community to replace the Booker T. Washington Branch. The location selected was adjacent to Birmingham's largest black housing project and three blocks from its largest black high school. The city built the Smithfield Branch to accommodate at least a few of the guidelines set by the Negro Advisory Committee in 1954; it was dedicated in April of 1956. The city constructed a smaller library for blacks near the Southside housing project in 1957.[48]

Birmingham's Negro Advisory Committee acted as advocates of black libraries as similar groups had in Huntsville and Montgomery. Birmingham was a larger city, however, and it had a longer tradition of black library service than other Alabama cities. By the 1950s, the central question in Birmingham was not whether the black community would have service, but what form that service would take. Rather than creating and sustaining institutions that paralleled the ones for whites that received full public support, the Negro Advisory Committee looked toward integration and equality of service. Months before the *Brown* decision, a year before the Montgomery Bus Boycott, and almost a decade before the Birmingham Demonstrations, these black Birmingham civic leaders presented a clear expression of their dissatisfaction with library segregation, calling for integration of the city's public libraries. Though they were unsuccessful in persuading the city to desegregate the libraries in 1954, their actions provide evidence of the changing attitudes within the leadership of black communities on the eve of the civil rights movement.

The history of segregated libraries is largely one of African Americans working to improve their lives and their social environments within the confines of segregation. Though impeded by social and economic barriers, black communities in Alabama proved strong and enthusiastic supporters of a black public library movement specifically and civic action in general. Black clergy, educators, club women, and librarians were the most active representatives of the communities. They organized support, raised funds, and pressured library boards and municipal governments into action.

Considering the disadvantages that segregation and a legacy of poor education placed upon southern African-American communities, it is remarkable that they maintained such an interest in libraries. Their efforts to initiate public library service were impaired by the economic and social subordination they experienced. The public library movement was, particularly among whites, a middle and upper class effort. Most often it was rooted in the work of women's civic organizations. These were book clubs and library societies created by the wives of merchants, bankers, and professionals, a class of women Carol Smith-Rosenberg calls the "bourgeois matrons."[49]

Thus, in creating a library movement parallel to that of whites, the black community was seemingly impaired not only by a lack of the public funding that white libraries enjoyed but also by a smaller middle class, by the white definition, from which to draw support. Only 3.3 percent of the black population in Montgomery County was classified as engaging in either professional or semi-professional occupations in 1940. In Huntsville, the percentage was 3.8. Black women in urban Alabama were far more likely to be employed than their white counterparts. Most often, they worked as domestic servants for white families.[50]

The black domestics and other African-American female workers lacked the leisure time many middle-class white women enjoyed, but they apparently shared the same inclination to engage in civic improvement. Leaders of black women's clubs were of the black elite, but unlike white groups, rank and file members were often working women of modest, even impoverished, backgrounds. The civic and religious organizations they formed stressed education, self-improvement, community improvement, also racial pride and racial advancement. Through their clubs and their churches, black women in Alabama proved enthusiastic and potent supporters of public libraries.[51]

Black professionals, though few in number, also played an important part. Among the few professions genuinely open to African Americans during the era of segregation were the ministry, teaching, and librarianship. Thus, it was individuals from these professions that provided much of the leadership in the creation of black social and cultural institutions, including public libraries. Black clergymen were among the African-American communities' most educated and most influential individuals. Under their direction black churches often provided "the organizational framework for most activities of the community—

economic, political, and educational endeavors as well as religious ones." In Huntsville and Montgomery, ministers and their congregations provided essential resources and leadership for the black public library movement. Educators also actively involved themselves in library development, since public libraries often assumed responsibility for the literary needs of black schools. The most conspicuous agents who advanced black public libraries were the black librarians. Individuals like Dulcina DeBerry in Huntsville and Bertha Pleasant Williams in Montgomery became pioneers who worked diligently with minimal resources to provide service to a large population that was unaccustomed to library service and that had never enjoyed equal educational opportunities.[52]

African-American business leaders provided additional direction for the black public library movement. Segregation often confined their financial activities to the black community. The economic and social bonds that connected them with their race also gave these individuals a stake in the well being of their African-American communities. Particularly in Birmingham and Huntsville, business people adopted library development as a worthwhile direction for their civic energies. Black business leaders applied their organizational skills and social standing toward establishing community library organizations that worked to initiate and sustain public libraries for African Americans.

The experience in Alabama's cities suggests that African Americans were supportive of their community institutions, raising money, making personal donations, and contributing their own physical labor in the interest of library service. Excluded from the social and cultural institutions of white society and lacking adequate public support, the black communities channeled their energies into creating their own civic infrastructures. African-American library founders rarely articulated the specific goals they had for black branches, nor did they express the motives that led them to act. But the institutions black civic leaders initiated, including their public libraries, served to promote unity among the members of the community. They reinforced a sense of collective identity and, according to Mary Sanford Brown, the community institutions enhanced the "economic health and social consciousness" of a group living under a restrictive social order. During the 1960s, however, black communities would turn their attention away from the "separate but equal" Negro library movement and toward erasing the color line between white public libraries and their own.[53]

# 4
# The Read-In Movement

*Desegregating Alabama's Public
Libraries, 1960–1963*

The desegregation of Alabama's public libraries was a product of the civil rights movement of the 1960s. It resulted from direct action by African-American civil rights workers coupled with federal intervention. The year after the United States Supreme Court's 1954 *Brown* decision, Montgomery's African-American community initiated a bus boycott designed to address abuses in the city's segregated public transportation system. It sparked a decade-long direct action campaign in communities throughout the region. A court order, rather than the economic pressure applied by the boycott, ultimately ended segregation on Montgomery's buses, however. The lesson for the civil rights movement was that direct action would have to create conflict of sufficient magnitude to change public opinion and induce federal intervention. Those working toward desegregation of public libraries took this lesson to heart. Southern blacks had worked to improve library service for their race throughout the first half of the twentieth century, but in 1960 they began to adopt the tactics of direct action, particularly the sit-in demonstration, to challenge the institution of library segregation itself.

Some reform-minded librarians had greeted the 1950s with an unwarranted optimism where public library segregation was concerned. In 1948, Emily Miller Danton, Birmingham Public Library's director, conducted a survey to gauge other southern libraries' practices in regard to black patrons and staff. Her interest stemmed from a debate in Birmingham over whether the library should allow black librarians to attend staff meetings. In the published version of the study in *Library Journal,* entitled "South Does Less Restricting," Danton wrote that southern cities were improving their services to blacks and that white librarians' attitudes were becoming more open to the idea of complete desegregation of library facilities. Still, only one among the twenty-one libraries she surveyed admitted blacks without restriction.[1]

The biracial Southern Regional Council conducted a more complete survey in 1954, finding that library desegregation was on the rise in the South. In the twelve years since Eliza Atkins Gleason's study of library service to African Americans, the number of integrated public libraries in the region had increased from four to fifty-nine. The figure was not as meaningful as it seemed in terms of the number of blacks served, however. For the most part, only those towns and cities with small black populations chose to integrate. Many were located "in the hills of Kentucky and the flatlands of western Texas, where Negroes compose 3%, 10%, perhaps 12% of all residents." In most southern cities where African Americans comprised significant numbers, and all of those in Alabama, the racial status quo prevailed. L. D. Reddick complained that "from Washington, D.C. to the Gulf of Mexico and from the Atlantic Ocean to the westernmost fringes of Texas and Oklahoma the public places are few and far between where a Negro may sit down and read a book." Because southern libraries lacked the will or capacity to enact change from within their own governing structures, southern public libraries, including those in Alabama, became ensnared in the angry and often dangerous direct action activities of the early 1960s.[2]

The library desegregation protests that began in 1960 were part of a larger struggle for civil rights in the United States. Public libraries became scenes of sit-in demonstrations not only in Alabama, but throughout the urban South. Libraries were popular targets for direct action because they were conspicuous public institutions most often located in the center of southern cities. Also, public libraries were ideally agencies of democracy and of culture, above such base impulses as prejudice. The exclusion of African Americans from these libraries presented a powerful image of the troublesome contradictions that characterized America's racial dilemma.

There was more to the library integration efforts than symbolism, however. At its core, the movement to desegregate public libraries in Alabama was an indigenous one driven by local concerns. By 1960, blacks were demanding access to the same civic institutions their white neighbors enjoyed. The activists who sought equal public library service, particularly the student demonstrators, were more educated than their parents and grandparents had been. Bernard Lee, an Alabama State College student and activist, vocalized this trend in 1960: "My grandfather had only a prayer to help him. I have a prayer and an education." It was only logical that schooled blacks like Lee would place a priority on securing equal access to their local public libraries.[3]

In 1960, a highly public sit-in demonstration in Danville, Virginia, resulted in a federal ruling that segregation in public libraries was unconstitutional, thereby setting the stage for public library protests throughout the South. On April 2, thirteen black high school students entered the segregated main library in Danville and refused to leave. Following their unsuccessful attempt to obtain library service, the students filed suit in federal district court. The fact that the library was housed in an antebellum home that had served as the last capitol of the Confederate government following its flight from Richmond gave the controversy a symbolic significance and evoked an emotional response from some whites. The federal district judge ruled in favor of the black teens, resulting in the judiciary's first express statement that library segregation was unacceptable. In a citywide advisory referendum, Danville's white citizens voted overwhelmingly in favor of closing the library to avoid integration. In 1960 and 1961, library protests spread to Petersburg, Virginia; Greenville, South Carolina; Memphis, Tennessee; and Jackson, Mississippi. The early "read-in" demonstrations often led to arrests and sometimes to library closures as in Danville. Occasionally, they resulted in violence. Library administrators in Alabama observed these events and began to prepare for the confrontation they feared would come to their own institutions. Among the Alabama cities to become involved in the library segregation debate between 1960 and 1963 were Mobile, Montgomery, Huntsville, Birmingham, and Anniston.[4]

## MOBILE, 1961

At the beginning of the civil-rights era, white Mobile remained dedicated to a policy of strict segregation. The Davis Avenue Branch served as the port city's only public library facility open to African Americans from 1931 until Mobile integrated its libraries in 1961. In 1954, the library board had reacted to the Supreme Court's decision in the *Brown v. Board of Education* case by reaffirming its commitment to preserving segregation in the public libraries. Under segregation, the city had attempted to maintain at least the appearance of an equitable arrangement, however; it even began an expansion of the Negro branch in 1960. In addition to whatever benign motives drove white Mobile to help sustain black library service, the maintenance of segregation was also a factor. Library director Arless B. Nixon wrote of the Davis Avenue library in 1952: "This branch library must be kept attractive if we are to keep the negroes from coming to the Main Library."[5]

The library board and Mobile's mayor had changed their minds on the issue of library segregation by the end of 1961. During the previous year, *Giles v. Library Advisory Committee of Danville, Virginia* established that segregation in libraries operated by state, city, or county governments was unlawful. In Danville, the city manager closed the public library rather than allow any kind of race mixing in the facility. When the library reopened it was only to provide service to those who already held library cards. The city claimed that the library was "overtaxed" by the demands of its patrons. The Federal District Court was unconvinced by the charade and it ordered Danville to integrate its library. In Mobile, the library board believed it was a matter of time before their own library became the scene of a sit-in or some other direct action on the part of the city's black citizens. The board members also knew, after the events in Danville, that if the issue of library segregation were pressed, their chances of prevailing in the federal courts were remote.[6]

In 1960, the board and the library staff began to prepare for the conflict they feared would come. At its March meeting, the board issued a statement to guide the actions of Mobile's white librarians should a demonstration occur. The library staff was not to serve African Americans, but was to allow them to remain in the library so long as they were "orderly in behavior." Recent events in Memphis motivated the board in its moderate response. In that city, police forcibly ejected demonstrators from the public library. The Mobile library board believed that such action only served the interests of the demonstrators. It was "desirous of avoiding giving [the activists] any chance for publicity. . . ."[7]

The demonstrations at the Mobile Public Library began one year later. In March of 1961, blacks began visiting the main library requesting service. In April, a group of African-American civic leaders calling themselves the "Citizens' Committee" submitted a petition to the city commission calling for the desegregation of the public library system. The group asserted that all of Mobile's citizens should be "permitted to have access to lounge, reading and all other accommodations and facilities of the main library and all branch libraries, bookmobiles, et cetera, sans any form of proscription based on race, color, or creed." The black leaders reminded the commission of the precedent set in the *Giles* decision, that the federal courts were on the side of Mobile's African-

American community. Another civil rights group, the Non-Partisan Voters League, met with library board chairperson S. P. Gaillard the following month to argue for library desegregation.[8]

The pressure applied to the library board continued to build, and by November of 1961 it was considering some type of revision of its segregation policy. The board members decided to consult the city commission before making any fundamental changes, however. They instructed Guenter Jansen, the library director, that until the library board could take further action, he should "use his best judgement" in handling any situation that might arise regarding the city's African-American population.[9]

The events of the following week forced the library board to accelerate its planning. Over two days, approximately twenty-four blacks staged sit-ins at the main library. As a part of their demonstration, the activists attempted to charge books, and also to use the library's lounges and drinking fountains. After the second day of demonstrations, Davis Avenue Branch librarian Virginia Smith called Jansen to inquire about the status of the board's plans for blacks. According to some of her patrons at the Negro branch, teachers at the African-American high school and junior high had announced to their classes that blacks were now free to use the main library. Jansen, who faced the prospect of droves of black youths appearing at the library's doorstep, called Frank B. Frazer, the library board chair, for instruction. The next morning, Frazer met with Mayor George E. McNally to solicit his opinion on the library situation. The mayor lent his approval to a revision of the library board's segregation policy; he "saw no objection to bona fide use of the library by Negroes."[10]

Frazer called a special meeting of the library board on November 13 to discuss the possibility of opening the main library to African Americans. He described the events of the past few days to the board; its members discussed the matter for about an hour. With the likelihood of continued visits to the main library by blacks, especially black students, with the mayor uninterested in defending segregation at the public library, and with no legal basis to justify their policy of exclusion, the board decided to adopt an interim policy allowing limited use of the main library by African Americans.[11]

The library board designed its new policy to allow black citizens to use the main library for reference work and, in special cases, to charge books. The board asserted that "the Davis Avenue Branch Library which has recently been substantially expanded, is designed to provide for the normal and reasonable needs of our Negro citizens. . . . " Blacks were to use their branch library for most services, as in the past. If they needed a book owned by the main library, they were still to request the item through the Davis Avenue Branch's librarian. But the board added that blacks could use the reference materials at the main library if they had a legitimate need. The board also permitted general circulation to African Americans at the main facility if there would be "undue delay" in transporting the requested books to the black branch or where "undue hardship from the standpoint of travel distance" resulted from requiring service at Davis Avenue. The determination of what constituted "undue delay" and "undue hardship" was left to the discretion of Jansen and the rest of the Mobile Public Library's staff. Their decisions were to be made based on the seemingly conflicting criteria of "the recent interpretations of the law by the Federal courts" and "the long-established customs of this community."[12]

Guenter Jansen's execution of the new policy resulted in a relatively quiet and peaceful demise of library segregation in Mobile. Jansen apparently had sympathy for the blacks in Mobile who sought integrated library service. His interpretation of the interim policy leaned toward a general inclusion of black patrons. According to segregationist opponents, Jansen actively encouraged black patronage, welcoming African Americans who called to inquire about the new policy. The librarian also began issuing library cards to blacks at the main facility, though the board had not expressly given him the authority to do so in their instructions. The entire affair was kept quiet. There was no publicity surrounding the desegregation of Mobile's library system and only black leaders were officially informed of the library board's action. By the beginning of 1962, Jansen and the library board had presented white Mobile with a fait accompli. According to the *Wilson Library Bulletin*, blacks and whites were "using the library together in complete harmony."[13]

Whites who actively opposed the library board's action were enthusiastic, but few in number. Their main criticism was the covert nature of the library's integration. One letter of complaint called the action a "clandestine agreement with Negro agitation groups." Another inquired, "How could this be done without any notice to the public?" It added, "If we do not want integration in our schools we must not allow it in our other institutions." The most vocal complainant, E. L. Cross, was invited to present his views to the library board. He railed that he had found the library "full of Negroes sitting at tables pretending to do reference work!" Cross suggested that Jansen was in league with civil rights groups and that the library board was being "brainwashed for integration," possibly by communists. Though the complainant insisted that he could get "thousands of signatures protesting this crime," it proved to be an empty threat. Mobile enjoyed a quiet and relatively early transition to integrated library service.[14]

## MONTGOMERY, 1962

Public library desegregation came with more difficulty in Montgomery than it had in Mobile. The white response to the boycott of the city buses in 1955 and 1956 provided evidence of interracial tension in the state's capital city that previously had lain hidden beneath the surface. By the end of the public transportation crisis, the politics of race had become an intrinsic part of civic life in Montgomery. Local white leaders found that they could use issues of race for their own political gain and they rushed to associate themselves with the forces of massive resistance. Many city officials joined the white Citizens' Council in 1955 and 1956 and the city government proved intransigent in its insistence on segregation of civic facilities. In 1959, the city commission voted to close all fourteen of Montgomery's parks in response to a desegregation order by the federal district court. It sold all of the animals in the city zoo and filled in the municipal swimming pool. When the federal district court ordered the city to desegregate its public library in 1962, the municipal government considered closing that institution as it had the city's parks. Ultimately, it settled on a plan of "vertical integration" designed to keep white and black patrons standing during their visits to the library. Their intention was to prevent the races from sharing library tables. The integration of the public library was an event of considerable public interest, marked by Klan activity at the library building and also by an outcry by the city's white moderates against the city's actions.

African-American college students began the challenge of the public library's segregation policy. Inspired by the student sit-ins in Greensboro, North Carolina, and in other southern cities, students from the all-black Alabama State College became active participants in local civil rights activity. In February of 1960, Bernard Lee led more than half of the Alabama State student body in a protest march and prayer meeting at the capitol building. As a part of the February protest, Lee and eight others staged a sit-in at the segregated snack bar at the Montgomery

County Courthouse. Leon Rice, one of the participants, promised that, "as soon as they serve us [at the lunch counter], and we've finished eating, then we'll go across the street to the public library." For their integrationist activities, Lee, Rice, and seven others were expelled.[15]

Two of the expelled Alabama State students, Elroy Emory and St. John Dixon, kept Rice's promise by attempting to patronize Montgomery's public library on May 17. They had decided to mark the sixth anniversary of the *Brown* decision by staging another sit-in at the cafeteria of the state capitol. After being rebuffed at the capitol building, the youths walked down Goat Hill to the city's Carnegie library. The librarians there refused to serve the two activists, referring them to the black Union Street Branch. The staff allowed them to fill out applications for library cards and no charges were filed.[16]

The event that ultimately resulted in the desegregation of Montgomery's public library system occurred two years later. On March 15, 1962, eighteen-year-old Robert L. Cobb, a recent graduate of Montgomery's Booker T. Washington High School, led five other youths in a forty-five minute sit-in at the main library. Though they denied association with any particular group, FBI sources asserted that the youths had received training in civil rights activism under Reverend Solomon Seay, Sr. and attorney Solomon Seay, Jr., leaders of the city's most important civil rights organization, the Montgomery Improvement Association (MIA), created in 1955 to direct the bus boycott.[17]

The activists met at a local black church and walked to the library. The group arrived at the new building on Lawrence Street, which housed both the public library and the city museum, about noon. Upon their entrance, a librarian inquired in a loud voice, "May I help you?" and then informed them that "we do not serve Negroes in this library." The youths split up; some used the card catalog, others sat at the tables. Cobb attempted to visit the museum and was refused entrance.[18]

Library director Farris Martin was away from the library, but returned upon learning of the demonstration. Martin called the young activists into his office where they held a "closed-door meeting." According to Martin, the youths were well dressed, polite, and apparently well educated. They would not directly answer Farris Martin's questions, however, and refused to give their names. One youth, whom the others referred to as their "secretary," made all of his replies to the library director in Spanish. During the confrontation, Martin told Cobb and the others that they would either have to leave the library or he would summon the police. The demonstrators stated that they would not comply. They continued their sit-in for several more minutes, but left before detectives from the Montgomery Police Department arrived.[19]

Cobb filed suit in federal district court in April 1962 seeking the desegregation of the Montgomery's main public library and its museum. African-American civil rights attorney Charles Conley represented Cobb in the suit with the assistance of Rufus Lewis, a prominent black leader in Montgomery, and Fred Gray, the city's foremost black lawyer. According to an FBI informant referred to in Bureau records as "T-1," the city desired to settle the case out of court. City attorneys knew there was no legal basis for library segregation. They also knew that the presiding judge would be unsympathetic to their position; Judge Frank M. Johnson Jr., was an independent-minded Republican from Alabama's hill country who was instrumental in dismantling segregation in Alabama.[20]

The city leaders offered to integrate their public library with a minimum of publicity, just as Mobile had done, but Cobb's lawyer insisted on a public trial. According to the FBI informant, Lewis and Gray were amenable to the city's solution. Charles Conley was not; he wanted a trial with full publicity and a judgement by Johnson. Apparently, the issue was a broader one than the integration of one Alabama library for Conley. The publicity and judicial precedent resulting from a trial would further the larger movement for equal access to public facilities. The city's attorneys made it clear that though they had little chance of success in a trial, they would have to create the appearance of mounting a vigorous defense "for political reasons." Lawyers on both sides also believed that if the library were integrated after a public court battle, the potential for interracial violence at the city library would be greatly increased.[21]

At the trial, the city based its defense on an argument that the library and museum were not actually segregated. According to city attorneys, Martin had prohibited the use of the library facilities to Cobb because he held no library card, not because of his race. They asserted that Cobb could have become a library member had he applied. There "were no color restrictions" in regard to membership. In fact there was "possibly one" African American who already held a library card for the main facility. Martin had only called the police on Cobb and the others, the city contended, because they posed a "disciplinary problem."[22]

Not surprisingly, Judge Johnson was unconvinced by the city's argument. In his August 7 decision, he ruled that the library and city museum were being operated on a racially segregated basis. Montgomery had more than forty-six thousand black citizens in 1962. Johnson found it inconceivable that there was only "possibly one" among this number that held a library card "unless there is and has been an effective exclusion of members of that race." He issued an injunction against the city commission, the library board, and the director barring racial discrimination at the Montgomery City Library.[23]

The next evening, August 8, the city commission met with the library and museum boards to discuss Judge Johnson's ruling. Commissioner Frank Parks made it known to the press that he would push for closing the city library rather than acquiescing to the court order. He intended to terminate service at the black branch on Cleveland Avenue, as well. Parks was not bluffing; he was the only remaining member of the previous commission that had closed all fourteen of Montgomery's parks in 1959 to prevent their integration. Though the participants refused to comment publicly on what had transpired at the August 8 meeting, it became apparent that more moderate voices had prevailed. The library would remain open.[24]

On the evening of August 8, shortly after the close of the secret meeting of the city officials, maintenance workers arrived at the main library and at the black Cleveland Avenue Branch, and they began removing all of the tables and chairs. Remaining tight-lipped regarding the city's plan of action, library board chair W. E. Goodwin quipped to reporters that workers might be removing the furniture to wax the floors. A cameraman from Montgomery's WSFA-TV captured the event; the parade of library furniture made the ten o'clock news.[25]

The library opened on the morning of August 9. The city had decided to comply with the court order by initiating "stand-up integration." It would allow blacks and whites to use the same library facilities. It would not provide the opportunity for the races to sit and read in the same space, however. No African Americans arrived to use the main library on the first day.[26]

At the city's new Negro branch on Cleveland Avenue, African-American children made the most of the "vertical integration." The branch had lost its seating facilities just as the main library had, but according to librarian Bertha Williams, "the kids made a mockery of it." The children brought folding chairs to the library and some carried typewriter tables from home.[27]

Cobb became the first African American to take advantage of the desegregation order on Saturday, August 11. At about 11:15 A.M., he entered the main library and asked for a membership card. The librarian approved his application. There was no disturbance. Cobb's visit was unexpected because it was generally understood that visits by members of Montgomery's black community would begin the following Monday.[28]

The general integration of the Montgomery City Library came on Monday, August 13, under the watchful eyes of Klansmen, police, and federal agents. African Americans began to appear at the main library on Lawrence Street shortly after 9:00 A.M., but the Klansmen had arrived already. According to FBI observers at the scene, known members of "Confederate Den 11" of the Knights of the Ku Klux Klan were in the immediate vicinity of the library as it opened, walking past the building on the sidewalk, cruising by in cars, and occasionally meeting in small groups at the street corner near the library building. The danger of violence at the city library was greatest at this point, because no uniformed police officers were present to protect the black patrons. Klansmen did not approach the arriving blacks, however, and Assistant Chief of Police Marvin Stanley arrived after several minutes with a contingent of uniformed officers. The police remained at the library for the rest of the day, observing the Klansmen and preventing them from gathering near the library.[29]

More than a dozen African Americans registered at the main library on August 13. Director Farris Martin stood at the door of the Montgomery City Library with a detective positioned nearby. Martin kept the doors locked, admitting patrons in ones and twos. He permitted only a few patrons in the building at one time, leaving people to wait outside before receiving permission to enter. According to the *Montgomery Advertiser*, whites using the library expressed no visible concern over the presence of blacks in the building. The new library members were "generally ignored by the white patrons." The only individuals Martin was compelled to eject from the building were a newspaper reporter and a television cameraman. Cobb was one of those served on the morning of August 13. He charged a copy of Shakespeare's *Much Ado About Nothing*.[30]

As blacks integrated the main library, white patrons began using the Cleveland Avenue Branch for the first time. Bertha Williams remembers that whites, many of whom were employees at the nearby Maxwell Air Force Base, began to visit and faced various forms of harassment by other whites. Policemen stood on the corner in front of the former black library writing down the automobile license tag numbers

Montgomery City-County Library, 1961. Klansmen gathered here in August of 1962 in opposition to the court-ordered integration of the facility. Courtesy Montgomery City-County Library.

of whites who used the facility. One angry white woman came into the Cleveland Avenue library and complained to Williams about being questioned by an officer about her presence there. Others received harassing telephone calls. According to Williams, "They got scared and stopped coming."[31]

The library integration sparked a lively debate in the editorial pages of the city's newspapers. Moderate whites believed that the removal of the tables and chairs was absurd and an embarrassment to the city. The policies of the public library were a reflection of the "cultural level" of the community. Moderates reasoned that even whites in Montgomery who were not "integrationists" or who even believed in white supremacy could at least tolerate Negro use of "a public facility to better their minds." Historian and Montgomery native J. Mills Thornton III argued that the commission had already "plundered the city of all its major recreational areas," and that with its action at the library it sought to "deny our citizenry access to its intellectual heritage." Writing in favor of the city's action was J. C. Kendrick, the executive secretary of the Montgomery white Citizens' Council; he also warned that the electorate would be unkind to politicians who failed to support segregation.

Montgomery's Cleveland Avenue Branch, 1961. On this corner, city police recorded license plate numbers of whites who patronized this former "Negro branch" following its integration. The white visitors received harassing phone calls shortly thereafter. Courtesy Montgomery City-County Library.

Another citizen heralded the commission's action, writing, "Hurrah!" for the removal of the library furniture. "Now let's go further and close and lock the doors . . . Let's keep a few places where we can still say *'White Only.'"*[32]

By the end of September 1962, the controversy had abated in Montgomery and interest in the public library situation had waned. Newspaper coverage ended in mid-August. On September 24, FBI observers reported that the danger of violence over the desegregation of the Montgomery City Library had passed. Blacks were using the main library freely. No disturbance had resulted and the white public no longer exhibited any visible interest in the matter. The board quietly returned the missing furniture to the libraries.[33]

## HUNTSVILLE, 1962

Racial integration in general came more gently in Huntsville than in other Alabama cities like Birmingham, Montgomery, and Selma, and the desegregation of the public library there was consistent with this trend. The federal presence in the Tennessee Valley helped to make it the most economically and racially stable region in the state. The population of Huntsville was more diverse in origin than most of Alabama, and a sizable number of its citizens were scientists and technicians employed in government-sponsored space-age projects. They had found little appeal in the race-baiting politics of George Wallace and others of his kind. As a result, the city was spared the "fire hose and snarling dog" scenes that sullied the civic reputations of Huntsville's neighbors.[34]

The library board desegregated the Huntsville Public Library in late 1962 at the prompting of its librarian, Richard J. Covey. Covey was Canadian by birth, but was raised in Oklahoma. He came to Alabama in 1956 to become library director at Gadsden. Huntsville's library board hired him in 1960 at the recommendation of departing librarian Eleanor Murphy. Two years after his arrival, Covey informed the library board that he had been named in an "omnibus integration suit" pertaining to the Gadsden Public Library. He warned that similar action was in store for Huntsville if nothing was done about its segregation policy. In response, the board quietly ended its exclusion of black readers at the main library. Judy Purinton, a student at the University of Alabama in Huntsville and part-time page during the early 1960s, remembers: "There was no confrontation or angry words in our library . . . just a quiet changing of the status quo."[35]

## BIRMINGHAM, 1963

Birmingham is a city whose history conjures images of marching children and police brutality. Civil rights leaders had banked on a violent response from the lame duck police commissioner Eugene "Bull" Connor in 1963 to create a drama designed to show the nation racial segregation at its ugliest. The ultimate result was the Civil Rights Act of 1964. Most civil rights workers indigenous to Birmingham did not carry such grandiose aims for their actions, however. Their objectives were more immediate. They sought the removal of degrading "white" and "colored" signs on dining rooms, rest rooms, and drinking fountains in downtown Birmingham. They wanted access to public accommodations, like lunch counters. They desired better educational opportunities for their children and better economic opportunities for the city's black workers. African Americans wanted the desegregation of civic resources, like parks, theaters, and the public libraries. Not all of the events of this day-to-day struggle captured national attention, but they did help to rectify old injustices and awaken white moderates to the need for civic reform and racial conciliation. The willingness of moderate whites to accept change by 1963 was more a result of judicial and economic duress applied by blacks than of a genuine repudiation of long held racial attitudes, however. The Birmingham Library Board and the city library director, Fant Thornley, reflected this moderate impulse in April by integrating the city's public libraries in response to two well-planned sit-in demonstrations by students from Miles College.

The Birmingham Library Board's best chance for a quiet desegregation of the libraries had come in 1954. In that year, the board's Negro Advisory Committee had called for an end to library segregation in the city and at least two of the library board members had expressed sympathy for the advisory committee's position. The board possessed the authority to change its segregation policy, since no state or local law required library segregation in Birmingham. The majority of the board remained committed to the exclusion of blacks from the main library and from "white" branches, however. The quality of race relations in Birmingham disintegrated quickly after 1954, leaving a city government that was, by 1960, unmistakably intransigent regarding matters of race.[36]

Bull Connor was elected in 1957 riding a wave of racial tension and along with J. T. "Jabbo" Waggoner, and Arthur Hanes, comprised a city commission that was committed to seeing that Birmingham remained "the most segregated city in America." Compromise on the subject of segregation in the city's public library system, or on any other racial matter in Birmingham, seemed remote by 1960. In that year, Harrison Salisbury of the *New York Times* reported from Birmingham that "every inch of middle ground has been fragmented by the emotional dynamite of racism" and there was evidence that the city government was even operating in collusion with the Ku Klux Klan to stem civil rights activism.[37]

In 1961, Reverend Fred Shuttlesworth, the leader of Birmingham's largest civil rights organization, the Alabama Christian Movement for Human Rights (ACMHR), sued the city in United States District Court, asking for the desegregation of Birmingham's recreational facilities. Judge H. Hobart Grooms ruled in Shuttlesworth's favor, ordering an end of segregation in the city's theaters, auditoriums, ball parks, playgrounds, and at "all types of entertainment, games, sports, amusement or recreation therein to which the public is admitted." The commission vowed to close all facilities that fell under the ruling, even Legion Field where The University of Alabama's Crimson Tide played football, rather than to integrate. As in Montgomery, the municipal government closed the city's parks and its swimming pools. It closed the municipal golf courses, filling in the holes with cement.[38]

There was evidence that the city commission might also close the public libraries if the issue of racial separation was pressed. The city's libraries were not subject to the court order that resulted from *Shuttlesworth v. Gaylord*. But when Commissioner Hanes was asked whether he would also close the schools and libraries to avoid desegregating, he replied: "If they integrate, it will be at gun point." Responsibility for the city's agencies was divided among the three commissioners. Bull Connor was the Commissioner of Public Safety, a post he used to make the Birmingham Police Department his "personal fiefdom," but the city's public libraries also came under his supervision. Though his appearances at library board meetings were extremely rare, Connor was an ex officio member of the board. Considering the racial climate in Birmingham and the influence arch-segregationist Commissioner Bull Connor had over the library system, the prospects for a voluntary integration of the public libraries seemed remote in 1961 and 1962.[39]

Against this backdrop, an African-American woman named Lola Hendricks visited Birmingham's central public library in June 1962. She requested a book. The circulation librarian refused to serve Hendricks, "because she was a Negro." The librarian invited her unwelcome patron to visit one of the city's Negro branches, instead. She told Hendricks that if neither of the black branches held the book, a black librarian could request that the item be sent from the main library to the branch.[40]

In July, Lola Hendricks filed suit in United States District Court seeking the desegregation of the public libraries. Her suit, supported by Shuttlesworth and the ACMHR, was combined with that of three other black citizens of Birmingham and an African-American minister from Louisville, Kentucky, asking for, besides integration of the libraries, the desegregation of the airport motel and all public buildings in the city. Among those named as defendants were Commissioners Connor, Hanes, and Waggoner, and also the individual members of the library board.[41]

While the litigants waited for a decision in the Hendricks case, the political situation in Birmingham changed dramatically. In the spring of 1963, voters rejected the strong-arm politics of Connor, Hanes, and Waggoner in favor of a more moderate government led by Albert Bout-

well. The closing of the parks and other recreational facilities had awak-
ened moderate whites to the need to reform their city government.
Also, Connor and the other commissioners had alienated white businessmen who wanted to make concessions to black leaders rather than
face economic boycotts and sit-in demonstrations. They were learning
that maintaining segregation in downtown stores and restaurants was
bad for business. It only worsened Birmingham's already tarnished civic
reputation and it drew the resentment of black consumers. The image-
conscious business leaders joined with an unlikely coalition of blacks,
labor unions, newspapers, and civic reformers to oust Connor's government in a runoff election on April 2.[42]

The demonstrations that the Southern Christian Leadership Conference (SCLC) initiated the next day, April 3, would change the face
of American race relations, but in the early days of the Birmingham
Campaign it seemed that the protest might be a failure. Considering
the recent election of the more conciliatory Boutwell government, even
sympathetic whites, including Attorney General Robert Kennedy, believed that the SCLC's actions were poorly timed. Boutwell responded
to the campaign: "I urge everyone, white and Negro, to calmly ignore
what is now being attempted in Birmingham." Most did; the protest
received little local or national press during the first half of April.[43]

Despite the initial shortage of popular support for the civil rights
protests in the city, students from Birmingham's black Miles College
carried out two sit-ins at the main public library, the first on or about
April 9 and the second on April 10.[44] Also on April 10, state Circuit
Judge W. A. Jenkins, Jr., enjoined Martin Luther King, Jr., and 132
other civil rights leaders from demonstrating. It was a low point in the
Birmingham movement. The SCLC was having difficulty recruiting
marchers, and the bail bond program was bankrupt. King was days
away from violating the injunction and intentionally going to jail in a
last-ditch effort to draw support for the Birmingham Campaign.[45]

Miles College students remained active during this difficult period.
They already had been deeply engaged in civil rights activity for three
years when King and SCLC came to Birmingham. Lucious H. Pitts,
the college president, actively encouraged Miles students to challenge
segregation, even holding group meetings at his home. In 1960, students from Miles and Daniel Payne Colleges gathered in Ingram Park
for a "Prayer Vigil for Freedom." Twelve were arrested and white vigi-
lantes assaulted one of the students and his family in retaliation for the
vigil. In 1961, seven hundred students from the school joined in adopt-

ing a five-page manifesto condemning the practice of de jure segregation and calling on the city commission to rescind Birmingham's segregation ordinances. The manifesto, distributed around Birmingham,
argued that segregation was "not in keeping with the ideas of democracy and Christianity," and warned that the students did not intend to
"wait complacently" for their civil rights.[46]

U. W. Clemon—a Miles student who would later become Alabama's
first African-American federal judge—was among the students who attempted to present the manifesto to the city commission. In 1963,
Clemon would participate in one of the protests at the downtown library, but he was just a first semester freshman at Miles during the
summer of 1961. He fell in with the group of young people by chance
as he was walking across the Miles campus, but once the students arrived at City Hall, they drafted Clemon to read the document to the
commissioners. Before he could begin, Safety Commissioner Bull Connor asked Clemon to identify himself. Upon learning that the student
was from Westfield—just outside the city limits—Connor asserted that
Clemon was an "outside agitator" and could not speak before the commission. Another student took his place. Clemon remembers that after
the meeting a policeman, whom he believed to be acting on Connor's
orders, told Clemon that he had "better be out of town by sundown."[47]

Miles College students followed up on the manifesto in 1962 by
promoting a "Selective Buying Campaign," a boycott of downtown
businesses designed to coerce businessmen into desegregating lunch
counters, rest rooms, and drinking fountains and to open sales jobs to
African Americans. The Miles students adopted the slogan, "Wear
Your Old Clothes for Freedom," and groups of young men from the
college walked the downtown sidewalks wearing Miles shirts as an in-
ducement for blacks to comply with the boycott. The campaign resulted in an eighty to 85 percent drop in Negro buying within its first
month.[48]

When the SCLC came to Birmingham in the spring of 1963, Miles
College students joined in its desegregation campaign, which its leaders
called "Project C." The students listened to speeches by King and other
civil rights leaders at mass meetings held at the Sixteenth Street Baptist
Church. The mass meetings aroused indignation and fortitude among
Birmingham blacks, particularly the youths who comprised the rank
and file of the Birmingham demonstrations. The speeches "stirred your
blood," former Miles student Shelly Millender recalls, and they left a
feeling that civil rights were "worth dying for."[49]

The following September, the Sixteenth Street church would be rocked by the deadly explosion of a Klansman's bomb, but during that spring it was the nucleus of the SCLC campaign in Birmingham. The students would return to the church on Sixteenth Street on mornings after the mass meetings to receive assignments from SCLC organizers Wyatt T. Walker and Andrew Young. Miles students carried out lunch counter sit-ins at four downtown stores on April 3. The following week their target would be the Birmingham Public Library.[50]

As a result of the segregation policy they sought to eliminate, none of the students or their leaders had ever been inside the downtown main library in Birmingham. They knew little about the facility and needed information regarding the location of the various departments and the general layout of the building. Wyatt Walker recruited Addine "Deenie" Drew, an adult advisor to the Miles students, to visit the downtown library in advance of the actual demonstration to obtain the information the protesters required. Drew was particularly "fair" in coloration and could easily pass as white. Drew's husband, John, was an insurance executive in the firm owned by Birmingham's African-American millionaire, A. G. Gaston. He and Addine were leaders among the black bourgeoisie. They were close friends of the Kings, and their home served, at times, as a headquarters for civil rights activity during the Birmingham Demonstrations.[51]

Walker instructed Drew to pose as a white society matron. Dressing the part in her blue and white silk dress and hat, Drew made her way to the Birmingham library. Walker had instructed a driver to let Drew off a block away from her destination, so as to maintain her anonymity. A frightened Addine Drew entered the library and walked its reading rooms and halls unhindered. She took note of all the departments and means of entrance and egress. From a pay telephone in the library she called Walker, who was at the SCLC headquarters at the A. G. Gaston Motel. Drew related what she had learned, and then she left.[52]

As visible participants in the civil rights movement, to some extent danger was always present for the Drews. For Addine, however, her lonely mission at the segregated downtown library was among the most frightening experiences of her life. As she walked back to the Gaston Motel by herself, Drew was so shaken that she had to "look down at my feet and tell them to keep walking."[53]

Drew had yet to complete her role in the affair, however. On or about April 9, she accompanied three Miles students in a sit-in at the Birmingham Public Library. Clemon was a sophomore in the spring of

Sit-in at the Birmingham Public Library in 1963. Left to right: Catherine Jones, Sandra Edwards, U. W. Clemon. Copyright *Birmingham News*, 2001. All rights reserved. Reprinted with permission.

1963. He, along with Sandra Edwards, Catherine Jones, and Addine Drew entered the library building. They did not request service of any kind or membership, but they sat and read as white patrons quietly stared. No police came, and the students left without incident.[54]

Walker ordered a second and larger contingent of students to sit in at the library on April 10. Meeting in the basement of the Sixteenth Street Baptist Church, Walker told the group of twelve to synchronize their watches and leave the church individually. They were to converge on the library at a specified time, entering from different directions. Walker appointed Shelly Millender—an ex-serviceman who was older than the others—as the spokesperson for the group.[55]

As Millender approached the library building through Lynn Park, two white men looked and gestured toward him. They began walking, taking a path to intersect with Millender's. "I was really afraid that day," Millender recalls. He remembers wishing that if he were to be beaten, he would have at least liked for the event to be captured by news cameras.[56]

Rather than attacking Millender, however, the men fell in behind as

Miles College student speaks to librarians during the April 1963 sit-in at the Birmingham Public Library. Copyright *Birmingham News*, 2001. All rights reserved. Reprinted with permission.

he entered the library. The other students arrived, and they dispersed throughout the building, sitting at tables and reading books. Millender went to the public service desk and asked to join the library. The two whites who had followed him, as it turned out, were reporters tipped off by Wyatt Walker. They began snapping photographs and television cameras ran as Millender spoke to the librarian on duty. She informed him that Birmingham had a library for blacks in the suburb of Smithfield and he should apply there. Millander remembers that he and the white librarian got into "quite a little skirmish in terms of rhetoric." Subsequently, he took a seat with some of the other students.[57]

The police came to the library, but seemed reluctant to jail the protesters. They consulted with one another and made telephone calls, but did not arrest the students. Eventually, the students left after staying at the library for about forty-five minutes. "We were there to get arrested," Millender explains. The crowd of young whites that met them

as they departed remained non-violent. Millender assumed it was because they were the studious sort, since they had been in the library.[58]

Fant Thornley, the director of Birmingham's library system, found
himself in a difficult position. He later told the board that he "did not
feel that the students had any bona fide desire for library service," that
they "were merely part of the demonstrations taking place throughout
the City." Thornley had a responsibility to execute the directives of the
library board, which had never rescinded its segregation policy. But the
Birmingham Public Library was already the subject of a case in federal
district court; it was only a matter of time before the library would be
integrated by federal injunction.[59]

The library director may have also sensed a weakening of the city's
and the board's resolve to preserve segregation. The defeat of Connor,
Hanes, and Waggoner in the April 2 runoff election meant that Thornley had less to fear from the city's hard-line segregationists. White
moderates in the city were clearly interested in civic reform and had
become more open to making concessions to black demands. Prior to
the election, there was a real danger that the incumbent city commission would choose to close the library rather than integrate it.

Thornley called a special meeting of the library board the next day,
April 11. He apparently related that the library had served the students in some fashion. Thornley asked for the board's approval of his
handling of the situation, and he asked for instructions should another
demonstration occur. Thornley explained that the Miles students were
quiet and decorous, and violated no library rules other than its customary exclusion of Negroes. Also, the students eventually left the library
"voluntarily and without incident or disturbance."[60]

The board discussed the matter "at some length," after which it
unanimously adopted a resolution integrating Birmingham's public library system. The board disapproved of the students' use of the library
"for sit-in demonstrations or for the agitation of racial incidents," but
nevertheless, it voiced its approval of Thornley's actions of the previous
day and it directed that "no persons be excluded from the use of the
public library facilities," on account of race.[61]

During the next month, the attention of African Americans in Birmingham, and of the nation, turned to the children's marches organized by the SCLC. Five days after the library sit-in, Connor, Hanes,
and Waggoner announced their refusal to surrender the governing of
the city to Boutwell until their judicial appeal of the April 2 election

was settled. Bull Connor jailed hundreds of young protesters and when the jails became full, his men turned German shepherds and high-pressure fire hoses on the marchers. Eventually, rioting and interracial violence took hold of the city.[62]

By July, the violence in Birmingham had temporarily abated, however, and blacks began using the formerly white public libraries in large numbers. At the July 18 library board meeting, director Thornley reported "a distinct increase in the number of Negroes using the library facilities." At the main library, blacks were applying for library cards, studying, reading, and "wandering over the entire building." But it was the formerly white branch in the industrial suburb of Ensley that was experiencing the most extensive patronage by black citizens. The Ensley Branch was closer to black neighborhoods than the main facility and Thornley asserted that it was the "focal point of the Negro drive for membership." During the previous week, half of the juvenile membership applications at the branch and a third of the adult applications were by African Americans. By August, the Wylam, North Birmingham, and Central Park branches were also serving blacks. By the time Thornley was subpoenaed to testify in the Hendricks case, which was finally heard in December, he could relate to the court that segregation at the Birmingham Public Library system was a thing of the past, that he saw African Americans using the downtown library every day.[63]

## ANNISTON, 1963

The threat of violence was omnipresent during the desegregation of the public libraries in Alabama, but the events in Anniston illustrated just how dangerous challenging library segregation could be. Anniston became the setting for one of the most disturbing incidents in American library history on September 15, 1963, when a white mob brutally assaulted two African-American ministers in front of the city's Carnegie Library during a desegregation attempt. The press' descriptions of the angry crowd driving the men from the steps of the public library with chains, clubs, and knives created a vivid image of the brutality with which some white southerners defended segregation. It was an image that had the potential to draw public attention to the national problem of racial discrimination in library service. The attack received little press outside the state, however, as the nation reeled over events in another Alabama city. On the same day as the violence in Anniston, four

African Americans enter Anniston's Carnegie Library circa 1938. The library
provided hours for black readers on Thursdays and on the first Sunday of each month.
In 1963, this building was the scene of the mob attack on the Reverends W. B.
McClain and Quintus Reynolds. Courtesy Anniston-Calhoun County Public Library.

black girls, Addie Mae Collins, Denise McNair, Carole Robertson, and
Cynthia Wesley, lost their lives in the bombing of the Sixteenth Street
Baptist Church in Birmingham.[64]

Anniston, located approximately sixty-five miles east of Birmingham,
emerged during the Reconstruction era as the New South's "Model
City," a utopian company town based on metal and textile production.
Henry Grady heralded the industrial and social developments there as
a shining example of the "New South Creed" in action. Blacks living in
"Model City" experienced the same occupational and residential segregation as in other southern industrial towns during the first half of the
twentieth century, but white Anniston still took pride in the quality of
race relations in their community. According to Grace Hooten Gates,
their racism was the paternalistic sort. They carried a sense that the
destiny of the African-American community, though distinct, was tied
to their own. This tradition carried through the century, and white racial moderates proved more powerful during the civil rights movement
in Anniston than in some other southern cities.[65]

By 1963, Anniston's civic leadership was unenthusiastic about actively defending segregation, particularly in its public library. Two years earlier, the city was the scene of violence against "freedom riders" traveling through the South to desegregate interstate bus transportation. A photograph of a burning Greyhound bus on the outskirts of the city hit the national press in 1961 and became one of the most recognizable images of the early years of the civil rights movement. Such publicity was bad for business and harmful to the city's image. In 1963, the city commission charged a biracial group, the Anniston Human Relations Council, with addressing the grievances of the black community and resolving differences between the races, including those related to segregation. Early on, the group made the integration of the city's Carnegie Library a priority; in late June it made contact with the Library Board of Trustees to discuss the policy of excluding black readers.[66]

During the next month blacks in Anniston actively began to challenge the segregation policy. Charles S. Doster, library board chair, wrote to the city commission on July 22 that during the previous week "a serious attempt was made to integrate the main library." Several African-American men had visited the library and applied for membership. Their applications were pending and Doster asked the city commission to decide what should be done with them. He asserted that each of the library board members believed that the basic question of library integration was a political one and that it "should be answered by the elected officials of the city," not by the appointed library board.[67]

Before the library board and the commission could meet to discuss the racial situation, another incident occurred. In August "a Reverend Jackson, Negro" visited the Carnegie Library and asked to examine the *Interpreter's Bible*. With the help of the acting librarian, Ann Everett, he located the multi-volume source in the reference section. Jackson took two volumes from the shelf and sat down at a table. The librarian reported later, "I told him that our library was not integrated; therefore, I could not allow him to use the books in the reading room." She offered the minister the use of one of the library offices. Jackson replied, "In other words, I cannot sit down in here and use [the reference books]?" When she replied in the negative, Jackson left.[68]

This time, the city reacted immediately. The Anniston Human Relations Council had been urging the city commission to integrate the library. As a gesture of good will, and with little legal alternative, a majority of the city commission voted to support a desegregation of the Carnegie Library by its Board of Trustees. The library board met on

August 22. Having received the backing of the commission, it resolved that "all persons will be served by the library" beginning on September 15, 1963. In a prepared statement, the board argued that Anniston's was one of three remaining segregated municipal libraries in Alabama. By continuing to exclude blacks, the board faced the probability of "a losing lawsuit and possible race riots and demonstrations." It was integrating "to avoid the horrible strife witnessed in Gadsden and Birmingham, the humiliating losing lawsuit that Montgomery experienced and the possible presence of Federal troops. . . ."[69]

Between August 22 and September 15, the library board cooperated with the Anniston Human Relations Council to orchestrate the integration of the library. Reverend W. B. McClain, a member of the biracial council, met with the board on September 10. They determined that McClain and Reverend Quintus Reynolds would be the first blacks to receive service at the Carnegie Library. The library board hired a police officer at its own expense to watch the library during the transition, but if the librarian saw that any trouble was beginning, she was to telephone Reverend McClain to warn him.[70]

The library board desired a quiet transition. It forbade the library staff from making any statements to the press and solicited assurances from the Human Relations Council that no newsmen would be present for the integration. The board reported to the mayor that "we do not anticipate any publicity in the absence of any problems." But as the plans were laid, rumors of the library's desegregation began to spread.[71]

McClain and Reynolds arrived at the Carnegie Library at approximately 3:30 P.M. on September 15, but word had already gotten out among radical segregationists. As the two ministers approached the steps of the library, a mob of angry whites emerged. They had been waiting on the sidewalks and in cars parked nearby. A white man grabbed McClain by the arm, wheeled him around and demanded "Where are you going?" He told the minister to go home. As McClain shook loose of his assailant's grasp, the man struck him. A group of about ten came up and began attacking the ministers with sticks and with their fists. One produced a length of chain and he used it to club Reverend Reynolds to the sidewalk. Reynolds managed to regain his feet and the two sprinted for their car, parked a half block east of the library.[72]

The mob continued to grow, reaching as many as seventy people. As McClain and Reynolds ran for their vehicle, the angry whites followed pelting them with stones and soft drink bottles. They found their automobile blocked in by other cars and as they attempted to maneuver from their parking space the crowd gathered around, rocking and pounding upon the vehicle. There was a sharp noise and the passenger-side window shattered. The ministers believed the noise to be a gunshot, that the bullet had passed directly between them. In the resulting confusion, they jumped from the car and began to run north along Quintard Avenue in the direction of the police headquarters. A black motorist spotted the two battered ministers. He stopped for them and drove them to the emergency room of the Anniston Memorial Hospital.[73]

Though the city had promised police protection, no Anniston police were on the scene until after the incident was over. They arrived moments later to find the mob still assembled. Police pushed the crowd away from the library and blocked off the street. Doctors treated McClain and Reynolds for cuts and abrasions. In addition to the wounds inflicted with the chain, Reynolds had been stabbed twice. The two were released after treatment.[74]

Law and order briefly broke down in the wake of the attack. In retaliation for the mob's actions, five angry black youths assaulted Frank Brown, a forty-five-year-old white man, at about 7:30 P.M. that evening. One of the youths struck the unfortunate man across the head with a soda bottle. As Brown collapsed to the sidewalk, the others crowded around and began kicking him. A black youth explained the attack: "We decided to kill the first white man we saw on 15th Street." The danger of interracial violence continued throughout the evening and at about 10:30, an unknown person opened fire on a Negro café, discharging three shotgun blasts before escaping the scene.[75]

The disintegration of order stunned law-abiding whites in Anniston. They were frightened by the retaliatory assault by the black youths and embarrassed that their Carnegie Library had been the scene of mob violence. The city commission vowed to restore order. Mayor Dear publicly apologized to McClain and visited Reynolds at his home where the minister lay recovering from his wounds. The mayor assured the two victims that the recent unpleasantness did not reflect the sentiments of white Anniston. He blamed the attack on a lack of police protection and offered a reward of a thousand dollars toward the apprehension of the responsible parties. The library board added a hundred dollars to the reward and Doster vowed: "We're not going to let a bunch of hoodlums run the library." The *Anniston Star* editor called September 15 "as dark a Sunday as this community has ever known" and found it cruelly ironic that such an act was perpetrated upon two respected preachers by "white thugs who would be far more uncomfortable in a library than in a jail." The *Star* added another five hundred dollars to the reward. The Women of the Grace Episcopal Church offered two hundred dollars and the Rotary Club gave fifty dollars toward the capture of those most responsible for the violence.[76]

Public Safety Commissioner Jack Suggs vowed to apprehend the perpetrators, but told reporters "he wanted it clearly understood that he did not approve of the integration of the public library." Suggs promised the policeman who cracked the case a week's vacation and fifty dollars as "a going away present." He defended his actions of September 15, explaining that the absence of a police contingent at the library was in response to a request from the library board. As a part of its plan to integrate without publicity, the board wanted no uniformed officers visible.[77]

Twenty-four hours after the attack on McClain and Reynolds, the library board and the Anniston Human Relations Council staged a peaceful desegregation of the Carnegie Library. The library board met with the biracial council and the city commission on the morning of September 16 to "discuss and plan a quiet and peaceful time when Negroes could be served by the library." That afternoon, McClain returned to the library along with another black minister, G. E. Smitherman. Reynolds's wounds prevented his participation. There were approximately twenty policemen on the scene. Library board members Charles S. Doster and Mrs. Lucian Lentz, Human Relations Council chair J. Phillips Noble, and City Commissioner H. Miller Sproull escorted the two ministers from the parking lot into the building. The ministers registered for library cards and checked out several books. They remained for fifteen to twenty minutes before leaving through the library's side door.[78]

Police carefully watched white bystanders. A few "apparent troublemakers" glowered at the ministers from across library tables that contained "little or no reading material." Others walked in and out of the building on pretended errands. Outside, small groups of whites gathered, but remained at least a half block from the library. Police were determined to keep order and no disturbance occurred.[79]

By October, the Carnegie Library had issued about forty-five library cards to African Americans; the librarian reported only mild disturbances. Librarian Ann Everett complained that on one occasion, black teens crowded the library and "monopolized" the tables and chairs, apparently testing the extent of their new library privileges. The library staff caught a white juvenile defacing library property; he had ripped the spines off of several books and scrawled "fight integration" on other books and on library shelf labels. Everett also noted that a black soldier had been spending each day in the library, staying until about 3:30 P.M. Everett believed that the soldier was testing library access at Anniston as a part of an armed services inventory of racial discrimination at public facilities near military bases. It appeared that the danger of violence had ended, but a police presence continued through the end of the year.[80]

Police apprehended nine suspects in relation to the racial violence of September 15. Authorities charged four whites for their roles in the mob activity at the library. Two of the whites had prior records relating to racial violence. Mike Fox was one of several men charged in Birmingham for a 1956 attack on African-American singer Nat King Cole. William Hardy Boyd had been convicted of assaulting two black women in Anniston with a pistol. Police booked five black youths for the retaliatory assault on Frank Brown. Police charged all nine with "assault with intent to murder," which carried a sentence of two to twenty years.[81]

None of the accused were convicted. At an initial hearing, McClain and Reynolds identified all four of the white suspects as being involved in the attack against them. Reynolds recognized Boyd as the individual who had struck him with the chain. The grand jury indicted only two of the nine suspects, however, one white and one black. The prosecutor eventually dropped the charges against both at the request of the victims, Brown, McClain, and Reynolds.[82]

Though overshadowed in the national press by the tragedy in Birmingham, the violence in Anniston sparked by the city's decision to integrate the Carnegie Library seriously shook the small industrial city. Civic leaders sought to foster good will with the black community and accepted its demand for equal library service. They hoped to avoid the lawsuits and bitter confrontations that characterized events in other southern cities. Library board members wanted a quiet, almost secretive integration. The board underestimated the resistance it would face in carrying out this plan, however, and left McClain and Reynolds to face an angry segregationist mob without police protection. The Carnegie Library had assumed symbolic significance in the local racial confrontation. The fury with which the mob defended segregation at Anniston's public library demonstrated that the advocates of white supremacy were less concerned about libraries as cultural and educational institutions than as disputed territory in the struggle to contain the civil rights movement at large.

Alabama was a focal point of the civil rights movement of the 1950s and 1960s, and the desegregation of public libraries in the state was a part of that effort toward social and legal equality. Before a backdrop of marches, sit-ins, riots, and bombings, African-American activists worked to bring integration to libraries because they were conspicuous public institutions of learning and of democracy. On this level the significance of libraries to blacks was largely symbolic. But the civil rights movement was actually an aggregate of hundreds of smaller local movements, each with its own politics and its own local priorities. The efforts on behalf of integrated public library service were in response to localized demands for equal access to community resources. In achieving this end, southern blacks adopted the sit-in demonstration to create an awareness of discrimination in libraries, and they prompted federal intervention by taking their complaints to the United States District Courts.

The response to library desegregation efforts by whites varied according to local politics and the individuals involved. In Mobile and Huntsville, library boards quietly desegregated their institutions. These cities sought to preserve their civic reputations and to avoid costly and embarrassing lawsuits. Sometimes their efforts were so quiet that the potential black patrons remained unaware of their newly acquired privileges. In Montgomery, library desegregation came only after a series of sit-ins, a highly public court action, and activity by the local Ku Klux Klan chapter. Birmingham desegregated its library after it became the subject of a lawsuit and the scene of a student protest. Events took a vicious turn in Anniston where mob violence prevented an attempt by two black ministers to integrate the Carnegie Library, despite the wishes of its board of trustees to acquiesce to black demands for integrated library service. The reaction of the intransigent among white Alabamians during the 1960s demonstrates that challenges to segregation in public libraries carried the potential for tension and for violence that exceeded the value they placed on libraries as cultural institutions or repositories of information. The agents of massive resistance believed that a threat to segregation anywhere in southern life represented a threat to their whole structure of defense. They adopted a racial domino theory characterized by a belief that if the public libraries fell other institutions, including the public schools, would be next.

# 5
# Librarians and the Civil Rights Movement, 1955–1965

In 1944, Swedish sociologist Gunnar Myrdal wrote that the United States faced a racial dilemma that pitted its underlying social values of democracy and self-determination against its practice of inequality in regard to African Americans. Librarians experienced the "American Dilemma," but they also carried a second conflict of values. Their code of professional ethics required librarians to promote intellectual freedom and access to information, a responsibility that was at odds with the practice of excluding black readers from "white" public libraries. The presence of library segregation held a mirror to the profession and tested librarianship's commitment to the values it professed to hold. This professional dilemma was less intense for African-American librarians, since it was the "white" institutions rather than theirs that most required racial reform. But for both black and white librarians, there were social, economic, and even physical dangers associated with open opposition to the prevailing racial order. The library organizations on the state and national levels had less to fear, but they were also unprepared to forcefully address issues as complex and as emotionally charged as race relations. Librarians lacked a tradition of organized resistance and were wary of becoming entangled in social issues of "local" concern.[1]

The experiences of Juliette Morgan, Emily Reed, and Patricia Blalock best illustrate the precarious position of public librarians in Alabama during the civil rights movement. These individuals challenged the forces of massive resistance, sometimes with tragic results. Also significant was the response of the American Library Association and the Alabama Library Association to the civil rights movement; both had great difficulty in coming to terms with matters of race. Even at the cost of its ALA chapter status, the state association excluded blacks from its membership until 1965, two years after all of the public libraries in urban Alabama had desegregated.

## JULIETTE HAMPTON MORGAN AND THE MONTGOMERY BUS BOYCOTT

Opposing the forces of massive resistance could be dangerous, even for native white southerners, as Juliette Morgan, a reference librarian at Montgomery's Carnegie Library, learned in 1955. Morgan was a "sensitive, delicate young woman from a fine old Alabama family." She was an educated and conscientious person who took exception to the racial customs into which she was born. As a result of her candid expressions of sympathy and admiration for civil rights workers during the Montgomery Bus Boycott in 1955, she became an object of scorn and of persecution by other whites in the city.[2]

Morgan was one of the few white race liberals in Montgomery who belonged to the Alabama Human Relations Council. This group of professional and business people in Montgomery held clandestine biracial meetings, working quietly to improve race relations in the city. The group was Alabama's affiliate of the Southern Regional Council. It was the state's most important, and Montgomery's only, interracial organization, "a meeting point for men and women of good will of both races," that advocated equal opportunity for African Americans. The council included notable Alabama New Dealers Clifford and Virginia Durr. Martin Luther King, Jr., also regularly attended the covert gatherings. According to Taylor Branch, "they were all sincere, and some were timid, or brilliant, or damaged."[3]

The group's leader, Episcopal priest Thomas R. Thrasher, conceded that the council could not hope to correct the racial discord that characterized his state in 1955, asserting, "We are too few and too weak." But during the Montgomery Bus Boycott the group emerged from its place in the shadows to sponsor the negotiations between city and bus company officials and the demonstrators. A few from this small contingent of race liberals spoke openly in favor of the position of King and the Montgomery Improvement Association. Morgan became the most visible of these.[4]

The boycott of the city buses that began in 1955 after the arrest of Rosa Parks deeply moved Juliette Morgan. She believed in the aims and the methods of Montgomery's African-American citizens who adopted passive resistance to address racial discrimination in the city's public transportation system. Unlike most people at the time, including the demonstrators themselves, Morgan understood that history was being made in her hometown.[5]

A week after the demonstration began, the reclusive and normally private librarian wrote a letter to the editor of the *Montgomery Advertiser* enthusiastically and eloquently lauding the efforts of the Montgomery Improvement Association and the rest of the participants in the bus protest. Referring to the use of taxis to transport troops in the defense of Paris during World War I, she asserted that "Not since the First Battle of the Marne has the taxi been put to as good use as it has this last week in Montgomery." Morgan compared the exodus of demonstrators walking from affluent Cloverdale back to Mobile Road to Gandhi's "Salt March" during India's struggle to secure independence from Britain. She reminded the readers of the *Advertiser* that American patriots had employed the boycott to demonstrate against George III.[6]

Morgan's final and most remarkable assertion was that history would record the Montgomery Bus Boycott as the city's most significant contribution to posterity. "One feels that history is being made in Montgomery these days," she wrote, "the most important in [the city's] career." This argument left most whites believing that Morgan was "something of a ninny." Montgomery had been the birthplace of the Confederacy. It was inconceivable to most people in 1955 and 1956 that a strike against the city buses would be a milestone on the path of America's changing racial conscience.[7]

The reaction of whites to Juliette Morgan's letter was both cruel and prolonged. Over a period of a year and a half, the librarian suffered constant harassment by whites, particularly young people, who threw rocks through the windows of her home where she lived with her mother. They insulted her on the streets and played tricks on her at the library. Miss Morgan received a string of lewd and threatening telephone calls both at home and at work. Her obvious sensitivity to these reprisals only served to encourage the perpetrators to do worse. In addition to the heartless pranks, segregationists brought pressure upon the city to fire Juliette Morgan on account of her racial views. Unable to cope with the unabating persecution, Morgan eventually took a leave of absence from her work at the city library.[8]

Shortly after, on the night of July 17, 1957, Juliette Morgan died. The exact cause of Morgan's demise has been the subject of speculation. It was generally believed that her death was a suicide, brought on by her extreme unhappiness as a result of the harassment she endured over the previous year and a half. Using interviews with individuals acquainted with the unfortunate librarian, Taylor Branch asserts in *Parting the Waters* that the death was a self-administered poisoning. The official certificate of death attributed the event to a sudden heart attack resulting from hypertension. Regardless of the precise physiological circumstances of Morgan's passing, the city's black citizens, including King, and its sympathetic whites, believed that Juliette Morgan had been persecuted to death because of her opposition to the racial status quo.[9]

A letter from Mary Y. Dobbins, one of Morgan's friends, appeared in the *Advertiser* on July 25. It described the librarian as a "rare spirit" who was "alive to the cause of justice." Dobbins asserted that her friend had been a "sensitive barometer, or conscience, for people like you and me." She conceded that Morgan's ideas were unpopular, perhaps even wrong, but "she was probably thinking along the lines that the rest of us will take for granted 50 years from now." Mary Dobbins concluded her remarks, writing that Juliette Morgan was "a flame that many cowardly people tried to extinguish, but she burned brighter for it."[10]

If white librarians in Alabama held any illusions that the high-minded nature of their occupation would protect them from the radical segregationists, those illusions were dispelled with the death of Juliette Morgan. Miss Morgan never publicly expressed the exact nature of her views in regard to discrimination by the library at which she was employed. But her experiences between December of 1955 and July of 1957 demonstrated what might happen to other white librarians who thought of doing so. Juliette Morgan would be the last white public librarian in the state to speak openly in favor of civil rights for black citizens during the movement years.

## EMILY WHEELOCK REED AND *THE RABBITS' WEDDING* CONTROVERSY

In their support of segregation, the practitioners of massive resistance created a climate of fear that fostered the censorship of library materials. The white Citizens' Councils, the Klan, even governmental officials clamored for the suppression of library materials they construed as sympathetic to integration. The prospect of book banning coupled the racial troubles of the era with librarians' professional ethics in a way that the controversy surrounding Morgan had not. In Alabama, the most visible illustration of the association between segregation and censorship came two years after Morgan's death, when the state legislature tried to remove the director of Alabama's public library agency from office because of her stand for intellectual freedom in the state. Like Morgan, Emily Wheelock Reed provided an example of what happened to librarians who challenged the radical segregationists.

The year 1958 marked a "watershed" in Alabama electoral politics, as massive resistance to civil rights openly became a major issue in state elections. In the gubernatorial race, Attorney General John Patterson and Circuit Court Judge George C. Wallace were the leading candidates. Patterson ran a "grim, hard-edged" campaign, preaching against crime and corruption, and for segregation. Patterson's race baiting was not his only appeal to voters. His father's murder in 1954 by Phoenix City gangsters lent authenticity to Patterson's rhetoric against organized crime. But the 1958 election also proved the power of the race issue in getting votes among white working and lower middle class Alabamians. Patterson promised them that there would be "no mixing of races" in Alabama, and he had proven credentials as a segregationist. During his term as Attorney General, Patterson banished the NAACP from the state, and his connection to the Klan was a poorly kept secret. At the same time, Patterson's campaign questioned George Wallace's dedication to segregation, asserting that Wallace had a history of waffling on the issue. Patterson defeated Wallace in a runoff election, and Wallace vowed never to be "outsegged" again.[11]

The importance of the race issue was not lost on the state legislature, either. Patterson supporters held the key legislative and committee posts, and they believed they had a clear mandate from Alabama's white voters to combat the state's integrationists, as well as the "outside agitators." So many pro-segregation bills were being introduced in 1958 and 1959 that the legislature formed a Joint Segregation Screening Committee to weigh the merits of each before they were submitted to the state House and Senate.

In 1959, Alabama's state library agency, the Public Library Service Division, and particularly its director Emily Reed, came under attack from the state legislature because law makers believed the agency was being used to disseminate books espousing racial integration and communism. The Alabama Public Library Service Division had been created during the Depression with the help of the Works Progress Administration. The division worked to expand library service in the state and it loaned books to public libraries. The controversy that surrounded the agency in 1959 centered around a children's book entitled *The Rab-*

*bits' Wedding* which, according to some legislators, advanced the practice of miscegenation. Pro-segregation politicians also opposed the Library Service's practice of disseminating "notable books" lists generated by the American Library Association, some of the works from which were sympathetic to the civil rights movement.

Led by Senator E. O. Eddins of Marengo County, segregationist legislators attempted to oust Miss Reed from her post as director of the Library Service, because of her inclusion of controversial works in her agency's book holdings and book lists, also because of her refusal to disclose her opinion in regard to racial segregation. The resulting highly publicized conflict demonstrated that white librarians in the South, like Emily Reed, and other library-minded citizens sometimes found it easier to oppose the forces of massive resistance where the issue was the banning of books used by white people rather than the more difficult intellectual freedom question of segregation in public library systems.

In 1958, Harper & Row published *The Rabbits' Wedding*, by Garth Williams, a book aimed at children between three and seven. The story is about two rabbits, one male and the other female, that play together in a meadow every day. Ultimately, the furry creatures decide that they want to marry. The other animals of the forest assemble for the rabbits' wedding and the two live happily ever after.[12]

The seemingly innocent story became the center of controversy in Alabama and in other southern states, not because of the subject matter or plot, but because of the colors the illustrator used to help the young readers distinguish between the two rabbits. The male rabbit is black and the female, white. *Orlando Sentinel* columnist Henry Balch railed against Williams's work: "As soon as you pick up the book, you realize these rabbits are integrated." He suggested that the book was an attempt to "brainwash" white children. In Alabama, Montgomery's organ of its local white Citizens' Council, the *Home News*, took up the book. In a column entitled "What Your Children Read," the Citizens' Council writer asserted facetiously, "What's Good Enough for Rabbits Should Do for Mere Humans," implying that the rabbit book was a subtle lesson in miscegenation. The article led Citizens' Council members to complain about the state Public Library Service, which held this book and made it available to public libraries throughout the state. The controversy that soon arose over the work pitted Senator Eddins against Library Service director Emily Reed.[13]

Senator E. O. "Big Ed" Eddins of Marengo County in Alabama's Black Belt was the son of a Confederate veteran and a staunch segrega-

In 1959, Alabama legislators attempted to oust state librarian Emily Wheelock Reed for circulating books they considered "integrationist," such as this one depicting the marriage of a black rabbit and a white rabbit. Used by permission of HarperCollins Publishers.

tionist. He was a six-foot-one-inch, 250-pound ex-marine, "a man you don't push around." He had fought in the First World War as a fifteen-year-old and had become an oil distributor in Demopolis before beginning his career as a state legislator in 1943. Eddins had been a friend to the agents of library development before the civil rights movement; he co-sponsored the first state appropriation for public libraries and then continued work toward adequate spending for library services. But by the mid-1950s, he had become known more for his strong stands on matters of race than for his efforts on behalf of libraries. In one of his more dramatic early attempts to address racial tension in the state, Eddins introduced a resolution in 1956 seeking federal funds to pay for a mass resettlement of black Alabamians in the North and the West.[14]

Emily Wheelock Reed assumed the directorship of the Public Library Service Division in 1957. She was born in Asheville, North Carolina. The state library board made much of her credentials as a native southerner when they hired Reed, but in fact she spent only her first year in Asheville and considered herself a Midwesterner. Reed graduated from Indiana University where she was elected to Phi Beta Kappa. She earned a library degree cum laude at Michigan. Reed had worked at the University of Michigan, Florida State University, the Detroit Public Library, a public library in Kauai, Hawaii, and most recently had worked for the state library agency in Louisiana before coming to Alabama. Gretchen Shenk, the interim director, predicted that Reed would soon become attached to Alabama "as everyone does who spends a while" in the state, but the new director was not so fortunate. Her career in Alabama was troubled and relatively brief.[15]

In a harbinger of the conflict to come, Reed found herself before Eddins and the state Senate's Interim Taxation Committee in March of 1959 being questioned about her agency's book holdings. She had appeared to discuss the Library Service's budget for the upcoming year, but Senator Eddins had other priorities. He had identified seven books dealing with "segregation and communism" and he took the opportunity of Reed's presence before the committee to ask her whether these books were being circulated by the library division. Reed replied that she did not know, but she promised to provide the requested information at a later time.[16]

In May of 1959, Reed appeared before Eddins again, this time in a meeting of the Senate Finance Committee. Reed had come to renew her appropriation request for the Library Service. Once again, Eddins questioned her about the practices of the library division, insinuating that the agency was disseminating information that flagrantly advocated race mixing.[17]

In an exchange that carried over into the state's newspapers, Eddins asserted that Garth Williams's book about the marriage of a white and a black rabbit was a particularly dangerous example of the kind of anti-segregationist material that Reed held at the state's library agency. Eddins posed for newspaper cameramen holding a copy of *The Rabbits' Wedding* and thundered to reporters that "this book and many others should be taken off the shelves and burned." He warned that there were other unacceptable books being circulated by the Library Service; some were "of the same nature" as the rabbit book and others were "communistic." When asked about the implications of his actions for freedom of expression, Eddins asserted that the South could tolerate but one viewpoint on race relations. "The integrationist doesn't have any right to express his opinion, not down here." Off the record, some of the senator's colleagues expressed their disapproval of Eddins's position to reporters, but they declined to publicly oppose Eddins for fear of being labeled "pro-integration."[18]

Emily Reed refused to remove *The Rabbits' Wedding* from circulation. When her agency originally purchased Williams's book in 1958, the cataloger confronted Reed with a vague warning that the work had the potential to bring trouble. Reed had dismissed the comment, seeing "no reason for tossing it out." She felt that children would enjoy the book and remembers, "I couldn't believe that anybody would get excited about rabbits, for heaven's sake!" Reed had not sought a conflict, but once she had added the book to the state library's collection, she felt an ethical responsibility to defend it against censorship. When Eddins demanded the removal of *The Rabbits' Wedding* in May of 1959, Emily Reed told him that she would not comply.[19]

This decision to keep Garth Williams's book put Emily Reed in a difficult position; along with her commitment to preserve intellectual freedom, she had her agency's financial needs to consider. Eddins had threatened to impede the approval of Reed's budget on account of her alleged advocacy of controversial books. She reacted to the senator's criticisms of the Williams's work, in particular, by asserting that the Library Service purchased it on the basis of favorable reviews from reputable sources and that she saw "nothing objectionable" in the work. She added that she even liked *The Rabbits' Wedding*. Reed argued that even if the book could be construed as pro-integration, the library agency had a responsibility to provide information "on all sides of a question." She emphasized that the Library Service also held books espousing racial separation, like *You and Segregation* by Herman E. Talmadge.[20]

Emily Reed refused to concede to Eddins's demands because, "it would not be morally right," but as a concession to the senator and the other segregationists who had complained about the book, she placed it on a special shelf created for racially controversial materials. Reed emphasized, however, that the book was not banned, that *The Rabbits' Wedding* was "available for anyone who wants to read it." She asserted that the book remained on the open shelves of some of the public libraries in Alabama and invited librarians who wanted the book for their own institutions to feel free to borrow it from the Library Service.[21]

The controversy surrounding the children's book quickly drew national attention. An observer noted in *Time* magazine that it seemed "incredible that any sober adult could scent in this fuzzy cottontale for children the overtones of Karl Marx or even of Martin Luther King." The Unitarian Fellowship for Social Justice in Boston passed a resolution that "thanked" Eddins for vividly illustrating the "futility of censorship" and the "irrationality and childishness of racism." The author of *The Rabbits' Wedding*, Garth Williams, issued a statement asserting that he wrote the book for children, not adults "who will not understand it." He scoffed at the idea that animals with white fur could be considered "blood relations" of white human beings. He "was only aware that a white horse next to a black horse looks very picturesque." Williams contended that his story was "only about soft furry love and has no hidden message of hate."[22]

The Alabama press was equally critical of Eddins. A segregationist editor for the *Birmingham News* wrote that "We have a good, a sound cause in our defense of segregation. . . . We haul many a prop out from under such a cause when we allow ourselves to appear ridiculous." Eddins's public stand against *The Rabbits' Wedding* had "made us just that." The *Montgomery Advertiser* simply made light of the senator's actions: "One bunny is white, like Senator Eddins's shirt, and one bunny is black, like Senator Eddins's tie. This combination the senator construes as propaganda to make race mixing palatable to tender minds."[23]

Sensing the unpopularity of his stand, Eddins backed away from his opposition to the children's book, but not from his feud with Emily Reed. The legislature approved the Library Service's budget despite the controversy. By the end of the summer, Eddins was denying that he had ever made "a public or private statement about the rabbit book."

He turned instead to the book lists the Library Service issued to Alabama's public librarians. As a part of its monthly newsletter, *Library Notes*, the library division included a list of "notable books" compiled by the American Library Association. Martin Luther King's account of the Montgomery Bus Boycott, *Stride Toward Freedom*, appeared on the list twice in 1959 and the Library Service held the work in its own collection. Senator Eddins took this book up, renewing his attack on Reed.[24]

In August 1959, Eddins delivered a speech on the Senate floor assailing Reed for her inclusion of the pro-integration work by King on the Library Service's book list. Eddins also complained to the upper house of the Alabama legislature that Miss Reed had refused to disclose her personal views regarding segregation. She had told Eddins that her "personal feelings had nothing to do with the way the agency was operated." She argued that her inclusion of the King book, or any other, on the list did not constitute an endorsement of the ideas expressed in the work. The senator disagreed. The Marengo County legislator told the Senate that he would seek a law to change the qualifications for the position of Public Library Service director. His intention was to remove Reed from office.[25]

On August 18, 1959, Eddins appeared before the Joint Segregation Screening Committee to present his bill. The committee had been created earlier that year to rule on the merits of the many segregationist measures being submitted to the legislature and to screen them before sending the bills to the full House and Senate for a vote. Eddins complained to the committee that the present rules prevented an Alabamian from becoming director of the Library Service. The position required an ALA-accredited masters degree in library science and Alabama had no school that offered such a degree. He neglected to mention that there were numerous librarians from Alabama who had gone out of the state for their professional education. Eddins sought to drop the library degree requirement and to limit the position to natives of Alabama.[26]

The Segregation Screening Committee voted to support Eddins's bill. The members of the committee made no secret of their motives. Representative Sim Thomas of Barbour County and committee chairman said it would be the "purpose and intent" of the bill to get rid of Miss Reed. When asked whether the bill would result in the director's dismissal, another member replied, "That was the whole idea wasn't it?"[27]

Over the course of the next several weeks, however, the Segregation Screening Committee and Eddins backed away from their insistence on Reed's immediate removal. The Screening Committee appointed a subcommittee to study the Library Service situation. Eddins, along with Lawrence K. "Snag" Andrews of Bullock County and Larry Dumas of Jefferson County comprised the new group. These legislators were unable to establish that they could legally remove Reed. The executive board of the Public Library Service had the ultimate responsibility for hiring and dismissing a director of their agency and any law the legislature might create would most likely only apply to the next director and not to Reed. Also, the committee was feeling the pressure being applied by the librarians and library-minded citizens in the state who were beginning to express their dissatisfaction with the attacks on their Library Service director.[28]

The professional librarians of Alabama had finally discovered an issue in which they felt comfortable engaging in debate. Emily Reed does not recall receiving any meaningful support from the librarians of the state during her controversial stand against the censorship of *The Rabbits' Wedding*. But when the legislature began debating the segregation subcommittee's Library Service bill in the late summer and fall of 1959, librarians around the state, mainly through their state library association, expressed their disapproval of Eddins's plans for their state library agency. They were particularly concerned about the measures changing the qualifications for the director's position. The president of the Alabama Library Association, Edna Earle Brown, obtained a public hearing before the Senate Judiciary Committee to express her objection to the work of the subcommittee. Several other librarians, led by former state library board member Mrs. J. E. Price, also made vocal appeals to the legislature.[29]

Attempting to save face, the subcommittee worked with the executive board of the Public Library Service to create a compromise bill. Eddins told the press that the reports that his bill was designed to oust Emily Reed were "in error." Retreating from his hard-line position, Eddins argued that his actual concern was over the fact that a graduate of an Alabama university could not meet the qualifications set for the Library Service post, since it required an ALA-accredited masters degree in library science. As a remedy, the subcommittee offered an addition to the current rules so that a candidate with a masters degree in education majoring in library science would be an acceptable choice for the director position. The compromise bill also gave the politically appointed executive board more authority over the director. For its part, the board agreed to take a more active role in supervising the creation of the *Library Notes* newsletter that had brought on the second phase of the controversy. The board agreed that the newsletter would be "prepared locally," rather than offering any book recommendations by the American Library Association.[30]

The state legislature passed the Library Service compromise bill leaving Emily Reed with her job. The subcommittee and the state library board offered an upbeat statement describing the compromise, asserting that "libraries in Alabama shall remain free and Alabama is not afraid of freedom of information. No books have been burned or banned in any state library in Alabama." Eddins hinted that the executive board of the state library agency might still fire Reed, however, and he apparently hoped that it would. The *Montgomery Advertiser* revealed that the director's most vocal advocate on the board, chairperson Mrs. J. U. Reeves of Mobile, would not be reappointed after her term expired at the end of September. This news gave credence to the senator's insinuation that Reed's days in office were numbered. But the board gave no indication that it had plans to remove its director.[31]

Emily Reed had weathered the controversy brought on by her commitment to the professional ethics of librarianship, but she chose to leave the state only two months after the compromise bill went to the legislature. The library service director was profoundly embarrassed that the state of Alabama, and her agency in particular, had been portrayed in such a negative light in the press. She had received newspaper clippings regarding the censorship controversy from as far away as London and Paris. Reed believed that the entire affair had impeded the progress she had hoped to make in library development in Alabama. With few vocal supporters of her stand within the state or national library community to bolster her, Reed took a measure of the blame for this perceived lack of progress upon herself. In January of 1960, the Library Service director announced that she would relocate to Washington. She had accepted a position with the District of Columbia Public Library as a consultant in adult education. Reed's decision was not under duress from the board, and at least to the public, she asserted that, "My leaving [Alabama] was not directly related to the incidents last year."[32]

The American Library Association's Intellectual Freedom Committee failed to support Emily Reed during the censorship controversy, but events in Alabama did help to shape the opinions of committee members on the issue of libraries and segregation. Dan Lacy wrote to committee chair Archie McNeal in October 1959 to express his desire that the Intellectual Freedom Committee take a more active role in southern censorship cases. "I must say I feel increasingly ashamed of myself," Lacy wrote, "that I have not before now spoken up about the need for ALA to take a stand on the harassment of Southern librarians in connection with their holdings of books in the field of race relations." He complained to McNeal that Alabama's state librarian had almost been fired for circulating ALA's own book list, making the association "directly and immediately affected." Lacy pointed out the need to publicly reaffirm ALA's "Freedom to Read" statement and that the committee might be more persuasive in its appeal to the South if it suggested that the segregationist point of view be represented in libraries outside the region. McNeal replied the he would support a statement by the committee, but warned that inappropriate action by ALA could actually make the position of southern librarians more difficult. The exchange foreshadowed the more public debate that would characterize the American Library Association in the next decade.[33]

The strife surrounding Alabama's Public Library Service Division in 1959 demonstrated that some librarians found it easier to defend white readers from censorship of pro-integrationist books than to take on the more complicated and deeply ingrained notion that black readers should be excluded from "white" libraries. Most librarians continued to avoid such controversies, however. The debate demonstrated that massive resistance to integration drew some white Southerners to defend segregation with the same measure their forebears had used to defend slavery; they attempted to curtail the free expression of information and ideas contrary to their own. But in 1959 most whites, or at least the most vocal of them, found censorship distasteful. To moderate whites and even to some dedicated segregationists, E. O. Eddins's actions seemed embarrassing, backward, and un-American. Clearly, Emily Reed could have defused the situation early by cooperating fully with Senator Eddins. Her refusal to take *The Rabbits' Wedding* out of circulation represented an important stand for the freedom to read in Alabama, however, and there was public support for it. But if the feud between Reed and Eddins was at the least a partial victory for intellectual freedom for whites, it left the library situation for blacks in Alabama no better.

## PATRICIA BLALOCK AND THE SELMA PUBLIC LIBRARY

Addressing the question of library service for black Southerners, Archie McNeal and other leaders of the American Library Association argued that, despite the difficulties and dangers involved, white librarians in the South were working quietly, but diligently, behind the scenes during the early 1960s to integrate their public libraries. Such was not the case in most Alabama cities. In Mobile, Montgomery, Birmingham, Gadsden, and Anniston protests or judicial action preceded the integration of the public libraries and these factors, more than a perceived ethical obligation moved librarians and library boards to act.

A notable exception to this trend occurred in Selma, Alabama, where Patricia Blalock, a white native Alabamian, worked toward a peaceful desegregation of the city's Carnegie Library, demonstrating librarians' potential to influence social change. Integration, in general, was a slow, painful process in Selma. The white Citizens' Council dominated local politics and the city became a focal point of civil rights activity in 1965 when Americans watched police forces savaging voting rights marchers on national television. Though equal access to most public accommodations in Selma was not easily won, the library had desegregated quietly and voluntarily in 1963 after the city librarian insisted that her library board repeal its policy of excluding African Americans. Hardline segregationists controlled Selma's library board and Blalock's ability to cajole them into integrating demonstrated the important part southern librarians could play in the civil rights movement in libraries.

Selma, the scene of America's most successful campaign for black voting rights, sits upon a bluff above a bend in the Alabama River. Located 50 miles west of Montgomery, in the "heart of the Black Belt," it is the seat of Dallas County. Before the Civil War, Selma was a center for river transportation from which the cotton grown in the rich black soil of the surrounding countryside was piloted down river to Mobile for export. It became a foundry town during the war, providing arms and ammunition for the Confederacy until it fell to Union raiders in 1865. Selma's economy continued to be based on agriculture in the years after the war and its politics remained largely the domain of "well-to-do patricians with long genealogies."[34]

By 1960, Selma had a population of approximately 28,400, a little more than half of which was African American. Race relations were based on a hundred-and-forty-year-long tradition of paternalism. African Americans were denied a political voice. Though they were in the majority, numerically, blacks comprised only 1 percent of the electorate by 1960. A "feudal society" prevailed on the farms and plantations of rural Dallas County and Selma, itself, was strictly segregated with distinct white and black communities. Though it had a larger black middle class than surrounding Black Belt towns, most who lived along the unpaved streets of black Selma were poor and had few opportunities for betterment.[35]

Most whites believed that the general state of race relations in their city was "quite amicable," however. Longtime white resident Claude C. Grayson asserted in 1948 that, "here in Selma the Negroes are contented and happy. . . . At present the negro is sitting on top of the world." Whites were surprised when organized expressions of dissatisfaction became apparent at the beginning of the civil rights movement. They assumed that the fault must lay with agitators from the outside.[36]

White Selma had reacted to the *Brown* decision and to the bus boycott in Montgomery by creating the state's first white Citizens' Council in 1955. The organization was more "respectable" than the predominantly lower-class Klan and it worked to preserve segregation without violence. There were 1,100 to 1,200 in attendance at the first meeting of the Dallas County Citizens' Council on November 29. The number included merchants, farmers, bankers, professionals, and politicians who gathered at the overflowing junior high auditorium to "learn the plans for applying stern economic pressure on Negro advocates of integration." A Selma attorney explained that whites held economic control of the city and that the work of the council could "make it difficult, if not impossible, for any Negro who advocates desegregation to find and hold a job, get credit, or renew a mortgage."[37]

The council became the "predominant force" in public life in Selma. It controlled municipal politics and public opinion. Membership was essential for those who held ambitions in local politics. It was a middle-class group and largely white collar. Influential whites led the council and they applied pressure on their own race as well as on blacks. The organization "drew a tight net of conformity" around white Selma, directing social and economic retaliation upon whites who displayed racial views inconsistent with the norm.[38]

There remained, however, numerous moderates in Selma and a small group of race liberals. Most of them felt isolated on the question of race relations, however, and feared to speak openly of their views. One of the few whites in Selma who actively opposed segregation in the Black Belt city was Patricia Blalock, director of the Carnegie Library.[39]

Blalock attributes her atypical racial views to her upbringing by racially moderate parents and her experiences as a medical social worker in rural Alabama. She was born and raised in Gadsden, Alabama, sixty miles northeast of Birmingham. Her family had been more liberal than most that surrounded her. Her grandfather, she explains, had been one of the first Populists in the area during the previous century and she remembers that she was "brought up" not to fear blacks. Blalock attended college at Montevallo. After graduating with a degree in Social Work, she took a job as a truant officer in the Black Belt town of Marion. In 1937, she moved to Selma and became a district supervisor for the State Crippled Children's Service. In her work for the agency, which was originally created to address the hardships of the 1936 polio epidemic, Blalock oversaw the administration of medical aid for twenty-eight central Alabama counties. It was a moving experience that Mrs. Blalock asserts instilled in her a need to treat all people with dignity.[40]

Patricia Blalock married, and when she had a daughter in 1946 she ended her work with disabled children. Six years later, the local librarian, "Miss Betty," recruited the former social worker to serve as a part-time assistant at the Carnegie Library. After serving in this capacity for about a decade, Mrs. Blalock agreed to serve temporarily in place of the library director who had fallen ill. When the library board learned that the director would be unable to return to her duties, it asked Patricia Blalock to accept the librarian position on a permanent basis. She was initially unsure. She stressed to the board that she had no formal library education, that all she knew of librarianship came from work experience. The board members expressed their faith in Mrs. Blalock's abilities and ultimately, she accepted the position. Patricia Blalock became director of the Carnegie Library in 1963.[41]

With Blalock's acceptance of the director's position, the board had hired a librarian with racial views that were inconsistent with its policy of serving only white patrons. In the years since the Carnegie Library was formed, there had been no formal public library service provided for African Americans. Selma lacked even the customary Negro branch created in other Alabama cities. According to local attorney and civil rights activist J. L. Chestnut, Jr., the occasional black Selmian was served from the back door of the Carnegie Library by the library's African-American maid. These were unofficial exceptions overlooked by sympathetic librarians. The status quo did not suit Patricia Blalock, however, and she began to press the issue of segregation almost immediately. The "first thing I did as director," she remembers, was to begin a dialogue with the board members on integration, "but it was pretty difficult."[42]

Chris Heinz, Selma's mayor, and Bernard Reynolds, Dallas County Probate Judge, were ex officio members of the library board. Unlike Bull Connor in Birmingham, Heinz and Reynolds took seriously their membership on the board, and they were regular attendants at its meet-ings. They were also orthodox segregationists. White moderates be-lieved Heinz would "rather see Selma blow away than to change any of its traditions." Mayor Heinz and Judge Reynolds were both leaders in Dallas County's white Citizens' Council. They were often on stage at Citizens' Council rallies and in 1955 they had made the nominations for the organization's first board of directors. Heinz even became chair-man of the council in 1965.[43]

Patricia Blalock faced the task of convincing Mayor Heinz, Judge Reynolds, and the rest of the members of the library board to consider integration at the library. In addition to the two ex officio members, the group consisted of three men and two women. They were civic lead-ers mostly from prominent families and included a Harvard-educated attorney, a certified public accountant, and a chair who was indepen-dently wealthy. "They were all fine people," the librarian recalls, "but they were just very strong about this [question of race], even the most liberal-minded, some of the ones that I was devoted to, who had the library interests at heart." The librarian raised the issue of integra-tion at her second meeting with the library board. Finding the group unresponsive, she visited individually with each member. Blalock ar-gued that integration should be the board's "top priority," and urged the members to begin work on a desegregation plan.[44]

Predictably, Mayor Heinz and Judge Reynolds were difficult to con-vince, but the librarian was insistent. Patricia Blalock recounts that she genuinely believed segregation to be wrong, but that she was also driven by a desire to avoid a disturbance at her library. Events in Alabama and throughout the South suggested that desegregation of public libraries was inevitable. Montgomery's city library had integrated the previous year under federal injunction. In April, Birmingham desegregated its library system after a student demonstration. Blalock argued to Heinz, Reynolds, and the other board members that to maintain their commit-ment to segregation at the Carnegie Library would lead to trouble and perhaps even closure of the library. She believed that integration would eventually come to Selma and argued to the board that "we need to get it done in a good way, and do it on our own."[45]

By mid-May, Blalock's entreaties to the board had assumed a new urgency. She believed a "push" by black demonstrators was imminent. Library board minutes record that she had received some "unusual telephone calls." The librarian wanted the board to produce a desegre-gation plan immediately. Meeting continued intransigence, Patricia

Blalock offered the library board an ultimatum. She recalls communicating to the board members, "I think we need very badly to get this library integrated, and I don't believe I can open up Monday until we've made a real decision." Mrs. Blalock remembers the board members as segregationists, but also as civic-minded individuals who genuinely cared about the Carnegie Library. They responded to the librarian's protest, agreeing to meet at her home on Monday, May 13 at eight in the morning, before the library was scheduled to open, to consider desegregation.[46]

In the face of the librarian's ultimatum, the library board acquiesced. The Monday morning meeting included the board and the entire library staff. After a lengthy discussion, the group began to form a plan it hoped would result in a quiet and peaceful integration of the Carnegie Library. The desegregation plan that resulted from the meeting, and from a second meeting held the following Friday, called for an imitation of the "vertical integration" used at the public libraries in Danville, Virginia, and in Montgomery. To prevent black and white patrons from sitting together, the staff would remove the chairs and store them in the library's basement. This was intended to be a temporary measure to "help the community to adjust to integration." The staff would return the furniture "as integration in the city progressed." The board voted to print new membership application cards requiring each applicant's name, address, and length of residence in Selma. The application would also call for two references. As an impediment to Selma's black citizens seeking use of their local library, the effectiveness of such a form would be negligible. But board members, particularly Mayor Heinz, were irritated by the participation of "outsiders" in Selma's civil rights activity, and they were looking for assurances that non-resident blacks would not interfere in the execution of their plans. The board also voted to close the Carnegie Library during the week of May 13 to May 19. Officially, the library was closed to take "inventory." Apparently, the board wanted time to carry out their desegregation plan and wanted to forestall any visits by blacks before the library could be integrated. The moves toward biracial service were to be kept quiet. Neither the board nor the staff was to make announcements to the newspapers nor even to black leaders. The librarian was uncomfortable with some of the terms of the plan, particularly the removal of the library furniture, but seeing the opportunity for peaceful desegregation of the library, she felt compelled to compromise.[47]

The Carnegie Library reopened uneventfully on May 20, 1963. Reverend Ralph Smeltzer visited the facility during the first days when it was still practicing "vertical integration." Smeltzer was a white Brethren preacher from Chicago and Southern California who came to Selma in 1963 in the hope of opening a dialogue between black and white leaders in the racially divided city. Smeltzer needed a place to write and went to the public library. Learning of the facility's temporary lack of furniture, he inquired about sitting in a corner or using a back room. He noticed footstools and asked to sit on one. A library worker eventually suggested that the minister sit at a low table in a corner "where no one would see him." Smeltzer recounted in his journal that the library staff was helpful and apologetic. The librarian explained the situation to Smeltzer and he was surprised to learn that she "seemed sympathetic to integration."[48]

Selma's librarian also believed that her staff should be integrated and soon after the board voted to desegregate the library, she hired the city's first African-American library assistant. Annie Molette had been the Carnegie Library's maid for many years and she had used her position to quietly provide library service to a small number of black Selmians from the Carnegie building's back door. Blalock told Molette that the library would hire a new maid, that she wanted Molette to begin doing actual library work and openly serving the public. According to Mrs. Blalock, her hiring of the African-American maid as a library worker was designed to "lay the groundwork for having some black employees."[49]

There was no rush of black patrons, since the African-American community was initially unaware of its new library privileges. African Americans were beginning to test the public facilities in Selma, however, including its library and they slowly began to arrive. By November, black patrons were a common sight.[50]

Patricia Blalock believed that, overall, the integration had been remarkably successful, but it was not without its problems. The white library staff members lacked enthusiasm for the changes their director was bringing in Selma, the integration and the promotion of their former maid. They respected Mrs. Blalock, but did not understand or agree with her racial views. Recognizing the discomfort of her employees, the director began holding daily meetings in which the staff could discuss problems that arose during the day. Blalock hoped that her staff could air its grievances within the context of the meetings. Discussing the library's problems "around the bridge table," she believed, would only make matters worse.[51]

Disgruntled white patrons sometimes expressed openly their disapproval of the Carnegie Library's new policy on integration. Surprised over the presence of African Americans in the library, a white woman "went into a tirade," and she asserted that she would rather see the library closed than to endure integration. One of Selma's leading citizens entered the library in 1963 and found black patrons reading at the tables and charging books. He became incensed and demanded of the librarian, "What's going on here!" Dissatisfied with her response, the white patron began making angry remarks to blacks using the library. His performance continued until a policeman arrived and informed the irate man that he would have to "move on."[52]

As integration progressed, Mayor Heinz and Judge Reynolds began to feel pressure from their constituents to reverse their decision regarding the library. They were seasoned politicians who understood keenly the political dangers of the board's actions. Heinz and Reynolds began calling the city librarian in the evenings for an update on how the integration was progressing. It was a particularly "worrisome" time for Mayor Heinz who told Blalock that he had received communications from white Selmians urging that he either re-segregate or close the Carnegie Library. Concerned about the mayor's backsliding, the librarian remembers suggesting to Heinz that he lay the responsibility with her: "Chris, I'll tell you what to do. Just tell them I did it . . . they can blame me. Tell them that you didn't have anything to do with it."[53]

It was a difficult time for the city librarian. She had to harden herself to the complaints of angry whites and to the disapproval of associates who did not share her views. The crisis did not last long, however, and the reactions of some whites helped to affirm her commitment to integration in the library. She describes one incident in which a patron—a white man who she thought to be "friendly" and "scholarly," but also "one of the worst racists in the world"—came into the library to find a line of blacks waiting to apply for library cards. He turned to Blalock and commented, "You know, that's not so bad." She believed she had cleared "a big hurdle" by winning the man's acceptance. Another white patron demonstrated his opposition to integration by tearing up his library card and vowing never to return. The librarian was heartened when the man arrived two weeks later to charge a book. She presented him with the pieces of his old library card, which she had clipped together and saved in case he returned.[54]

The voluntary integration of the Carnegie Library in Selma by its board in 1963 represented an anomaly in local race relations. It is remarkable that a city that met civil rights marchers with clubs and cattle prods, and that had the state's first and most active white Citizens' Council would desegregate any of its public facilities in the absence of organized duress. In May 1963, however, the members of the city's library board, two of whom were also the county's leading segregationists, quietly and peaceably integrated the public library at the insistence of the city librarian. The board concluded that interracial service at the Carnegie Library did not represent as socially dangerous a situation as race mixing in schools or as threatening a proposition as equal voting rights. But it also mattered that the white librarian was the individual pressing for change. Unmistakably southern in bearing, manners, and speech, Patricia Blalock was one of *them*. She was a long-time resident of the community, a respected citizen and friend, and though she did not share the board members' racial views she "understood how they were brought up." Changing the library board's membership policy at the insistence of a native white Alabamian was more amenable to segregationists like Heinz and Reynolds and less politically damaging than integrating at the behest of black demonstrators, "outside agitators," and federal judges. Blalock's performance demonstrated that southern librarians could be effective agents of social change, even in the most inhospitable political environments.

## THE AMERICAN LIBRARY ASSOCIATION

The American Library Association (ALA) had little influence in the events that resulted in library desegregation in Alabama, and the support it provided for librarians like Juliette Morgan, Emily Reed, and Patricia Blalock was negligible. At the beginning of the 1960s, ALA was not the aggressive defender of intellectual freedom that it became by the end of the decade. ALA members were unsure if it was the place of a library association to become involved in regional questions of race relations. Some feared that public action on behalf of southern public librarians would only jeopardize the quiet but steady gains they believed the librarians were making on their own.

The news accounts of library sit-ins and the controversy surrounding Emily Reed attracted the attention of the library association by 1960, ending the long silence of the library profession on the "segregation problem." Members debated the association's role in the civil rights movement in libraries for six years. It proved a defining time for the organization. The dialogue caused ALA to reorder its priorities and reexamine perceived professional values, making it a more socially relevant body. Change did not come quickly enough, however, for ALA to exert any meaningful influence in regard to public library segregation in Alabama.

The American Library Association created its Intellectual Freedom Committee (IFC) in 1939 to address censorship issues and threats to freedom of expression, but the committee, and the association at large, remained silent on the subject of library segregation until after Emily Reed's ordeal. The controversy over *The Rabbits' Wedding* and ALA's failure to support Reed and others like her embarrassed IFC member Dan Lacy into opening a dialogue with Archie McNeal and the other committee members on matters of race and libraries in October of 1959.[55]

In 1960, news media coverage of the sit-in protests in the public libraries of Danville, Petersburg, Memphis, and Greenville brought the issue of library segregation to the notice of the ALA membership at large. Association president Benjamin Powell created a Civil Liberties Committee and called on the group to consider a public statement of ALA's position on the matter. Though Powell asserted that the association's "attitude with respect to freedom of libraries should be clear," he believed that segregation was a provincial matter and that the association should not "attempt to intrude on local jurisdiction." In the *Wilson Library Bulletin*, John Wakeman followed the ALA announcement with an editorial absolving the association of responsibility in the area of library segregation. Change had to begin at the local level, Wakeman contended. ALA was already as effective against racial discrimination as "its structure" permitted.[56]

In the December issue of *Library Journal*, Eric Moon, the journal's new editor, and Rice Estes, the Pratt Institute librarian and a Southerner, took issue with the position of Powell and Wakeman, beginning a debate over library segregation in ALA that would last for the next three years. Estes complained that the library profession was inconsistent in its opposition to information freedom challenges: "When a book is banned in the smallest hamlet, there is a vigorous protest. . . . But when a city takes away the right of citizens to read *every* book in the public library, we say nothing. The problem has suddenly become 'local,' and a very good alternative for 'untouchable.'" He asserted that he knew how complex the racial issue was, being a native South Carolinian, but that the national library organization had to speak out on behalf of the southern librarians; they were not free to speak for themselves on account of the "reprisals and political retaliation" that might result. Estes challenged Wakeman's argument that ALA had been effective regarding racial discrimination in libraries. He argued that it had been "completely ineffective about the issue." It had never lauded the efforts of civil rights activists, lent its name as amicus curiae to any group bringing a desegregation suit, or even passed a resolution stating its position on library segregation.[57]

In an editorial entitled "The Silent Subject," Moon echoed Estes's position and also complained that the library profession had generally ignored the issue of segregation. He argued that "any librarian looking at our library periodicals over the past five or six years" would find no indication that a "segregation problem" existed. Moon found two items on *The Rabbits' Wedding* controversy in general periodicals, but contended that, with the exception of Wakeman's recent editorial, library journals did not cover segregation-related issues.[58]

At the 1961 Midwinter meeting of the association, Herman Fussler and the rest of the Civil Liberties Committee submitted the library discrimination statement Powell had called for the previous year. It took the form of a proposed addition to the Library Bill of Rights. The statement asserted that "The rights of an individual to the use of a library should not be denied or abridged because of his race, religion, national origins or political views." The association adopted the addition in a near-unanimous vote. It left unanswered the question of what actions, if any, ALA would take to advance its professed belief in intellectual freedom for southern blacks.[59]

In a May *Wilson Library Bulletin* article, black librarians responded to ALA's recent statement, asserting that the association should begin to consider how it could "implement" its opposition to library segregation. Atlanta University's library school dean, Virginia Lacy Jones, contended that the association should be a model for the profession in race relations. It should hire blacks at ALA headquarters. She argued for more black speakers at conferences and more African Americans leading important committees. Other black contributors asserted that ALA should take aggressive measures in regard to southern public libraries. The African-American librarians suggested that, besides including blacks in the Intellectual Freedom Committee, ALA should make legal aid available to activists arrested for sitting in at public libraries. They also argued that the library association should pressure the federal government to withhold library funds from municipalities that segregated their libraries.[60]

For Archie McNeal, University of Miami library director and IFC chair, the methods proposed by the black librarians and by Eric Moon, Rice Estes, and others concerned with civil rights, would be dangerous and counterproductive. He warned that an aggressive stance by ALA would only hamper progress being made by quiet but right-minded southern librarians. Professionals in the region were making measurable progress, McNeal asserted, but only because their efforts were unpublicized and performed within the local power structure. Strong statements or actions by outsiders would only worsen hot tempers and would draw the attention of segregationists to libraries. Likewise, any pressure on the federal government to eliminate funds to southern libraries would jeopardize the tenuous progress being made in extending library service to rural blacks. Ultimately, McNeal argued, the responsibility for desegregating libraries lay with southern blacks rather than northern librarians. The most effective way to bring change was for African Americans to take offending whites into federal court.[61]

The membership of the American Library Association continued to wrangle over the library segregation issue through 1962. At the Midwinter conference in Chicago, ALA's executive board rejected an IFC recommendation that the association withhold institutional membership from libraries that excluded blacks. Instead, it issued a mild "Declaration of belief, encouragement and confident expectation." The declaration expressed the association's opposition to segregation, lauded gains made by southern librarians, and expressed an understanding that some librarians were unable to integrate their libraries because of state and local laws. When the ALA Council met in Miami the following summer, it refused to validate the executive board's declaration, instructing it to create a stronger statement.[62]

The "endless debate and quibbling" that characterized the 1962 conference ultimately resulted in a statement that urged offending libraries to integrate rather than barring them from institutional membership, as the IFC had suggested. It encouraged librarians to work toward equality of access in their libraries. The statement also called for a study of the segregation problem in libraries. Critics called the 1962 measure "unequivocal," but it did settle the question of the library association's self-perceived role in the civil rights movement in libraries. ALA was publicly opposed to library segregation and it would attempt to determine the extent of the problem, but the association would not directly participate in the movement to end segregation in libraries.[63]

The library segregation controversy did not end with the 1962 statement, however. The library association charged International Research Associates, Inc., a New York research organization, with surveying the extent of black access to public libraries. The research agency found that library segregation was on the decline by 1963. The South was making more rapid progress desegregating its libraries than it was in other public facilities, like schools, swimming pools, and buses. According to the researchers, libraries were easier to integrate, because they attracted a more educated class of people who were less likely to hold violently pro-segregationist views. Despite the advances being made, however, the access report revealed that library segregation was still common in the rural South and remained "widespread and severe" throughout Deep South states like Alabama.[64]

Interested ALA members had expected this type of revealing examination of the openly racist exclusions practiced by segregated libraries in the South. Many were unprepared, however, for the research agency's findings regarding "indirect" discrimination in public libraries outside the South. The absence of de jure segregation in American cities did not preclude other forms of discrimination, according to the report. While the branch libraries of a city "may be formally integrated," the researchers contended, "they may act informally as instruments of discrimination." In all but one of the non-South cities covered in the study, researchers found evidence of racial discrimination in the provision of library service. The *Access to Public Libraries* report implied that de facto residential segregation in urban America resulted in the creation of neighborhood branches that were either predominantly white or predominantly black. The white neighborhoods were more likely to have library branches than African-American neighborhoods and the resources of the white branches were more extensive. The researchers asserted that the "cumulative effect" was "a clear pattern of discrimination against non-white neighborhoods." In Detroit, for example, white neighborhoods were twice as likely to have a branch as non-white neighborhoods. White neighborhoods in Philadelphia were six times more likely to have a branch than non-white.[65]

At the 1963 conference in Chicago, the survey was "easily the most controversial item of business to be considered." Librarians from outside the South, particularly those from the cities covered in the study, were incensed. They denounced the research procedures employed in the survey and called for new studies. Others condemned the report as an attempt to sidetrack ALA in the area of civil rights. For white and black southern librarians, the controversy only provided evidence that their northern colleagues were dedicated to eradicating racial discrimination in library service, except when it took place in their own libraries. Edward G. Holley of the University of Houston Library contended that "any research team which implicates those in the power structure of an organization gets short shrift." Virginia Lacy Jones scolded the access study's critics, asserting that library discrimination was a national, rather than a southern, phenomenon and it was "time the North woke up to it."[66]

The association continued to debate questions of race after the 1963 controversy, but with little effect as far as libraries in Alabama were concerned. It reconsidered sanctions against ALA member libraries that practiced segregation in 1965 and again in 1966, but the measures suggested were largely irrelevant. The Civil Rights Act, passed in 1964 in the wake of the Birmingham Campaign, had already made such exclusions from public facilities patently illegal. In Alabama, the four largest cities, along with Gadsden, Selma, and Talladega, had already integrated their libraries as a result of civil rights activity and of the efforts of southern librarians when the *Access to Public Libraries* was presented to ALA in 1963.[67]

Through the first three years of the 1960s, the American Library Association represented a well-intentioned body of librarians genuinely distressed over the question of library segregation. The association's exclusion of segregated chapters—like Alabama's—was a decisive action toward integrating the associational membership, but not toward desegregating libraries, themselves. The issue of race proved too complex, and clear remedies too difficult to find, for the association to become an effective agent in the movement for equitable access to public libraries in Alabama and in other southern states. Members debated whether ALA could engage in political activism and whether it was the place of a professional organization to interfere in matters of "local" concern. Leaders could not reach a consensus on whether aggressive action by ALA would only sabotage the efforts of librarians in the region, like Patricia Blalock in Selma, who worked quietly toward peaceful integration, and some members were unwilling to confront the reality of de facto segregation outside the South.

The experience caused the association to reexamine its thinking on the responsibilities implied by its code of professional ethics. In their separate histories of ALA and intellectual freedom, Evelyn Geller and Louise S. Robbins make clear that the library association was not always the active partisan for freedom of expression and access to information that it is at the beginning of the twenty-first century. The civil rights movement was an important leg of the "sometimes ponderous journey" of ALA's development on the intellectual freedom issue. The association's debate regarding segregation in Alabama and other southern states was ALA's "first lesson in activism," according to Robbins, and the movement is partly responsible for the library association's emergence as a champion of intellectual freedom. Ultimately, the existence of library segregation in the South had a larger influence on the American Library Association than ALA had on it.

## THE ALABAMA LIBRARY ASSOCIATION

Library leaders organized the Alabama Library Association (Ala.L.A.) on November 21, 1904, in Montgomery. Its objectives were "the promotion of libraries and library interests" in the state and to create an "esprit de corps" among Alabama librarians. The association located its headquarters in Montgomery's newly constructed Carnegie Library on Perry Street. The organization adopted a constitution at its first meeting; it provided that "Any person desirous of promoting the objects of the Association shall be eligible for membership." In reality, the group was only open to whites. There was no official statement barring African Americans, but it became the practice of the library association to ignore applications submitted by blacks.[68]

In 1951, Alabama Library Association president Gretchen Shenk prompted the organization's first moves toward integration, but her efforts were unsuccessful. Under Shenk's leadership, the association created a biracial committee to study the possibility of admitting African-American librarians. The group held a meeting on April 12 at Montgomery's Carnegie Library to "determine whether Negro librarians wished to join the Ala.L.A., and to discuss problems which are evident in any bi-racial group." Ten black librarians attended along with six whites. The African-American group expressed its desire to participate in the activities of the state library organization and to enjoy full membership privileges. The meeting had little effect. African-American school librarian Carrie Robinson attended and remembers that it was clear that the library association members were unready to accept her and the other blacks. She remarks on the "ease with which some members of the Alabama Library Association demeaned prospective black members." According to Robinson, William Stanley Hoole, library dean at The University of Alabama, demanded during Shenk's failed attempt to integrate, "Who is stuffing these Negroes down our throats? I want you to know that I represent a conservative institution." The Bi-Racial Committee dissolved the following year.[69]

In 1963, the association once again had a president sympathetic to racial integration. Richard Covey, who had helped to integrate his library in Huntsville in 1962, received letters of application from six librarians at Tuskegee Institute during the spring of 1963. They were professionals with substantial educational credentials. Three were department heads. Covey replied to the Tuskegee group, "You might know that there has never been a Negro member of the Association. We have, by custom, never offered anything but rather weak excuses." He asserted that the segregation policy had been "most irksome" to him and he promised to submit the matter to the Executive Council for a vote. He would reply as soon as the council had decided.[70]

Covey wrote to the members of the Executive Council on April 11 (coincidentally this occurred the same day that the Birmingham Public Library was integrated). The association president described the qualifications of the applicants and reminded the council of the association's inclusive membership clause opening the group to "any person" who supported the organization's objectives. "It is false to operate" under the constitution, he wrote, "if we do not mean it." Covey argued that if the Alabama Library Association wanted to remain segregated, "let us say so," otherwise the council should make a statement integrating the organization "and stand behind it." Earlier decisions to remain segregated rested on an argument that blacks could not be accommodated at conference hotels and meeting places on account of local segregation ordinances. But Covey contended that the actions of individual cities was not an excuse for the library association to shun its own responsibilities. He instructed the council members to submit their votes on the Tuskegee applications by mail.[71]

Covey was unable to get a quorum in his mail ballot. There were four affirmative votes, three votes against admitting the black librarians, four abstentions, and the remaining council members failed to reply. One of the negative votes came from Farris Martin, the Montgomery librarian who grudgingly integrated his facility under federal injunction. Martin warned Covey that "with Mobile integrated, Montgomery under injunction," and "Birmingham under duress" the racial climate was too dangerous to begin admitting blacks to the library association. He believed that the ALA access survey and the Mississippi and Louisiana chapters' withdrawal from ALA provided further evi-

dence that Covey's timing was poor. Taking up the issue of desegregation of the membership might "tear both the Executive Council and the
whole Alabama Library Association asunder."[72]

At the annual meeting the council voted to "delay" a decision on the
Tuskegee applications and to change the constitution so the associa-
tion could officially deny membership to future applicants if it wished.
Covey wrote to the Tuskegee librarians explaining the council's actions.
He asserted that he was "not at all satisfied" with the outcome and ad-
mitted that he was "a little ashamed" by the affair.[73]

In December of 1964, the Alabama Library Association finally desegregated. The Civil Rights Act, passed earlier in the year, made segregation in public accommodations illegal, and the library association
could no longer use its traditional excuse that segregation laws prevented biracial conventions. Also, the American Library Association
had applied pressure on associations like Alabama's, forbidding its officers from participating in the activities of segregated organizations. Of
more immediate importance to Alabama's association, the federal government had begun to instruct its employees not to take part in organizations that excluded blacks. This meant the loss of the association's
current president, Maxwell Air Force Base librarian Robert W. Severance, and several incoming council members.[74]

In a letter to the membership that appeared in *Alabama Librarian*,
the president explained the council's decision to integrate. He asserted
that the association was "*not* engaged in attempting to solve racial problems" and hoped that a "minimum of publicity" would accompany the
change. The library associations in Alabama and Georgia had lost their
chapter status in ALA in 1956 as a result of their refusal to desegregate.
Severance added in his letter that Ala.L.A. would not immediately seek
to rejoin ALA, even though the desegregation made it eligible for membership. He explained that some members of the Alabama Library Association were resentful of the actions ALA had taken in regard to state
library organizations in the South; they opposed the "application of
force by outside agencies."[75]

The Alabama Library Association held its first integrated convention in Mobile during the following spring. Freed to participate in the
meeting by the state association's decision to desegregate, Eric Moon,
the controversial editor of *Library Journal*, delivered the principal address. His speech, "The Central Fact of Our Times," covered civil
rights and the responsibilities of the library profession. The *Alabama*

*Librarian* described the talk as "well-received" adding, "You do not have to agree with the man to admire him." About forty African-American librarians joined the association during the first two months of integration. According to Moon, fifteen to twenty of them were in attendance at the convention and they were represented in "just about all the meetings." He asserted that there was "not too much open mingling of the races," but that the black librarians he talked to seemed "generally pleased" with the conference atmosphere and had experienced no significant problems.[76]

After a decade of banishment, the Alabama Library Association rejoined ALA in July 1965. The membership of the state library organization had approved the union 124 to 3 in a mail ballot. The civil rights years had been tumultuous ones for librarianship in Alabama, but it was clear that its library association, as a segregated organization, was in no position to provide leadership in matters of race. The group's own internal struggle regarding membership provided evidence that the association reacted to, rather than participated in, the changes in race relations in Alabama, and the association had no observable influence on the events of library desegregation. In fact, after all of the state's major cities had integrated their libraries, the Alabama Library Association still excluded black librarians.

As a group, the state's librarians exhibited no clear pattern of genuine support of library desegregation. Black librarians were excluded from the decision-making process and they could not exert measurable influence on "white" libraries. In general, white public librarians understood the volatility the subject of race engendered in the Deep South and they sought to avert conflict in their institutions. The state library association was consumed with a quiet debate over its own segregationist practices and it successfully avoided the issue of public library integration.

Most white librarians in the state were moderates and largely apolitical on the subject of race; they were neither fervent segregationists nor vocal supporters of civil rights. Outright integrationists like Patricia Blalock were exceptional, and likewise, Alabama provides no examples of librarians who demonstrated extreme forms of massive resistance. Librarians' attitudes toward blacks were as varied and as difficult to explain as the complex relationships between white moderates and blacks in the general population. Their racial attitudes incorporated notions of paternalism, but also of professional responsibility. The civil rights movement was a time of anxiety for them, but for some the fear of changing racial mores was acute.

Ultimately, it is easier to understand why many Alabama librarians did not lead their libraries toward desegregation than to explain why some did. Professional ethics stood little chance against a tradition that overpowered white conscience, democratic values, even Christian teachings. Most who believed segregation wrong could not imagine actively opposing it. For native southerners, it meant questioning what they had been taught in school, at church, and at home, challenging the "natural order" of things. Supporting integration meant allying with the enemy, not the southern blacks, but the "hypocritical" white outsiders. It meant risking ostracism and possibly worse. Within their own profession and their own state, Alabama librarians saw in Juliette Morgan and Emily Reed examples of what happened to individuals who challenged the agents of massive resistance.

The deeply ingrained racial attitudes of white Southerners were becoming less impregnable by the 1960s, however, and library directors responded to the changes in race relations. Patricia Blalock was a genuine integrationist who ended exclusions at Selma's Carnegie Library in advance of any civil rights demonstrations or federal intervention. More common were individuals like Guenter Jensen of Mobile, Richard J. Covey of Huntsville, and Fant Thornley of Birmingham who reacted to duress by black activists and to judicial pressure by leading their libraries toward integration. They held moderate racial views and proved more interested in the well being of their institutions than in protecting racial separation. Some—like Thornley—were occupied by merely keeping the library doors open during a time when local politicians would rather have seen public libraries closed than integrated. But events demonstrated that the efforts of black protesters were ultimately more important to the cause of equal access to public libraries than the impulses of librarians on the state and national level to fulfill their professional values.

# Conclusion

Affecting millions of blacks, the exclusion of African-American readers from public libraries undermined intellectual freedom in American libraries more than any other factor during the twentieth century. Neither the segregation of libraries nor their integration has been treated adequately in scholarly literature, however. The study of such events in Alabama is an appropriate starting point, since Alabama is a state whose history is closely associated with the emergence of de jure racial separation and one that became a crucible of the black struggle for basic civil rights in America. The Alabama experience provides an extreme example of racial discrimination in American public library service, one that reflects the changing pattern of race relations that characterized the United States, and particularly the South, during the first sixty-five years of the twentieth century.

Both segregation and the southern public library movement were products of the Progressive movement spawned by the modernization which the South experienced at the turn of the century. The legally sanctioned separation of blacks from whites, which Jack Temple Kirby called the region's "seminal reform," established a social order under which Southerners could create new industries, employ new technologies, and found new institutions while maintaining white supremacy. Segregation thus provided a social framework within which progressives could build libraries and other organizations for educational and cultural improvement in the New South.[1]

Beginning in 1918, white Alabamians began to lend their support to the creation of library facilities for African Americans. This support was conditional, however; black facilities had to be inexpensive and they had to adhere to the customs of the racially segregated society. As a result African-American readers had separate buildings, usually small rented spaces or modest structures, and small collections, invariably inferior to those held by white libraries. While the main libraries often lent books to the Negro branches to meet "special needs," racial separation was sometimes carried to extremes, as for example in Birmingham where white administrators determined that once black hands had touched a book it could not return to general circulation.

Between 1900 and 1940, white philanthropy and federal library aid made significant contributions to the public library movement in the South. New Deal programs in Alabama ushered in a time of expansion for public library service and resulted in the creation of a state library agency. But the benefits of these programs were enjoyed mostly by whites. The success of the Julius Rosenwald project in Walker County —where black readership overtook that of whites—had demonstrated that where agents from outside the region provided resources for the provision of black library service substantial gains could be made. But in administering the Works Progress Administration and Tennessee Valley Authority library programs federal officials acquiesced in local racial customs, and they often did not include black library development in their plans.

Black communities created their own public library movement to parallel the one southern whites had started at the beginning of the century. In the 1940s and 1950s African-American civic and religious organizations, educators, clergy, business leaders and librarians led an indigenous effort to develop libraries for their race. They worked within the prevailing social order to enhance their civic infrastructures and improve their social environment. African-American librarians were pioneers in their profession and in their communities, providing library services to a large population unaccustomed to library access.

During the early 1960s blacks began working toward integrating white public libraries rather than accommodating themselves to the realities of segregation. They applied the methods of direct action, staging sit-in protests in public libraries and filing desegregation suits in the federal courts. Young blacks were particularly active in the movement. Often better educated than their parents, they were increasingly impatient to secure access to their local cultural resources. In southern cities the public library was a conspicuous public institution, one of many that activists targeted. The emphasis that black civil rights workers placed on the integration of public libraries throughout the segregated South demonstrated that to them the public library was not a "marginal" cultural institution but an intrinsic part of a community's educational infrastructure. Because of their professed democratic nature public libraries that practiced segregation became symbols of the American racial dilemma.

The reaction of whites in Alabama to civil rights activities in libraries varied according to the political and racial climates in the cities involved and the character of their civic leadership. Recognizing that defending library segregation was legally untenable, some cities integrated their public libraries quietly, almost covertly, to avoid conflict. Other cities held out longer for reasons of politics or conviction. Although the prospect of library integration was less frightening to whites than the desegregation of schools, swimming pools and buses, race mixing in public libraries was still a dangerous proposition. The most violent example of this occurred in Anniston in 1963 when an angry white mob armed with chains, knives and bottles viciously attacked the black clergymen who were attempting to integrate the Carnegie Library.

Among Alabama librarians, active opposition to library desegregation was rare. Before the civil rights movement most were constrained by local racial customs, Jim Crow laws and, often, by their own racial attitudes. Their reactions to the movement for civil rights were inseparably linked to their complex and widely varying beliefs in regard to race; racial attitudes among Alabama's white librarians ranged from Farris Martin's brooding racism, to Patricia Blalock's integrationist notions of human dignity. Most librarians fell between the two poles; they were within the broad category of white Americans known as racial moderates.

The chair of the American Library Association's Intellectual Freedom Committee, Archie McNeal, argued that professionals such as these were making laudable progress on their own in regard to the extension of library service to southern blacks. But in the cities of Alabama, most library directors led their institutions toward integration only after the libraries became the subject of sit-in protests or federal pressure.

Events related to library segregation bear relevance to broader discussions of public library movements, librarians and intellectual freedom, and the relationship between racial and ethnic minorities and public libraries. Therefore the history of southern public libraries, including those in Alabama, serves as a model for studying issues of general professional significance from an alternative perspective, and it suggests new subjects for study.

One of the most heated scholarly debates in library history has been over the motives that drove public library movements in the United States. One school of thought, represented most visibly in the works of Jesse Shera, Sidney H. Ditzion, Phyllis Dain and Elaine Fain, suggests, in general terms, that the creators of popular libraries in the nineteenth and early twentieth centuries designed their institutions as agents of social improvement. These authors emphasize the role of public libraries in the education and general betterment of the working class, paying particular attention to the democratic, or at least the paternalistic, nature of the institutions. The revisionists, who include Michael Harris, Dee Garrison and Peter Mickelson, argue that libraries were built by an elite bent on social control. These authors see the patricians who built libraries as agents of conservatism who defended the status quo and promoted Anglo-American values and culture at the expense of diversity and self-determination.

In their support of segregated public libraries for African Americans early library boosters and librarians in urban Alabama exhibited motives described by both schools of thought. These whites believed in the potential of libraries to improve the lives of black people, were proud of their Negro branches, and lent their support to the efforts of black public library movements so long as they in no way suggested social equality. The sense of obligation that led them to provide educational and cultural opportunities for African Americans and their equal commitment to racial order reflected their complex and sometimes contradictory attitudes toward race relations and libraries. But these irresolute positions were consistent with the ambiguous nature of southern progressivism and white paternalism, and they demonstrated that in Alabama, at least, the desire for social improvement and the impulse toward social control were not mutually exclusive.

The history of library segregation also relates closely to the changing values of librarianship. In their respective studies of librarianship and intellectual freedom, Evelyn Geller and Louise Robbins depict a profession whose convictions in regard to the free access to information evolved over the course of America's library history. In 1876, when the American Library Association was created, library leaders endorsed the notion that their profession should play the role of moral censor. Professionalism meant protecting the reading public from salacious or otherwise inappropriate materials and guiding patrons to literature of quality. By 1939, however, librarianship had shed its identity as a censor, and ALA created a Library Bill of Rights. This expression of the profession's belief in the freedom to read reflected an increasing emphasis on democracy in America that accompanied the rise of European totalitarianism. After World War II American librarians continued to promote a role for libraries as agents of pluralism and democratic living, but their support for these ideals was largely passive, expressed in words rather than actions.

Just as external forces had brought ideological changes to librarianship during the 1930s and 1940s, the civil rights movement of the 1950s and 1960s left an indelible mark on the profession as it continued its "odyssey of self-definition." As part of that odyssey, librarians gradually revised their understanding of what intellectual freedom meant. What began as a general condemnation of the banning of books became a more encompassing commitment to enhance access to information, including the promotion of information equity.[2]

The troubles that surrounded Emily Reed and others similarly situated, like Ruth Brown of Oklahoma, led librarians to see a relationship between segregation and the suppression of information. The sit-in protests of blacks in cities like Birmingham, Mobile and Montgomery pushed issues of information equity into the national library dialogue and led ALA to examine racial discrimination in public libraries, not just in the South but in other parts of the country as well, where de facto segregation, economic disadvantages and discriminatory practices led to inequalities in library service.

Although the part the American Library Association played in the integration of public libraries was small, the internal debate over race resulted in a re-examination of the role of librarians, broadening the profession's commitment to expand access to information and making it a more vocal advocate of its ideals. There can be little doubt that the tumultuous events in Alabama and other southern states that resulted in the demise of library desegregation also brought important changes to ALA and to the way librarians thought about intellectual freedom. For Louise Robbins, the civil rights movement was librarianship's "first lesson in activism" as librarians became caught up in the spirit of social change, leading some to a belief in social responsibility that occasionally led the focus away from pluralism and objectivity.[3]

In addition to the question of professional values, library segregation speaks to the relationship between public libraries and the African-American communities they serve. The historical effort to create black libraries provided an example of communities enhancing their own cultural and educational resources in a climate of social distress and economic disadvantage. The result was the emergence of racially distinct institutions that sought to encourage blacks and to instill racial pride, especially in young people. Black libraries offered materials by black authors such as DuBois, Hughes, and Wright, which helped provide a sense of group identity, and black librarians served as role models for children and as educational leaders for their communities. The experience in Alabama also demonstrated that black library efforts could benefit from resources from outside the community and that blacks responded to improved library service with increased library use.

The civil rights movement ended de jure desegregation, enfranchised southern blacks and diminished overt racial discrimination but left unsolved the more difficult problems of black poverty and racism. Many blacks, now as earlier, have been unsatisfied or disillusioned with racial progress in America, and as a result there has been a resurgent movement to promote the social benefits of strong, coherent African-American communities with their own distinct institutions. Since the 1960s, a few observers, most notably E. J. Josey, have proclaimed the social importance of library work, in particular, for black communities. In this environment the work of public librarians assumes the character of social reform that harkens back to the branch libraries in ethnic communities during the era of progressivism that emphasized practical help for immigrants. It also leads to the African-American public library movement that emerged under segregation.

As a result, there is a continuing need to examine library services for minority populations within a historical context. Some of the fundamental issues associated with black library movements under segregation have an enduring relevance to the role of public libraries in today's disadvantaged and racially homogenous neighborhoods. There has been little scholarship in this area, however, partly because race poses as complex an issue at the end of the twentieth century as it did in the middle of the century.

Ultimately, the history of segregation and civil rights in Alabama's public libraries is a study of social institutions in a state where America's racial dilemma was particularly acute. Libraries were places of public interaction, and white southerners segregated them to maintain white supremacy. Both the oppressors and the oppressed held social priorities that defined the form and purpose of segregated libraries. As Alabama's library history unfolded these priorities made public libraries instruments of social improvement and social control, objects of community action, targets for civil rights protest, and battlegrounds in the struggle to preserve white supremacy. For Alabama librarians, library desegregation provided evidence of their internal conflicts between professional values and a southern identity. Circumstances linked public libraries to the state's racial troubles, and the development of black library service became an indicator of social progress.

# Notes

Notes to Chapter 1

1. Jesse H. Shera, *Foundations of the Public Library: The Origins of the Public Library Movement in New England, 1629–1855* (Chicago: University of Chicago Press, 1949), 156–99, 200–244; Sidney Ditzion, *Arsenals of a Democratic Culture: A Social History of the American Public Library Movement in New England and the Middle States from 1850–1900* (Chicago: American Library Association, 1947), ix.

2. Mary Edna Anders, *The Development of Public Library Service in the Southeastern States, 1895–1950* (D.L.S. diss., Columbia University, 1958), [unpaginated abstract].

3. Ibid, 44, 63–64, 236.

4. Dewey Grantham, *Southern Progressivism: The Reconciliation of Progress and Tradition* (Knoxville: University of Tennessee Press, 1983), 50; Sheldon Hackney, *Populism to Progressivism in Alabama* (Princeton, NJ: Princeton University Press, 1969), xiv–xv, 331.

5. Anders, *Development of Public Library Service in the Southeastern States,* 52, 63–64; Marilyn J. Martin, *From Altruism to Activism: The Contributions of Women's Organizations to Arkansas Public Libraries* (University of North Texas, Ph.D. diss., 1993), vii, 73, 195–96.

6. Alabama Library Association, *Proceedings of the First Meeting of the Alabama Library Association* (Montgomery, AL: Brown Printing Company, 1905), 11–12, 65–68; Jean Le Furgey Hoffman, "The Alabama Library Association, 1904–1939: A History of its Organization, Growth and Contribution to Library Development" (Florida State University, M.S. thesis, 1962), 15–25; Thomas M. Owen, "Address on Organization of Alabama Library Association," Alabama Library Association Papers, W. S. Hoole Special Collections Library, University of Alabama, Tuscaloosa; In addition to the library associa-

tion, Thomas M. Owen led the development of the Alabama Department of Archives and History—the nation's first state archives—in 1901.

7. Robert H. Wiebe, *The Search for Order, 1877–1920* (New York: Hill and Wang, 1967), 111–32, 166; Grantham, *Southern Progressivism*, 126; Jack Temple Kirby, *Darkness at the Dawning: Race and Reform in the Progressive South* (Philadelphia: Lippincott, 1972), 4; See also, John W. Cell, *The Highest Stage of White Supremacy: The Origins of Segregation in South Africa and the American South* (Cambridge: Cambridge University Press, 1982); and William A. Link, *The Paradox of Southern Progressivism, 1880–1930* (Chapel Hill: University of North Carolina Press, 1992).

8. Birmingham, Library Board, *Triennial Report*, 1925–27; Brooks Stewart to Dr. R. R. Moton, Aug. 28, 1930, Mobile Public Library, Mobile, AL.

9. Marjorie Longenecker White, *The Birmingham District: An Industrial History and Guide.* (Birmingham, AL: Birmingham Historical Society, 1981), 1–63; Bobby M. Wilson, "Racial Segregation Trends in Birmingham, Alabama," *Southeastern Geographer* 25 (May 1985): 31.

10. Birmingham, Library Board, *Fiftieth Anniversary, Birmingham Public Library*, 1959; William T. Miller, "Library Service for Negroes in the New South: Birmingham, Alabama, 1871–1918," *Alabama Librarian* (Nov.–Dec. 1975): 7.

11. Henry McKiven, Jr., *Iron and Steel: Class, Race, and Community in Birmingham, Alabama, 1875–1920* (Chapel Hill: University of North Carolina Press, 1995), 41, 42, 49–50, 53; Robert J. Norrell, "Caste in Steel: Jim Crow Careers in Birmingham, Alabama," *Journal of American History* 73 (1986): 669–94.

12. John Fitch, "Birmingham District: Labor Conservation," *Survey* 27 (Jan. 6, 1912): 1532, 1540; Miller, "Library Service for Negroes in the New South," 7.

13. Miller, "Library Service for Negroes in the New South," 7; Birmingham, Library Board, *Fiftieth Anniversary.*

14. Eliza Atkins Gleason, *The Southern Negro and the Public Library* (Chicago: University of Chicago Press, 1941), 18–19.

15. Birmingham, Library Board, "Minutes," Jan. 8, July 25, Aug. 2, Aug. 14, 1918, Archives Dept., Birmingham Public Library, Birmingham, AL; Miller, "Library Service for Negroes in the New South," 8.

16. *Birmingham News*, Oct. 8, 1918; Birmingham *Age-Herald*, Oct. 8, 1918; Birmingham *Age-Herald*, Oct. 27, 1937; Birmingham, Library Board, "Minutes," July 29, 1918, Aug. 2, 1918, Aug. 14, 1918.

17. Birmingham, Library Board, "Minutes," Aug. 2, 1918.

18. Birmingham, Library Board, "Minutes," Mar. 13, 1918; Birmingham *Age-Herald*, Aug. 1, 1918; Miller, "Library Service for Negroes in the New South," 7; Annie Greene King, "Library Service and the Black Librarian in

Alabama," in *The Black Librarian in the Southeast*, ed. Annette L. Phinazee (Durham: North Carolina Central University, 1980), 21.

19. John Wilkins, "Blue's 'Colored' Branch: A 'Second Plan' that Became a First in Librarianship," *American Libraries* 7 (1976): 256–57; Birmingham, Library Board, "Minutes," July 29, 1918, Aug. 14, 1918.

20. Birmingham, Library Board, "Minutes," July 29, 1918, Aug. 14, 1918.

21. Birmingham, Library Board, "Minutes," Feb. 12, 1919, May 2, 1919, May 14, 1919; Carl Milam to Reginald Gaines, May 2, 1919, Archives Dept., Birmingham Public Library, Birmingham, AL.

22. Carl Milam to Reginald Gaines, May 2, 1919, Archives Dept., Birmingham Public Library, Birmingham, AL; Carl Milam to Reginald Gaines, May 15, 1919, Archives Dept., Birmingham Public Library, Birmingham, AL.

23. L. W. Josselyn to Reginald Gaines, June 20, 1919, Archives Dept., Birmingham Public Library, Birmingham, AL.

24. L. W. Josselyn to Reginald Gaines, Sept. 22, 1919, Archives Dept., Birmingham Public Library, Birmingham, AL; Bertha Williams, interview by author, May 23, 1996, Montgomery, tape recording.

25. Birmingham, Library Board, "Minutes," May 11, 1921, Nov. 18, 1922, Sept. 6, 1924; Birmingham Public Library, "Work of the Branches, 1920," Director's Files, Archives Dept., Birmingham Public Library, Birmingham, AL; Bureau of Business Research, School of Commerce and Business Administration, University of Alabama, *Alabama County Statistical Abstracts* (University, AL: University of Alabama Press, 1943), 161–63.

26. Birmingham Public Library, "Work of the Branches, 1920," Director's Files, Archives Dept., Birmingham Public Library, Birmingham, AL; Birmingham Public Library, *Triennial Report, 1935–1936–1937*, 27, 30, 41, 42; Earline Cureton Driver to L. W. Josselyn, 1921, Director's Files, Archives Dept., Birmingham Public Library, Birmingham, AL; Birmingham, Library Board, "Minutes," Aug. 8, 1923, Oct. 10, 1923, Dec. 8, 1926, Aug. 10, 1927, Aug. 9, 1933; Birmingham, Library Board, *Annual Report*, (1925), 18, 19, 20.

27. Birmingham, Library Board, *Triennial Report* (1935–37), 30; "City's Increasing Thirst for Knowledge Revealed in Annual Library Report," Undated Clipping [1920s], Public Information Subject Files, Alabama Department of Archives and History, Montgomery, AL; Bureau of Business Research, *Alabama County Statistical Abstracts*, 161–63; Louis Vandiver Loveman, *Alabama Book of Facts and Historical Statistics* (Gadsden, AL: Loveman, 1975), 58. The illiteracy rate in Alabama was 26.2 percent in 1930.

28. Birmingham *Age-Herald*, Oct. 27, 1937.

29. Charles Grayson Summersell, *Mobile: History of a Seaport Town* (University, AL: University of Alabama Press, 1949), 1–3, 15–24.

30. Blacks comprised about half of Mobile's population by 1812. See Summersell, *Mobile*, 11; Bureau of Business Research, *Alabama County Statistical Ab-*

*stracts*, 217–22; Louis Vandiver Loveman, *Alabama Book of Facts and Historical Statistics* (Gadsden, AL: Loveman, 1975), 33; Summersell, *Mobile*, 39; Melton McLaurin and Michael Thomason, *Mobile: The Life and Times of a Great Southern City* (Woodland Hills, CA: Windsor, 1981), 118.

31. McLaurin and Thomason, *Mobile*, 119; E. T. Belsaw to Dr. Dunbar H. Ogden, June 15, 1928, Mobile Public Library, Mobile, AL.

32. "Brief History of the Mobile Public Library," Vertical Files, Mobile Public Library, Mobile, AL; Mobile *Register*, Feb. 6, 1919; Robert Sidney Martin, ed., *Carnegie Denied: Communities Rejecting Carnegie Library Construction Grants, 1898–1925* (Westport, CN: Greenwood Press, 1993), 158; Mobile, Board of Commissioners, "Resolution," Dec. 8, 1925, Mobile City Archives, Mobile, AL; R. V. Taylor (Finance Commissioner, City of Mobile), "To the People of Mobile," Jan. 27, 1926, Mobile City Archives, Mobile, AL.

33. Harry T. Hartwell (Commissioner) to Dr. E. T. Belsaw (Inter-racial Committee Chair), June 23, 1926, Mobile Public Library, Mobile, AL.

34. Dr. E. T. Belsaw to George Fearn, Jr., (President, Library Board), Dec. 11, 1926, Mobile Public Library, Mobile, AL; E. T. Belsaw to George Fearn, Jr., June 15, 1928, Mobile Public Library, Mobile, AL; Dr. E. T. Belsaw to George Fearn, Jr., June 15, 1928, Mobile Public Library, Mobile, AL.

35. E. T. Belsaw to George Fearn, Jr., June 15, 1928, Mobile Public Library, Mobile, AL; Mobile, Library Board, "Minutes," June 28, 1928, Mobile City Archives, Mobile, AL; George Fearn, Jr., to A. E. Bostwick (Director, St. Louis Public Library), July 16, 1928, Mobile Public Library, Mobile, AL. The groups represented at the June 28, 1928, board meeting were the inter-denominational organization of local black churches, the Interracial Committee of the Mobile Chamber of Commerce, and the Negro Auxiliary of the Mobile Chamber of Commerce.

36. Frederick G. Bromberg to Stewart Brooks (President, Library Board), June 7, 1929, Mobile Public Library, Mobile, AL.

37. Stewart Brooks to Frederick G. Bromberg, June 18, 1929, Mobile Public Library, Mobile, AL; Frederick G. Bromberg to Stewart Brooks, June 19, 1929, Mobile Public Library, Mobile, AL.

38. George Fearn, Jr., to American Library Association, July 6, 1928, Mobile Public Library, Mobile, AL; George Fearn, Jr., to A. E. Bostwick, July 11, 1928, Mobile Public Library, Mobile, AL.

39. Ibid.

40. George Fearn, Jr., to A. E. Bostwick, July 11, 1928, Mobile Public Library, Mobile, AL; A. E. Bostwick to George Fearn, Jr., Dec. 24, 1926, Mobile Public Library, Mobile, AL; Carl Milam (Secretary, ALA) to George Fearn, Jr., July 13, 1928, Mobile Public Library, Mobile, AL; A. E. Bostwick to George Fearn, Jr., July 14, 1928, Mobile Public Library, Mobile, AL; Mobile, Library Board, "Minutes," May 2, 1929, Mobile City Archives, Mobile, AL.

41. Vincent F. Kilborn (City Attorney) to Board of Commissioners, City of

Mobile, June 10, 1929, Mobile City Archives, Mobile, AL; Robert H. Smith, "Supplemental Brief in *James F. Maury, Jr. v. Board of Commissioners of the City of Mobile, et al*, in Circuit Court of Mobile County, Alabama," Vertical Files, Mobile Public Library, Mobile, AL; Untitled chronology of *Maury v. Board*, Vertical Files, Mobile Public Library, Mobile, AL.

42. "Davis Avenue Branch—Mobile Public Library. History," May 1970, Vertical Files, Mobile Public Library, Mobile, AL; Birdie Turner James, "History and Development of Public Library Service to Negroes in Mobile, Alabama, 1931–1959" (M.S. thesis, Atlanta University, 1961): 20; Mobile *Press*, Sept. 17, 1948; Mobile, Library Board, "Memorandum," [1930], Vertical Files, Mobile Public Library, Mobile, AL; Stewart Brooks to Dr. R. R. Moton (Principal, Tuskegee Institute), Aug. 28, 1930, Mobile Public Library, Mobile, AL.

43. Lila May Chapman to Stewart Brooks, Nov. 14, 1929, Mobile Public Library, Mobile, AL; James, "History and Development of Public Library Service to Negroes in Mobile," 24–5.

44. Stewart Brooks to Lila May Chapman (Director, Birmingham Public Library), Nov. 22, 1929, Mobile Public Library, Mobile, AL; Mobile, Library Board, "Minutes," July 9, 1931, Mobile City Archives, Mobile, AL.

45. James, "History and Development of Public Library Service to Negroes in Mobile," 25; McLaurin and Thomason, *Mobile*, 113; Marie Bankhead Owen, *The Story of Alabama: A History of the State* (New York: Lewis Historical Publishing Co., 1907), 341.

46. *New York Times*, Aug. 8, 1932.

Notes to Chapter 2

1. Donald G. Davis, Jr., "The Rise of the Public Library in Texas, 1876–1920," in *Milestones to the Present: Papers from Library History Seminar V*, ed. Harold Goldstein (Syracuse: Gaylord, 1978), 166–83.

2. Edwin R. Embree and Julia Waxman, *Investment in People: The Story of the Julius Rosenwald Fund* (New York: Harper, 1949), 5–28, 37–51; Thomas W. Hanchett, "The Rosenwald Schools in North Carolina," *North Carolina Historical Review* 65 (Oct. 1988): 387–89.

3. Embree and Waxman, *Investment in People*, 67; Louis R. Wilson and Edward A. Wight, *County Library Service in the South: A Study of the Rosenwald County Library Demonstration* (Chicago: University of Chicago Press, 1935), v, 29–30.

4. Berkeley North Hackett, "Walker County, Alabama, 1850 to 1950: A Migration Study" (M.S. thesis, University of Alabama, 1974): 8–9.

5. Hackett, "Walker County, Alabama," 19, 50; John Martin Dumbhart, *History of Walker County* (Thornton, AR: Cayce Publishing Co., 1937), 41–43.

6. Hackett, "Walker County, Alabama," 52–53; Dumbhart, *History of Walker County*, 43; Works Progress Administration, *Gainful Workers by Occupa-*

*tional Groups and By Race in Southeast, 1930* (Birmingham, AL: Works Progress Administration of Alabama, 1938), 100.

7. Jasper *Mountain Eagle*, Nov. 26, 1930, Jan. 14, 1931; Willie Fagan Calkins, "The Walker County Library," (M.A. thesis, University of Alabama, 1934), 8–11; Wilson and Wight, *County Library Service in the South*, 30.

8. Julius Rosenwald Fund, "General Plan," [n.d.], Vertical Files, Carl Elliott Regional Library, Jasper, AL.

9. The library for African Americans later relocated to the local black Industrial High School in Jasper.

10. J. Alex Moore to Jackson Towne, Jan. 31, 1930, Vertical Files, Carl Elliott Regional Library, Jasper, AL; Wilson and Wight, *County Library Service in the South*, 30; Calkins, "The Walker County Library," 12; Jasper *Mountain Eagle*, Jan. 14, 1931.

11. Walker County Public Library, "Library History," [n.d.], Vertical Files, Carl Elliott Regional Library, Jasper, AL; Walker County Public Library, "Annual Report for Libraries Receiving Julius Rosenwald Fund Aid," 1933, Vertical Files, Carl Elliott Regional Library, Jasper, AL.

12. Jasper *Mountain Eagle*, Jan. 14, 1931; Willie Fagan Calkins, [notebook of librarian,] Oct. 9, 1931, Vertical Files, Carl Elliott Regional Library, Jasper, AL; Wilson and Wight, *County Library Service in the South*, 30. Jordan became librarian of the Davis Avenue Branch in Mobile in May 1931. She was replaced in Walker County by Louise Williams of Oklahoma, then one month later by Louada Meadows, a native of Alabama.

13. Elizabeth Toombs to S. L. Smith, Aug. 10, 1934; Elizabeth Toombs to S. L. Smith, May 31, 1935, Vertical Files, Carl Elliott Regional Library, Jasper, AL; Wilson and Wight, *County Library Service in the South*, 31; Calkins, "Walker County Library," 20.

14. Walker County Library, "Annual Report," 1931–35, Carl Elliott Regional Library, Jasper, AL. The black librarian did not share completely in the good fortune of Walker County's black population. She experienced the wage discrimination that characterized the segregated South. Jordan started at $1,200 a year, just over half the amount of the white librarian's salary and 22 percent less than the average library assistant in Walker County.

15. Walker County Library, "Annual Report," 1931, 1932, 1933, 1934, 1935, Carl Elliott Regional Library, Jasper, AL; Wilson and Wight, *County Library Service in the South*, 89–90, 96.

16. Walker County Library, "Newsletter," July 2, 1936.

17. Edward Barrett Stanford, *Library Extension Under the WPA: An Appraisal of an Experiment in Federal Aid* (Chicago: University of Chicago Press, 1944), 33–36; Martha H. Swain, "A New Deal in Libraries: Federal Relief Work and Library Service, 1933–1943," *Libraries & Culture* 30 (Summer 1995): 266.

18. Anders, *Public Library Development in the Southeast*, 131, 135; Untitled report on the Alabama Public Library Service Division by Lois L. Rainer, Di-

rectors' Files (Marie Bankhead Owen), ADAH; Michael S. Blayney, "'Libraries for the Millions': Adult Public Library Services and the New Deal," *Journal of Library History* 12 (Summer 1977): 235; Mildred Harrison, interview by Annabel Stephens, Oct. 30, 1995, tape recording.

19. E. A. Chapman (WPA Library Section Chief) to J. Studabaker (Commissioner, US Office of Education, Federal Security Agency), Feb. 5, 1940, WPA Papers, NARA; Swain, "A New Deal in Libraries," 266, 270.

20. Mary Weber (Director, Division of Professional and Service Projects, WPA) to I. C. Heck (State Comptroller, Alabama), Dec. 2, 1939, Directors' Files (Owen), ADAH; Marie Bankhead Owen (Director, ADAH) to Sallie F. Hill, Dec. 4, 1939, Directors' Files (Owen), ADAH; APLD, "Minutes," Oct. 25, 1939, Directors' Files (Owen), ADAH; Harrison, interview.

21. E. A. Chapman to Dutton Ferguson (Negro Services, Division of Employment, WPA), Feb. 2, 1940, WPA Papers, NARA, Washington, DC; Harrison, interview; Dulcina DeBerry, "The History of 'Dulcina DeBerry' Branch Public Library," Huntsville Public Library, Huntsville, AL.

22. Roger Biles, *The South and the New Deal* (Lexington: University Press of Kentucky, 1994), 115–16.

23. Harrison, interview; Flossie Powell to Florence Kerr, Nov. 3, 1941, WPA Records, NARA; Margaret Butcher to Marie Bankhead Owen, May 14, 1937, Directors' Files (Owen), ADAH; Marie Bankhead Owen to Margaret Butcher, May 17, 1937, Directors' Files (Owen), ADAH.

24. Dalzie M. Powell to Florence Kerr, Mar. 1941, WPA Records, NARA; Florence Kerr to Dalzie M. Powell, Mar. 21, 1941, WPA Records, NARA; Lois Rainer Green to Dalzie M. Powell, Mar. 31, 1941, WPA Records, NARA; Dalzie M. Powell to Florence Kerr, Apr. 21, 1941, WPA Records, NARA; Florence Kerr to Dalzie M. Powell, Apr. 25, 1941, WPA Records, NARA.

25. Mary Mallory, "The Rare Vision of Mary Utopia Rothrock: Organizing Regional Library Services in the Tennessee Valley," *Library Quarterly* 65 (1995): 70–71; Elizabeth P. Beamguard, "Alabama Public Library Development," (prepared for the Alabama Historical Association, Apr. 24, 1970) 8; John Chancellor, *The Library in the TVA Adult Education Program* (Chicago: American Library Association, 1937), 16.

26. Marguerite Owen, *The Tennessee Valley Authority* (New York: Praeger, 1973), 19; Charles M. Stephenson (Social and Economic Division, TVA) to T. Levron Howard (Social and Economic Division, TVA), July 13, 1935, TVA Records, NARA, Atlanta Branch.

27. Mallory, "Mary Utopia Rothrock," 65, 70–71; Chancellor, *The Library in the TVA Adult Education Program*, 18.

28. Harry L. Case (Director of Personnel, TVA) to John Oliver (Acting General Manager, TVA) May 21, 1951, TVA Records, NARA, Atlanta Branch; Harry L. Case to George F. Gant (General Manager, TVA), May 24, 1950, TVA Records, NARA, Atlanta Branch; Mary Edna Anders, *The Tennessee Val-*

*ley Library Council, 1940–1949: A Regional Approach to Library Planning* (Atlanta: The Southeastern Library Association, 1960), 2; Mallory, "Mary Utopia Rothrock," 65, 70–71.

29. TVA, "Report of the Authority's Library Extension Program," Apr. 1939, TVA Records, NARA, Atlanta Branch; Anders, *Tennessee Valley Library Council,* 2, 5; Chancellor, *The Library in the TVA Adult Education Program,* 45.

30. Nancy L. Grant, *TVA and Black Americans: Planning for the Status Quo* (Philadelphia: Temple University Press, 1990), xxix; TVA, Interracial Relations Committee of Personnel Department, "Statement of Negro Problems of the Authority," Jan. 5, 1935, NARA, Atlanta Branch.

31. Charles M. Stephenson (Social and Economic Division, TVA) to T. Levron Howard (Social and Economic Division, TVA), July 13, 1935, TVA Records, NARA, Atlanta Branch; J. Max Bond (Supervisor of Negro Training, TVA) to C. W. Farrier (Assistant Coordinator, TVA), Feb. 25, 1936, TVA Records, NARA, Atlanta Branch; Grant, *TVA and Black Americans,* 57, 58, 92.

32. Frances P. Howard, "A Survey of Library Agencies in the Muscle Shoals Area," Apr. 1, 1939, TVA Records, NARA, Atlanta; "Review and Appraisal: Wilson Dam Library Program," May 2, 1942, TVA Records, NARA, Atlanta.

33. Ibid.

34. "TVA Libraries," 1937, TVA Records, NARA, Atlanta; Howard, "Survey of Library Agencies in the Muscle Shoals Area," 27.

35. Huntsville, Library Board, "Annual Report," 1941, Huntsville Public Library, Huntsville, AL; Gordon R. Clapp (Assistant Director of Personnel, TVA) to Harold H. Earthman (U.S. House of Representatives) Aug. 15, 1946, TVA Records, NARA, Atlanta Branch; TVA Training Section, "Budget Estimates," 1938, Huntsville Public Library; "Library Service for the Guntersville Area. Three Year Budget Estimates," Huntsville Public Library; TVA, "Report of the Authority's Library Extension Program," TVA Records, NARA, Atlanta Branch; Regional Library Service, "Monthly Report," March 1939, Huntsville Public Library.

36. Steering Committee, Regional Library Service, "Progress Report," Aug. 20, 1937, Huntsville Public Library; Horace S. Moses, "A Regional Library in Transition," *Library Journal* 67 (Sept. 1, 1942): 713; Huntsville, Library Board, "Annual Report," 1941, Huntsville Public Library; Negro Rural School Fund, *The Negro Rural School Fund, Inc. (Anna T. Jeanes Foundation), 1907–1933* (Washington, DC: Negro Rural School Fund, 1933), 7–10.

37. Huntsville, Library Board, "Annual Report," 1941, Huntsville Public Library; Steering Committee, Regional Library Service, "Progress Report," Aug. 20, 1937, Huntsville Public Library; Horace S. Moses, "A Regional Library in Transition," *Library Journal* 67 (Sept. 1, 1942): 713.

38. TVA Training Section, "Budget Estimates," 1938, Huntsville Public Library; "TVA Libraries, As Described by TVA Librarians at a Conference held July 27, 1937, at Knoxville, Tennessee," NARA, Atlanta.

39. Marlene Hunt Rikard, "An Experiment in Welfare Capitalism: The

Health Care Services of the Tennessee Coal, Iron and Railroad Company" (Ph.D. diss., The University of Alabama, 1983), 80, 83, 110, 162, 245; Mollie Beck Jenkins, "The Social Work of the Tennessee Coal Iron and Railroad Company" (M.A. thesis, The University of Alabama, 1929), 1; Fitch, "Labor Conservation," 1532, 1540; George Brown Tindall, *Emergence of the New South* (Baton Rouge: Louisiana State University Press, 1967), 300; Williams, interview.

40. American Cast Iron Pipe Company, *People and Pipe: Fifty Years of Pipe Progress at Acipco* (Birmingham, AL: Acipco, 1955), 44–45; American Cast Iron Pipe Company, *Acipco: A Story of Modern Industrial Relations* (Birmingham, AL: Acipco, 1920), 7; American Cast Iron Pipe Company, *Manual for Acipco Employees* (Birmingham, AL: Acipco, 1948), 8; S. D. Moxley, "The Material and Spiritual Progress at Acipco And What Part the Women of Acipco Have Played in This Progress," 1954, W. S. Hoole Special Collections Library, The University of Alabama, Tuscaloosa.

41. Acipco, *Story of Modern Industrial Relations*, 14; Kenneth R. Daniel, "People and Pipe, A Brief History of the Cast Iron Pipe Industry in Alabama with Special Reference to the Company founded by the Late John J. Eagan," 1964, W. S. Hoole Special Collections Library, The University of Alabama, Tuscaloosa.

42. *Acipco News*, June 1940; Birmingham, Library Board, "Minutes," Oct. 2, 1939.

43. Wayne J. Urban and Jennings L. Wagoner, Jr., *American Education: A History* (New York: McGraw-Hill, 1996), 258–59; Birmingham, Library Board, "Minutes," Oct. 2, 1939.

44. Biles, *The South and the New Deal*, 119–20; John Salmond, *A Southern Rebel: The Life and Times of Aubrey Willis Williams, 1890–1965* (Chapel Hill: University of North Carolina Press, 1983), 60, 122, 126–27, 132.

45. United States. National Youth Administration for Alabama, "Narrative Report of Negro Activities," Dec. 1939 in *New Deal Agencies and Black America in the 1930s* ed. by John B. Kirby (Frederick, MD: University Publications of America, 1983); V. T. Spraggs to Mary McLeod Bethune, Sept. 8, 1939 in *New Deal Agencies and Black America;* Betty Lindley, *A New Deal for Youth: The Story of the National Youth Administration* (New York: Viking Press, 1938), 50; United States. National Youth Administration for Alabama, "Narrative Report of Negro Activities," Apr. 1939 in *New Deal Agencies and Black America.*

46. Stanford, *Library Extension Under the WPA*, 43–44.

47. Birmingham, Library Board, "Minutes," Oct. 2, 1939; American Cast Iron Pipe Company, *Manual for Acipco Employees* (Birmingham, AL: Acipco, 1948), 27–31; *Acipco News*, June 1940.

48. Richard Anderson Bowron, "American Cast Iron Pipe Company: A Study of an Industrial Democracy" (M.B.A. thesis, University of Pennsylvania, 1948): 19; American Cast Iron Pipe Company, *Manual for Acipco Employees* (Birmingham, AL: Acipco, 1948), 27–31.

49. Birmingham Public Library, *The Birmingham Public Library: A Ten Year Summary, 1937–1947* (Birmingham, AL: Birmingham Public Library, 1948), 19; Birmingham Public Library, "Slossfield Branch Library, At Your Service," Vertical Files, Birmingham Public Library, Birmingham, AL; Birmingham, Library Board, "Minutes," Apr. 12, 1944, May 12, 1948.

50. *Birmingham News*, Apr. 13, 1944; Birmingham Public Library, "Welcome to the Slossfield Branch of The Birmingham Public Library," June 21, 1964, Vertical Files, Birmingham Public Library, Birmingham, AL.

Notes to Chapter 3

1. Aldon D. Morris, *The Origins of the Civil Rights Movement: Black Communities Organizing for Change* (New York: Free Press, 1984), 3–5.

2. Bureau of Business Research, University of Alabama, *Alabama County Statistical Abstracts*, 203; Mary Sanford Brown, "Introduction," in *Dulcina DeBerry: Door Opener* by Missouri L. Torrence (Huntsville: AL: Golden Rule, 1996), ix.

3. Patricia H. Ryan and Peter Cobun, *Historic Huntsville: A City of New Beginnings* (Woodland Hills, CA: Windsor, 1984), 12, 13, 23; "History of Huntsville's Public Library," Huntsville Public Library, Huntsville, AL; "History of the Huntsville-Madison County Public Library, 1818–1955," Huntsville Public Library; "Huntsville Public Library," Historical Collection, Huntsville Public Library; *Lockheed Retirees Newsletter*, June 1995; George S. Bobinski, *Carnegie Libraries: Their History and Impact on American Public Library Development* (Chicago: American Library Association, 1969), 222; Huntsville *Mercury Banner*, Mar. 1, 1914, Apr. 27, 1915; *Huntsville Times*, Dec. 28, 1969, March 12, 1993; Carnegie Library Governing Board of Huntsville, Alabama, "Constitution and By-Laws," Huntsville Public Library; Huntsville, Library Board, "Annual Report," 1941, Huntsville Public Library; Gordon R. Clapp to Harold H. Earthman, Aug. 15, 1946, TVA Records, NARA, Atlanta.

4. Missouri L. Torrence, *Dulcina DeBerry: Door Opener* (Huntsville, AL: Golden Rule, 1996), 13, 18, 24; *Huntsville Times*, Mar. 12, 1991.

5. Torrence, *Dulcina DeBerry*, 26, 29–30.

6. Anne G. Maulsby, "The Dulcina DeBerry Branch Library, Huntsville, Alabama, 1940–1968," Huntsville Public Library, 1; Torrence, *Dulcina DeBerry*, 30.

7. Dulcina DeBerry, "Accomplishments of the Winston Street Branch Library of Huntsville, Alabama from 1940 to 1943," Huntsville Public Library; Maulsby, "DeBerry Branch Library," 1; *Huntsville Times*, Mar. 12, 1991.

8. DeBerry, "Accomplishments"; Maulsby, "DeBerry Branch Library," 1; Torrence, *Dulcina DeBerry*, 33–34.

9. Torrence, *Dulcina DeBerry*, 35.

10. DeBerry, "Accomplishments"; *Huntsville Times*, Aug. 3, 1950.

11. Horace S. Moses, "A Regional Library in Transition," 713; Dulcina DeBerry, "The History of 'Dulcina DeBerry' Branch Public Library," 1954, Huntsville Public Library; Torrence, *Dulcina DeBerry*, 34.

12. DeBerry, "History of 'Dulcina DeBerry' Branch"; DeBerry, "Accomplishments"; Torrence, *Dulcina DeBerry*, 42–45.

13. Maulsby, "The Dulcina DeBerry Branch," 2.

14. Horace S. Moses, "Annual Report to the Huntsville Public Library Board," 1941, Huntsville Public Library; Horace S. Moses, "A Regional Library in Transition," 713; Maulsby, "The Dulcina DeBerry Branch," 2.

15. "Ninth Annual Library Musical, Program," May 8, 1949, Huntsville Public Library; *Huntsville Times*, May 6, 1949; Torrence, *Dulcina DeBerry*, 54–58.

16. *Huntsville Times*, May 2, 1943; Maulsby, "Dulcina DeBerry Branch," 2–3; DeBerry, "History of the 'Dulcina DeBerry' Branch," Huntsville Public Library; Huntsville, Library Board, "Minutes," Sept. 14, 1943, Huntsville Public Library.

17. "Library Service in Madison County," 1944, Huntsville Public Library; Imogene Morgan, "Report, Regional Library Service," Nov.–Dec. 1949, Huntsville Public Library; Huntsville Public Library, "This is Your Library," [n.d.], Huntsville Public Library; DeBerry, "History of 'Dulcina DeBerry' Branch"; Torrence, *Dulcina DeBerry*, 61.

18. Elizabeth Parks Beamguard, "Report of Regional Library Service in Madison and Jackson Counties," Nov.–Dec. 1950, Huntsville Public Library; Beamguard, "Report on Service to Madison County," Dec. 1951, Huntsville Public Library; *Huntsville Times*, Sept. 14, 1965; Beamguard to Huntsville Library Board, May 29, 1952, Huntsville Public Library.

19. DeBerry, "History of the 'Dulcina DeBerry' Branch," Huntsville Public Library; Torrence, *Dulcina DeBerry*, 79; Huntsville, Library Board, "Minutes," Mar. 27, 1956; Dorothy Webb (Director) to Mrs. Charles Hendley Feb. 29, 1956, Huntsville Public Library; Huntsville, Library Board, "Minutes," Feb. 20, 1968, Aug. 1968.

20. DeBerry, "Accomplishments"; Brown, "Introduction," ix; Moses, "A Regional Library in Transition," 713.

21. Montgomery *Daily Post*, Oct. 26, 1860; Marie Bankhead Owen, *A History of the State*, 334; Montgomery *Alabama Journal*, June 5, 1960, Apr. 20, 1972; Juanita McClain Owes, "Brief History of the Montgomery City-County Public Library," Montgomery City-County Public Library; *Montgomery Advertiser*, May 2, 1949, Aug. 23, 1950, Aug. 26, 1951.

22. Williams, interview; Montgomery, Library Board, "Minutes," June 20, 1947, Montgomery City-County Library, Montgomery, AL; "Your Public Library," 1946–47, Montgomery City-County Library.

23. Montgomery, Library Board, "Minutes," June 20, 1947.

24. Montgomery, Library Board, "Minutes," June 20, 1947, July 18, 1947;

Williams, interview; Bertha Thomas McClain, *Montgomery Then and Now as I Remember* (Montgomery: Walker Printing, 1960), 51.

25. Montgomery, Library Board, "Minutes," July 18, 1947; Library Board to John L. Goodwyn (Mayor), July 18, 1947, Montgomery City-County Library; Williams, interview; *Montgomery Advertiser*, July 26, 1947; "Opportunities for Recreation in Montgomery Libraries and Museums," 1948, Montgomery City-County Library.

26. Williams, interview; Nellie Glass, "Librarian's Report," July 9, 1948, July 29, 1948, Montgomery City-County Library.

27. Nellie Glass, "Librarian's Report," Mar. 12, 1948, July 29, 1948, Montgomery City-County Library; Nellie Glass, Untitled Manuscript, 1949, Montgomery City-County Library; Williams interview.

28. Williams, interview.

29. Ibid.

30. Ibid.

31. *Montgomery Advertiser*, June 26, 1947; Montgomery *Alabama Journal*, Dec. 7, 1948; Montgomery, Library Board, "Minutes," Jan. 27, 1949; Montgomery *Examiner*, Jan. 10, 1952; Nellie Glass, Untitled Narrative, Jan. 1954, Montgomery City-County Library.

32. Williams, interview; Nellie Glass, Untitled Narrative, Jan. 1954, Montgomery City-County Library.

33. Williams, interview.

34. Montgomery Public Library, "Annual Report," 1948–49, Montgomery City-County Public Library; Montgomery Public Library, "Your Library Report," 1950–51, Montgomery City-County Library; Montgomery *Examiner*, Jan. 10, 1952; Montgomery *Alabama Journal*, July 16, 1951.

35. Montgomery *Examiner*, Jan. 10, 1952; Williams, interview; Montgomery, Library Board, "Minutes," Mar. 11, 1953, Oct. 20, 1953, Montgomery City-County Library.

36. Nellie Glass, "Librarian's Narrative Report," Aug. 13, 1952, Apr. 8, 1953; Nellie Glass to Zenovia Johnson, Sept. 11, 1952, Montgomery City-County Public Library; Montgomery, Library Board, "Circulation Report," 1954–55, Montgomery City-County Library; Montgomery, Library Board, "Annual Report," 1955–56, Montgomery City-County Library; Montgomery, Library Board, "Annual Report," 1956–57, Montgomery City-County Library.

37. Dixie Lou Fisher, "Montgomery Bond Issue Passes for New Library—Museum," *Alabama Librarian* 7 (July 1956), 18; Montgomery *Advertiser*, May 13, 1956, Feb. 18, 1959, May 5, 1960, May 8, 1960, Feb. 8, 1994; Montgomery *Alabama Journal*, Feb. 17, 1959; Montgomery, Library Board, "Circulation Report," 1959–60, Montgomery City-County Library; Teresa Temple interviewed by author, Mar. 8, 1996, Montgomery, AL, tape recording.

38. Birmingham, Library Board, "Minutes," July 9, 1953; Negro Advisory

Committee, "Plan of Action Proposed by Advisory Board on Library Service to Negroes from Aug. 1, 1953 to Aug. 1, 1954," 1953.

39. Advisory Committee, "Plan," 1953.

40. Ibid.

41. Advisory Committee, "Plan," 1953; C. W. Hayes to Mervyn H. Sterne, Sept. 17, 1953, Archives Dept., Birmingham Public Library.

42. Vivian F. Bell to Advisory Committee [1954], Archives Dept., Birmingham Public Library.

43. Birmingham, Library Board, "Minutes," Jan. 5, 1954.

44. Negro Advisory Committee to Mervyn H. Sterne, Mar. 31, 1954, Archives Dept., Birmingham Public Library; C. W. Hayes to Sallie M. Anderson, Jan. 25, 1954, Archives Dept., Birmingham Public Library; Fant Thornley to Library Board, Feb. 20, 1954, Archives Dept., Birmingham Public Library; Birmingham, Library Board, "Minutes," Feb. 25, 1954.

45. Advisory Committee to Mervyn H. Sterne, Mar. 31, 1954, Archives Dept., Birmingham Public Library.

46. Ibid.

47. Advisory Committee to Mervyn H. Sterne, Mar. 31, 1954, Archives Dept., Birmingham Public Library; Richard Kluger, *Simple Justice: The History of Brown v. Board of Education and Black America's Struggle for Equality* (New York: Knopf, 1976), 275, 523–24.

48. Mervyn H. Sterne to C. W. Hayes, Apr. 5, 1954, Archives Dept., Birmingham Public Library; Birmingham, Library Board, "Minutes," Mar. 11, 1954, Jan. 5, 1954; Birmingham *Post-Herald*, Nov. 26, 1955, Dec. 19, 1955, Mar. 31, 1956, Jan. 11, 1957, Apr. 16, 1957; *Birmingham News*, Oct. 10, 1953, Apr. 11, 1955; "Smithfield Branch, Birmingham Public Library," [n.d.] Smithfield Branch, Birmingham Public Library.

49. Carol Smith-Rosenberg, *Disorderly Conduct: Visions of Gender in Victorian America* (New York: Knopf, 1985), 29–64.

50. Bureau of Business Research, University of Alabama, *Alabama County Statistical Abstracts*, 200, 229.

51. William Warren Rogers, et al. *Alabama: The History of a Deep South State* (Tuscaloosa: University of Alabama Press, 1994), 378, 385.

52. Morris, *Origins of the Civil Rights Movement*, 4–5.

53. Robin D. G. Kelley, *Race Rebels: Culture, Politics, and the Black Working Class* (New York: Free Press, 1994), 52; Brown, "Introduction," ix–x.

## NOTES TO CHAPTER 4

1. Emily Miller Danton, "South Does Less Restricting," *Library Journal* (July 1948): 990–92; Birmingham, Library Board, "Minutes," Aug. 11, 1948.

2. Anna Holden, "The Color Line in Southern Libraries," *New South* 9 (Jan. 1954): 3–11; *The Christian Science Monitor*, Feb. 18, 1954; "No Segrega-

tion Here: Negro and White Children Share Library Facilities in a Growing Number of Southern Towns," *Library Journal* 80 (Nov. 15, 1955): 2633; L. D. Reddick, "Where Can a Southern Negro Read a Book?" *New South* 9 (Jan. 1954): 5–11.

3. "The South," *Time* (Mar. 21, 1960): 21.

4. *Birmingham News*, May 7, 1960; Chicago *Defender*, June 4, 1960, Sept. 24, 1960; Jackson *Daily News*, June 15, 1960; Pittsburgh *Courier*, July 23, 1960; *Washington Post*, Sept. 14, 1960; Washington *Evening Star*, Sept. 24, 1960; "The News," *Library Journal* 85 (Nov. 1, 1960): 3964; "The Danville, Virginia, Public Library," *Wilson Library Bulletin* 36 (June 1962): 798. Danville opened its library in September, but only for circulation. The library also began requiring a registration fee and a four-page application form for members. Petersburg reopened after four months and Greenville after two weeks.

5. Mobile, Library Board, "Minutes," Aug. 9, 1961, Mobile City Archives; Arless B. Nixon (Library Director) to Charles A. Baumhaur (City Commissioner), Mar. 24, 1952, Mobile City Archives; Mobile, Library Board, "Minutes," May 18, 1954, Mobile City Archives.

6. *Giles v. Library Advisory Committee of Danville, Virginia* 5 Race Rel. Rep. 1140 (1960).

7. Mobile, Library Board, "Minutes," Mar. 25, 1960; Joe Templeton (Library Director) to Staff of the Main Building and Toulminville Branch, Mar. 28, 1960, Mobile City Archives.

8. Mobile, Library Board, "Minutes," Mar. 7, 1961; Citizens' Committee to Board of City Commissioners, Apr. 18, 1961, Mobile City Archives; J. L. LeFlore (Citizens' Committee) to S. P. Gaillard (Chair, Mobile Public Library Board) May 2, 1961, Mobile City Archives; Mobile, Library Board, "Minutes," May 9, 1961.

9. Mobile, Library Board, "Minutes," Nov. 7, 1961.

10. Mobile, Library Board, "Minutes," Nov. 13, 1961; Frank B. Frazer (Chair, Library Board) to George E. McNally (Mayor), Nov. 14, 1961; Patsy Busby Dow, "Joseph N. Langan: Mobile's Racial Diplomat" (M.A. thesis, University of South Alabama, 1993): 38–40.

11. Mobile, Library Board, "Minutes," Nov. 13, 1961.

12. Frank B. Frazer to Guenter Jansen (Library Director), Nov. 13, 1961, Mobile City Archives.

13. E. L. Cross to Charles S. Trimmer (City Commissioner), Jan. 8, 1962, Mobile City Archives; "Alabama Library Serves Negroes," *Wilson Library Bulletin* 36 (Mar. 1962): 504, 506.

14. E. L. Cross to City Commissioners, Jan. 5, 1962, Mobile Public Library; Robbie Jarrell to City Commissioners, Jan. 9, 1962, Mobile City Archives; E. L. Cross to Frank B. Frazer, Jan. 21, 1962, Mobile City Archives; Frank B. Frazer to E. L. Cross, Jan. 23, 1962, Mobile City Archives; George E. McNally (Mayor) to E. L. Cross, Jan. 31, 1962, Mobile City Archives; Charles

Trimmer (City Commissioner) to E. L. Cross, 15 Jan. 1962, Mobile City Archives.

15. J. Mills Thornton III, "Challenge and Response in the Montgomery Bus Boycott of 1955–1956," in *The Walking City: The Montgomery Bus Boycott, 1955–1956*, ed. David J. Garrow (Brooklyn, NY: Carlson, 1989), 355; *Gilmore v. Montgomery* 4 Race Relations L. Rep. 977 (1959); "Races," *Time* (Jan. 4, 1960): 19; Taylor Branch, *Parting the Waters: America in the King Years, 1954–63* (New York: Simon & Schuster, 1988), 280–83; "The South," *Time* (Mar. 21, 1960): 21. Governor Patterson and the state board of education fired Alabama State history professor Lawrence Reddick, alleging that he fomented the courthouse sit-in and the march. The American Association of University Professors censured Alabama State for this action.

16. *Montgomery Advertiser*, May 18, 1960.

17. Montgomery *Alabama Journal*, Mar. 15, 1962; Airtel, SAC (Special Agent in Charge), Mobile to Director, FBI, 3/15/62, Negro Sit-In Demonstration, Montgomery City Library, Racial Matters, Bureau File 157-6-61-83; *Montgomery Advertiser*, July 25, 1962; Ralph D. Abernathy, "The Natural History of a Social Movement: The Montgomery Improvement Association," in *The Walking City*, 99–172.

18. *Montgomery Advertiser*, July 25, 1962; *Robert L. Cobb v. Montgomery Library Board*, 1962; Montgomery *Alabama Journal*, Mar. 15, 1962.

19. Airtel, SAC, Mobile to Director, FBI, 3/15/62, Negro Student Sit-In Demonstration, Montgomery City Library, Racial Matters, Bureau File 157-6-61-83; *Montgomery Advertiser*, Mar. 16, 1962, Apr. 28, 1962; Montgomery *Alabama Journal*, Mar. 15, 1997; "Read-In at Montgomery," *Wilson Library Bulletin* (May 1962): 722.

20. Teletype, SAC, Mobile to Director, FBI, 6/19/62, Negro Sit-In Demonstration, Montgomery City Library, Racial Matters, Bureau File 157-6-61-103; Memorandum, SAC, Mobile to Director, FBI, 6/30/62, Negro Sit-In Demonstrations, Montgomery City Library, Racial Matters, Bureau File 157-6-61-111; Tinsley E. Yarbrough, *Judge Frank Johnson and Human Rights in Alabama* (Tuscaloosa: University of Alabama Press, 1981), vii–viii, 2–3.

21. Teletype, SAC, Mobile to Director, FBI, 6/19/62, Negro Sit-In Demonstration, Montgomery City Library, Racial Matters, Bureau File 157-6-61-103; Memorandum, SAC, Mobile to Director, FBI, 6/30/62, Negro Sit-In Demonstrations, Montgomery City Library, Racial Matters, Bureau File 157-6-61-111.

22. Memorandum, SAC, Mobile to Director, FBI, 7/2/62, Negro Sit-In Demonstration, Montgomery City Library, Racial Matters, Bureau File 157-6-61-110; *Montgomery Advertiser*, July 25, 1962; *Cobb v. Montgomery Library Board*, 1962.

23. *Cobb v. Montgomery Library Board*, 1962; *Montgomery Advertiser*, Aug. 8, 1962; Airtel, SAC, Mobile to Director, FBI, Negro Student Sit-In Demonstration, Montgomery City Library, Racial Matters, Bureau File 157-6-61-119.

24. Montgomery *Alabama Journal*, Aug. 8, 1962; Airtel, SAC, Mobile to Director, FBI, 8/8/62, Negro Student Sit-In Demonstrations, Montgomery City Library, Racial Matters, Bureau File 157-6-61-124; Airtel, SAC, Mobile to Director, FBI, 8/17/62, Negro Student Sit-In Demonstrations, Bureau File 157-6-61-127.

25. Airtel, SAC, Mobile to Director, FBI, 8/8/62, Negro Student Sit-In Demonstration, Bureau File 157-6-61-124; Montgomery *Alabama Journal*, Aug. 9, 1962; *Montgomery Advertiser*, Aug. 9, 1962.

26. *Montgomery Advertiser*, Aug. 9, 1962.

27. Williams, interview.

28. *Montgomery Advertiser*, Aug. 12, 1962.

29. Teletype, SAC, Mobile to Director, FBI, 8/13/62, Negro Student Sit-In Demonstration, Montgomery City Library, Bureau File 157-6-61-120; Airtel, SAC, Mobile to Director, FBI, 8/17/62, Negro Student Sit-In Demonstration, Montgomery City Library, Bureau File 157-6-61-127; Montgomery *Alabama Journal*, Aug. 13, 1962.

30. Montgomery *Alabama Journal*, Aug. 13, 1962; *Montgomery Advertiser*, Aug. 14, 1962; Teletype, SAC, Mobile to Director, FBI, 8/13/62, Student Sit-In Demonstration, Montgomery City Library, Bureau File 157-6-61-120.

31. Williams, interview.

32. *Montgomery Advertiser*, Aug. 13, Aug. 14, Aug. 16, Aug. 17, Aug. 18, Aug. 19, 1962.

33. Memorandum, SAC, Mobile to Director, FBI, 9/24/62, Negro Student Sit-In Demonstration, Montgomery City Library, Bureau File 157-6-61-131.

34. "Civil Rights," *Time* (Sept. 20, 1963): "Alabama: Civil Rights Battlefield," *Time* (Sept. 27, 1963): 17.

35. *Huntsville Times*, Oct. 2, 1960, Dec. 28, 1969; Huntsville, Library Board, "Minutes," May 15, 1962; Judy Purinton to P. Toby Graham, Sept. 18, 1996.

36. Negro Advisory Committee to Mervyn H. Sterne, Mar. 31, 1954, Archives Dept., Birmingham Public Library; Birmingham, Library Board, "Minutes," Jan. 5, 1954; Mervyn H. Sterne to C. W. Hayes, Apr. 5, 1954, Archives Dept., Birmingham Public Library; Edward Shannon LaMonte, *Politics and Welfare in Birmingham, 1900–1975* (Tuscaloosa: University of Alabama Press, 1995), 163.

37. Rogers, et al., *Alabama*, 555–56; Martin Luther King, *Why We Can't Wait* (New York: New American Library, 1963), 43.

38. William A. Nunnelley, *Bull Connor* (Tuscaloosa: University of Alabama Press, 1991), 112–15; *Shuttlesworth v. Gaylord* 202 F Supp. 59 (N.D. Ala. 1961).

39. Nunnelley, *Bull Connor*, 116; *Birmingham News*, Dec. 12, 1961; Rogers, *Alabama*, 55.

40. Birmingham *Post-Herald*, July 11, 1962.

41. Ibid.

42. Glenn T. Eskew, "The Alabama Christian Movement for Human Rights

and the Birmingham Struggle for Civil Rights, 1956–1963," in *Birmingham, Alabama, 1956–1963: The Black Struggle for Civil Rights* ed. David Garrow (Brooklyn, NY: Carlson, 1989), 63–64, 92; Branch, *Parting the Waters*, 703–05.

43. Branch, *Parting the Waters*, 711; Martin Luther King, Jr., *Letter from Birmingham City Jail* (Philadelphia: American Friends Service Committee, 1963), 3.

44. There is disagreement among some of the participants of the two sit-ins regarding the exact dates and which group went to the Birmingham Public Library first. Newspaper and Library Board minutes document a sit-in on Apr. 10. This was almost certainly a group led by Shelly Millender, since the number of participants (twelve) matches that given in the print accounts of the Apr. 10 protest. I have placed the other sit-in on or about Apr. 9, since U. W. Clemon believes that Millender's group went to the library 'the next day' following his own visit. Also, it stands to reason that Wyatt Walker would have planned a sit-in prior to, rather than after, the official integration of the public libraries, which occurred on Apr. 11; Birmingham, Library Board, "Minutes," Apr. 11, 1963.

45. Birmingham *Post-Herald*, Aug. 30, 1982; Branch, *Parting the Waters*, 730; David Garrow, *Bearing the Cross: Martin Luther King, Jr. and the Southern Christian Leadership Conference* (New York: Morrow, 1986), 236–37.

46. U. W. Clemon, telephone interview by author, May 24, 2001, tape recording; Eskew, "Alabama Christian Movement for Human Rights," 50–51, 65, 68–69; Lee E. Baines, "Birmingham 1963: Confrontation over Civil Rights," in *Birmingham, Alabama*. Garrow, ed. 169.

47. Clemon, interview.

48. Garrow, *Bearing the Cross*, 199; Shelly Millender, telephone interview by author, June 13, 2001, tape recording; Nunnelley, *Bull Connor*, 121–22.

49. Clemon, interview; Millender, interview.

50. Clemon, interview; Millender, interview; Garrow, *Bearing the Cross*, 236–37.

51. Addene Drew, interview, [nd], Southern Women's Archive, Archives Dept., Birmingham Public Library; Addene Drew, telephone interview by author, June 17, 2001, transcript; Garrow, *Bearing the Cross*, 255-57.

52. Drew, interview; Drew, interview, [nd].

53. Drew, interview.

54. Clemon, interview.

55. Millender, interview; Birmingham, Library Board, "Minutes," Apr. 11, 1963.

56. Millender, interview.

57. Millender, interview; Birmingham, Library Board, "Minutes," Apr. 11, 1963.

58. Millender, interview; Birmingham, Library Board, "Minutes," Apr. 11, 1963.

59. Birmingham, Library Board, "Minutes," Apr. 11, 1963.

60. Birmingham, Library Board, "Minutes," Apr. 11, 1963.

61. Birmingham, Library Board, "Minutes," Apr. 11, 1963, June 13, 1963.

62. Birmingham *Post-Herald*, May 2, 1963, May 4, 1963, May 6, 1963, May 7, 1963, May 8, 1963, May 10, 1963, May 13, 1963; Steven E. Barkan, "Legal Control of the Southern Civil Rights Movement," *American Sociological Review* 49 (Aug. 1984): 559–60.

63. Birmingham, Library Board, "Minutes," July 18, 1963, Aug. 8, 1963, Dec. 3, 1963.

64. Stephen Cresswell, "The Last Days of Jim Crow in Southern Libraries," *Libraries & Culture* 31 (Summer/Fall 1996): 561; Branch, *Parting the Waters*, 889–90.

65. Grace Hooten Gates, *The Model City of the New South: Anniston, Alabama, 1872–1900* (Tuscaloosa: University of Alabama Press, 1996), 3–4, 32, 174–76, 188; *Atlanta Constitution*, June 10, 1883.

66. Anniston, Library Board, "Minutes," June 25, 1963, Anniston-Calhoun County Public Library, Anniston, AL.

67. Charles S. Doster (Chair, Library Board of Trustees) to City Commission, July 22, 1963, Anniston-Calhoun County Public Library.

68. Ann Everett (Librarian) to Charles S. Doster, Aug. 19, 1963, Anniston-Calhoun County Public Library.

69. Charles S. Doster to Claude Dear (Mayor), Aug. 22, 1963, Anniston-Calhoun County Public Library; Anniston, Library Board of Trustees, "Minutes," Aug. 22, 1963, Sept. 12, 1963.

70. Anniston, Library Board of Trustees, "Minutes," Sept. 12, 1963; *Anniston Star*, Sept. 16, 1963.

71. Charles S. Doster to Claude Dear, Aug. 22, 1963, Anniston-Calhoun County Public Library; Anniston, Library Board of Trustees, "Minutes," Sept. 12, 1963; *Atlanta Constitution*, Sept. 16, 1963.

72. *Anniston Star*, Sept. 16, 1963, Sept. 18, 1963.

73. *Anniston Star*, Sept. 16, 1963; *Atlanta Constitution*, Sept. 16, 1963.

74. Birmingham *Post-Herald*, Sept. 16, 1963; *Anniston Star*, Sept. 21, 1963.

75. *Anniston Star*, Sept. 16, Sept. 19, Sept. 20, 1963.

76. Birmingham, *Post-Herald*, Sept. 16, 1963; *Anniston Star*, Sept. 16, 1963, Sept. 18, 1963; Anniston, Library Board of Trustees, "Minutes," Sept. 16, 1963; Rotary Club of Calhoun County, "Resolution," Sept. 17, 1963.

77. *Anniston Star*, Sept. 16, Sept. 17, Sept. 18, 1963.

78. Anniston, Library Board of Trustees, "Minutes," Sept. 16, 1963; Birmingham *Post-Herald*, Sept. 17, 1963; *Anniston Star*, Sept. 17, 1963.

79. *Anniston Star*, Sept. 17, 1963.

80. Anniston, Library Board of Trustees, "Minutes," Oct. 7, 1963, Oct. 10, 1963, Nov. 11, 1963.

81. *Anniston Star*, Sept. 20, Sept. 21, 1963.

82. *Anniston Star*, Nov. 13, 1963. The grand jury indicted Billy Franklin Young, white, and Isiah Harris, Jr., black.

## Notes to Chapter 5

1. Leon F. Litwack, "Hellhound on My Trail: Race Relations in the South from Reconstruction to the Civil Rights Movement," in *Opening Doors: Perspectives on Race Relations in Contemporary America*, ed. by Harry J. Knopke, Robert J. Norrell, and Ronald W. Rogers (Tuscaloosa: University of Alabama Press, 1991), 4–5.

2. "Report on Montgomery a Year After," *New York Times Magazine* (Dec. 29, 1957): 37.

3. David J. Garrow, "Introduction," in *The Walking City: The Montgomery Bus Boycott, 1955–1956* ed. Garrow (Brooklyn, NY: Carlson, 1989), xxiii; Thomas R. Thrasher, "Alabama's Bus Boycott," in *The Walking City*, 66; Thomas J. Gilliam, "The Montgomery Bus Boycott of 1955–56," in *The Walking City*, 237; Garrow, *Bearing the Cross*, 51; Hollinger F. Barnard, ed., *Autobiography of Virginia Foster Durr* (Tuscaloosa: University of Alabama Press, 1985), 277; Branch, *Parting the Waters*, 127.

4. Thrasher, "Alabama's Bus Boycott," 66–67; Garrow, "The Origins of the Montgomery Bus Boycott," in *The Walking City*, 617.

5. *Montgomery Advertiser*, Dec. 12, 1955; Martin Luther King, Jr., *Stride Toward Freedom: The Montgomery Story* (New York: Harper & Row), 85.

6. *Montgomery Advertiser*, Dec. 12, 1955; Branch, *Parting the Waters*, 144; Gilliam, "The Montgomery Bus Boycott of 1955–56," 233.

7. *Montgomery Advertiser*, Dec. 12, 1955; Branch, *Parting the Waters*, 144.

8. "Report on Montgomery," 37; Branch, *Parting the Waters*, 144; *Montgomery Advertiser*, July 18, 1957.

9. "A Report on Montgomery," 37; Branch, *Parting the Waters*, 144; Alabama Center for Health Statistics, Certificate of Death, Juliette Hampton Morgan, July 16, 1957; King, *Stride Toward Freedom*, 85.

10. *Montgomery Advertiser*, July 25, 1957.

11. Anne Permaloff and Carl Grafton, *Political Power in Alabama: The More Things Change . . .* (Athens: University of Georgia Press, 1995), 69–90; Rogers, *Alabama*, 571.

12. Garth Williams, *The Rabbits' Wedding* (New York: Harper & Row, 1958).

13. *Time*, June 1, 1959; *Montgomery Home News*, Feb. 26, 1959.

14. Montgomery *Alabama Journal*, Aug. 12, 1959; Greensboro *Watchman*, Apr. 4, 1963; *Birmingham News*, Apr. 4, 1976; "Surname File," ADAH; *Who's*

*Who in Alabama*, vol. 2 (Birmingham, AL: Sayers Enterprises, 1969), 130; *Montgomery Advertiser*, Mar. 2, 1956.

15. Emily Wheelock Reed, interviewed by author, Oct. 29, 1997, Baltimore County, MD, tape recording; *Montgomery Advertiser*, Aug. 10, 1957.

16. Montgomery *Alabama Journal*, Mar. 13, 1959.

17. *Birmingham News*, May 22, 1959; Birmingham *Post-Herald*, May 23, 1959.

18. *Birmingham News*, May 22, 1959; Birmingham *Post-Herald*, May 23, 1959; Clark E. Center, Jr., "Rabbits, Martin Luther King, and the Alabama Public Library Service," (unpublished paper, 1992): 4. See also, Center, "Of Rabbits, Martin Luther King, Jr., and the Alabama Public Library Service," *Alabama Librarian* (Winter 1996): 16–20.

19. Reed, interview.

20. *Birmingham News*, May 23, 1959; Birmingham *Post-Herald*, May 22, 1959, Jan. 11, 1960; Reed, interview.

21. Ibid.

22. *Time*, June 1, 1959; *Montgomery Advertiser*, May 24, 1959; *Birmingham News*, May 22, 1959.

23. *Birmingham News*, May 23, 1959; *Montgomery Advertiser*, May 24, 1959.

24. *Montgomery Advertiser*, Aug. 14, 1959; *Birmingham News*, Aug. 16, 1959, Aug. 18, 1959.

25. Ibid.

26. *Birmingham News*, Feb. 5, 1959, Aug. 18, 1959, Aug. 19, 1959; Birmingham *Post-Herald*, Aug. 19, 1959.

27. Birmingham *Post-Herald*, Aug. 19, 1959; *Montgomery Advertiser*, Aug. 19, 1959.

28. Birmingham *Post-Herald*, Aug. 19, 1959; *Montgomery Advertiser*, Aug. 23, 1959; *Birmingham News*, Aug. 25, 1959; Center, "Rabbits," 12–13.

29. Reed interview; Edna Earle Brown, "President's Overview Report For 1959–1960. Alabama Library Association Convention, Apr. 9, 1960," *Alabama Librarian* (July 1960): 54; *Montgomery Advertiser*, Oct. 1, 1959.

30. *Journal of the Senate of the State of Alabama, Regular Session, 1959* (Montgomery, AL: Skinner Printing & Office Supply, 1959), 1589–90; *Montgomery Advertiser*, Aug. 23, 1959, Sept. 17, 1959, Sept. 18, 1959, Oct. 1, 1959; *Birmingham News*, Sept. 17, 1959.

31. *Montgomery Advertiser*, Aug. 23, 1959; *Birmingham News*, Sept. 17, 1959. Reed remembers her board as being helpful throughout the controversy. The members remained "friendly," though not in complete agreement with her position.

32. *Montgomery Advertiser*, Jan. 10, 1960, Mar. 13, 1960; *Birmingham News*, Apr. 7, 1960; Birmingham *Post-Herald*, Apr. 6, 1960; Reed, interview. One board member did encourage Reed to find another position, fearing for the director's personal safety.

33. Dan Lacy to Archie McNeal, Oct. 16, 1959, American Library Association Archives, University of Illinois, Urbana-Champaign; Archie McNeal to Dan Lacy, Oct. 19, 1959, ALA Archives.

34. Stephen L. Longenecker, *Selma's Peacemaker: Ralph Smeltzer and Civil Rights Mediation* (Philadelphia: Temple Press, 1987), 13–17; J. L. Chestnut, Jr., and Julia Cass, *Black in Selma: The Uncommon Life of J. L. Chestnut, Jr.* (New York: Farrar, Straus and Giroux, 1990), 3, 4; Robert M. Mikell, *Selma* (Charlotte, NC: Citadel Press, 1965), 3.

35. Alabama Department of Public Health, *Alabama's Population, 1930–1980* (Montgomery: Alabama Department of Public Health, Special Services Administration, Bureau of Vital Statistics, 1983), 77; Mikell, *Selma*, 3; Longenecker, *Selma's Peacemaker*, 18; Amelia Boynton Robinson, *Bridge Across Jordan* (Washington, DC: Schiller Institute, 1991), 56; Chestnut, *Black in Selma*, 19–37.

36. Patricia Blalock, interview by author, Mar. 4, 1997, Birmingham, AL, tape recording; Chestnut, *Black in Selma*, 7; Claude C. Grayson, *Yesterday and Today: Memories of Selma and its People* (New Orleans: Pelican Press, 1948), 89.

37. Rogers, *Alabama*, 548; Chestnut, *Black in Selma*, 82–83.

38. Longenecker, *Selma's Peacemaker*, 37; Chestnut, *Black in Selma*, 82–84.

39. Longenecker, *Selma's Peacemaker*, 29, 33, 106; Chestnut, *Black in Selma*, 222–23.

40. Blalock, interview, Mar. 4, 1997; Patricia Blalock, telephone interview by author, Dec. 17, 1997, transcript.

41. Ibid.

42. Blalock, interview, Mar. 4, 1997; Chestnut, *Black in Selma*, 220.

43. Blalock, interview, Mar. 4, 1997; Selma, Library Board, "Minutes," May 13, May 17, June 18, 1963, Public Library of Selma-Dallas County; Longenecker, *Selma's Peacemaker*, 6, 106, 115; Charles Fager, *Selma, 1965* (New York: Charles Scribner's Sons, 1974), 171; Chestnut, *Black in Selma*, 83.

44. Selma, Library Board, "Minutes," May 13, May 17, 1963; Blalock, interview, Mar. 4, 1997; Blalock, interview, Dec. 17, 1997.

45. Blalock, interview, Mar. 4, 1997.

46. Blalock, interview, Dec. 17, 1997; Blalock, interview, Mar. 4, 1997; Selma, Library Board, "Minutes," May 13, 1963.

47. Selma, Library Board, "Minutes," May 13, May 17, 1963; Longenecker, *Selma's Peacemaker*, 32; Blalock, interview, Mar. 4, 1997.

48. Longenecker, *Selma's Peacemaker*, 32.

49. Blalock, interview, Mar. 4, 1997; Blalock, interview, Dec. 17, 1997; Chestnut, *Black in Selma*, 220.

50. Longenecker, *Selma's Peacemaker*, 32.

51. Blalock, interview, Mar. 4, 1997; Blalock, interview, December 17, 1997.

52. Blalock, interview, Mar. 4, 1997.

53. Ibid.

54. Ibid.

55. Dan Lacy to Archie McNeal, Oct. 16, 1959, ALA Archives; Archie McNeal to Dan Lacy, Oct. 19, 1959, ALA Archives.

56. John Wakeman, "Segregation and Censorship," *Wilson Library Bulletin* 35 (Sept. 1960): 63–64.

57. Rice Estes, "Segregated Libraries," *Library Journal* 85 (Dec. 5, 1960): 4418–21.

58. Eric Moon, "The Silent Subject," *Library Journal* 85 (Dec. 1960): 4436–37; Louise Robbins, *Censorship and the American Library: The American Library Association's Response to Threats to Intellectual Freedom, 1939–1969* (Westport, CN: Greenwood Press, 1996), 107–08, 111–12; DuMont, "Race in American Librarianship," 502.

59. Everett T. Moore, *Issues of Freedom in American Libraries* (Chicago: American Library Association, 1964), 73; Robbins, *Censorship and the American Library*, 112.

60. Virginia Lacy Jones, Milton S. Byam, Spencer G. Shaw, and Miles M. Jackson, "Segregation in Libraries: Negro Librarians Give Their Views," *Wilson Library Bulletin* 35 (May 1961): 707–10.

61. Archie McNeal, "Integrated Service in Southern Public Libraries," *Library Journal* (June 1, 1961): 2045–48.

62. Eric Moon, "Integration and Censorship," *Library Journal* 87 (Mar. 1, 1962): 904–05; Robbins, *Censorship and the American Library*, 117–18.

63. Ibid.

64. International Research Associates, Inc., *Access to Public Libraries* (Chicago: American Library Association, 1963), 25, 48; "The Access to Public Libraries Study," *ALA Bulletin* 57 (Sept. 1963): 742–45.

65. International Research Associates, Inc., *Access to Public Libraries*, 53, 57, 59–60.

66. "Access to Public Libraries Study," 742–45; DuMont, "Race in American Librarianship," 502–03; Robbins, *Censorship and the American Library*, 120.

67. Robbins, *Censorship and the American Library*, 120; International Research Associates, Inc., *Access to Public Libraries*, 128.

68. Marie Bankhead Owen, *The Story of Alabama*, 286–87; "A Proposed Alabama Library Association, Circular No. 1," Alabama Library Association Papers, W. S. Hoole Special Collections Library, The University of Alabama, Tuscaloosa; "The Alabama Library Association, Circular No. 2, Officers 1904–05; Announcement, and Constitution," Alabama Library Association Papers.

69. Alabama Library Association, Bi-Racial Committee, "Report," Apr. 12, 1951, Public Information Subject Files, ADAH; Robinson, 49; Barbara Bishop and Kayla Barrett, "Librarians for Anybody, Anywhere," unpublished paper. The author would like to express gratitude to Barbara Bishop and Kayla Barrett for providing a copy of their paper on the desegregation of the Alabama Li-

brary Association. A published version of their work will appear in *Libraries & Culture*.

70. Carolyn L. Redden (Assistant Serials Librarian, Tuskegee) to Mrs. James A. Bentley (President, Alabama Library Association), Mar. 27, 1963, Alabama Library Association Papers; Louise E. Riley (Assistant Circulation Librarian, Tuskegee) to Mrs. James A. Bentley, Apr. 2, 1963, Alabama Library Association Papers; Fannye J. Harris (Head, Circulation Division, Tuskegee) to Mrs. James A. Bentley, Apr. 3, 1963, Alabama Library Association Papers; Freddye M. Burns (Head, Cataloging Division, Tuskegee) to Mrs. James A. Bentley, Apr. 4, 1963, Alabama Library Association Papers; Annie G. King (Head, Reference Division, Tuskegee) to Mrs. James A. Bentley, Apr. 4, 1963, Alabama Library Association Papers; Frances F. Davis (Reserve Librarian, Tuskegee) to Mrs. James A. Bentley, Apr. 4, 1963, Alabama Library Association Papers.

71. Richard J. Covey to Members of the Executive Council of the Alabama Library Association, Apr. 11, 1963, Alabama Library Association Papers.

72. Richard J. Covey to Annie King, May 21, 1963, Alabama Library Association Papers; also eleven undated replies to Covey from the Executive Council members, Alabama Library Association Papers.

73. Richard J. Covey to Annie King, 21 May 1963, Alabama Library Association Papers.

74. "Minutes of the Executive Council, Alabama Library Association, Dec. 4, 1964," *Alabama Librarian* 16 (Jan. 1965): 3; Alabama Library Association, Executive Council, "Minutes," Jan. 15, 1965, May 6, 1965, Alabama Library Association Papers; Executive Council to Sybil Baird, 17 May 1965, Alabama Library Association Papers.

75. Robert W. Severance, "To the Membership," *Alabama Librarian* 16 (Jan. 1965): 3.

76. Eric Moon, "The Central Fact of Our Times," *Alabama Librarian* 16 (Oct. 1965): 3–9; Eric Moon, "Movement in Mobile," *Alabama Librarian* 16 (July 1965): 13; "Membership News," *Alabama Librarian* 16 (Apr. 1965): 5.

## NOTES TO CONCLUSION

1. Kirby, *Darkness at the Dawning*, 2–3.
2. Robbins, *Censorship and the American Library*, 1.
3. Ibid., 107.

# Bibliographic Essay

Virginia Lacy Jones, director of Atlanta University's library school, wrote in 1962, "One phase of American library history that has been neglected is the struggle of the Southern Negro to secure public library service." Nearly thirty-five years later, library historians can repeat this sentence with similar conviction. The published literature on segregation and civil rights in libraries that does exist is divisible into four categories. The first is contemporary studies written during the formative period of black librarianship in the South. These were published between 1900 and 1953. The second category is the contemporary literature relating to the issue of integration. Much of this deals with the American Library Association's own racial angst. This was published after the 1954 *Brown* decision and before 1972. The third category is the historical analysis of the subject written by library scholars after 1975. These are the rarest. The final category of published literature is general historical works. In addition to the published works, however, and perhaps the most important informational resources for the historian of library development are the primary materials, including manuscripts, official records, and oral histories that provide firsthand accounts of events.

## CONTEMPORARY LITERATURE ON SEGREGATED LIBRARIES, 1913–1953

William F. Yust, librarian at Louisville and later Rochester, exemplifies the paternalistic racist of the early twentieth century. In his paper, "What of the Black and Yellow Races?" read before ALA in 1913, Yust asserted that integrated service was detrimental to whites and blacks.

Furthermore, it was a violation of southern custom. He contended that most blacks did not require libraries, but where there was service blacks were quick to take advantage of it, and as a result made "commendable progress." The best solution, according to Yust, was "colored branches" operated by black assistants, but under the supervision and control of white administrators, *ALA Bulletin* 7: 159–67.

Louis Shores queried eighty cities in 1930 to determine the existence and quality of library service to blacks in those places. In Alabama, only Birmingham responded as providing service to blacks. Birmingham Public Library replied that there was a single "Negro branch" with 8,950 volumes for 9,567 readers. Circulation was 69,448 volumes and the branch employed two library assistants. Anniston and Mobile answered as specifically having no facilities for African Americans. Shores asserted that service to blacks should be part of every library program. To attain this goal the South needed additional Rosenwald funds, more black librarians, and the commitment to solicit black readership, *Library Journal* 55 (1930): 150–54.

Later that year Shores led a "Negro Library Conference" at Fisk University. Highlights of the conference were papers by Clark Foreman of the Rosenwald Fund, ALA Field Agent for the South Tommie Dora Barker, and America's first black library director, Thomas F. Blue. It was the first gathering of its type and indicated a push for black service in the region as a whole.

During the Depression years the Julius Rosenwald Fund was the most important impetus to the extension of black library service. Louis Round Wilson and Edward A. Wight appraised the Fund's County Library Demonstrations in their 1935 *County Library Service in the South* (Chicago). They placed their study in the context of the southern social and economic conditions that affected library service to the region. The South had a "historical lag" in education brought on by a persisting frontier culture. Efforts to improve education were hindered by the region's general lack of wealth, which the authors attribute to the pervasiveness of sharecropping and tenancy. Segregation exacerbated the problem. It necessitated a dual system of public services that wasted limited resources. Library development lagged in the South, but for blacks the situation was particularly poor. Over 80 percent of southern blacks lacked service of any kind. The authors called for additional resources, improved facilities, library education, and extension work for African Americans. Interest in black libraries should be "cultivated and stimulated in every way possible," they asserted. In the end, Wilson and

Wight were critical of the Rosenwald demonstrations, particularly of their planning and administration. They asserted that where blacks were concerned all the counties involved provided inadequate collections and ineffective distribution of books. Still, Wilson and Wight supported the concept of countywide service, and they believed that the Rosenwald efforts marked a recognition that libraries could be an agent for social and educational improvement.

Willie Fagan Calkins's history of the Walker County Public Library from 1927–1933 provides an example of a Rosenwald Demonstration. Walker County was the first in Alabama to provide countywide access to African Americans. Such were the terms of the Rosenwald Fund. Calkins recounts the opening of the "negro branch," identifies its librarians, and lists the stations designated for use by blacks. The paper also provides circulation information divided by race (Masters thesis, Univ. of Alabama, 1934).

In a paper presented to the Southeastern Library Association in 1936, George T. Settle of the Louisville Free Public Library, asserted that there were only two ways to reach blacks with public library service. Southerners could allow unrestricted access to all libraries, or they could provide separate facilities of high quality. The region, he argues, was "not accepting either proposition" (Nashville, 1936).

Eliza Atkins Gleason's *The Southern Negro and the Public Library* (Chicago, 1941) is the first Library Science Ph.D. dissertation completed by an African American. It provided what is still the most complete history of African-American library development in the South. Gleason's work also forcefully defines the legal basis for free public library service for blacks and it actively advocates library desegregation. According to the prevailing legal precedent of the day, *Plessy v. Ferguson* (1896), local governments could exclude blacks from libraries if they provided separate arrangements that were substantially equal. Gleason contends that southern governments could not afford to duplicate their white library service at an equal rate. She suggested that federal courts could make segregation financially untenable by enforcing the "separate but equal" doctrine to the letter. This was the approach broadly applied by the NAACP to fight segregation until the *Brown* decision. Gleason argued that creating one first-rate integrated system per community was in the interest of everyone.

Querying twenty-two southern libraries in 1948, Birmingham Public Library director Emily Miller Danton found a liberalization of racial attitudes among librarians. A critical reading evidences a situation less desirable, however. Most libraries queried occasionally permitted limited access to their main library, but this could mean as little as loaning books to the black branches. All but two hired blacks; this only means black librarians served black libraries. Only two respondents made integrationist statements, and at the time the study was published, Danton's own library was firmly entrenched in the segregationist tradition, "South Does Less Restricting," *Library Journal* 73 (1948): 990-02.

## Contemporary Literature on Segregated Libraries, 1954–1972

The 1954 *Brown* decision was a salient expression of changing racial attitudes in America. The legal breakthrough came four years earlier with the *Sweatt v. Painter* decision when the Supreme Court ruled that in providing "separate but equal" facilities, governments had to consider not just dollars spent and resources provided, but other "intangible" characteristics. The logical conclusion, expressed in *Brown*, was that separation is inherently unequal. In 1955, the Montgomery Bus Boycott marked the beginning of a direct action campaign lasting more than a decade. As the nation began to question the morality of de jure discrimination, librarians wrote about the place of their own institutions within this social transition. The library profession, like the rest of the nation, was divided over the events and the meaning of the civil rights movement.

In "The Color Line in Southern Libraries," Anna Holden responded to a 1953 report of the Southern Regional Council. The report asserted that the number of southern communities extending full service to blacks in their main libraries increased from sixteen in 1941 to fifty-nine in 1953. According to Holden, however, these numbers were not as hopeful as it might seem. She contended that integration was taking place chiefly in areas with low black populations. She argued that communities in the hills of Kentucky, in the flatlands of western Texas, and the Valley of Virginia integrated while no communities in the deep South had done so, *New South* 9 (1954): 3–4, 11.

In the same issue of *New South*, Atlanta University Librarian L. D. Reddick called for integration in "Where Can a Southern Negro Read a Book?" In the South, he asserted, the public places were "few and far between where a Negro may sit down and read a book," even though his taxes supported the library and paid the librarian who told him "curtly or apologetically: 'We do not serve Negroes.'" Even where service was provided, Reddick argued, it was through neighborhood branches incapable of meeting the needs of large urban clienteles dwelling at widely separated locations throughout southern cities. Providing exceptional segregated service was not the answer either; it would be "sheer waste." By eliminating the color line, he contended, a million blacks could receive library service "without the outlay of a single dime" (5–11).

In his "Can We Afford to Ignore the Negro?" Thomas F. Parker called for improved library service for urban blacks based on the need for self-education. His argument harkens back to the message of social uplift espoused by turn-of-the-century "progressive" librarians. Blacks could compensate for inadequate educational backgrounds with "collateral reading." Self-education would help them "break out" of the dismal economic situation many African Americans faced after the Great Migration to northern cities. Libraries built branches for the convenience of the suburbs, not the disadvantaged inner cities. Municipalities needed branches near public transportation and required more books teaching basic skills. Parker believed that the nucleus of the answer was already present in the "Negro branches." He stressed the importance of their black librarians who understood community needs, knew community leaders, and were received without the suspicion that whites might expect. This sounds like an argument for library segregation. But it also foreshadows a recurring emphasis on the benefits of strong black communities. Parker's model accounts for positive role models and racial pride. It also suggests that northern librarians saw their own "Negro branches" as somehow more defensible than those in the South, *Library Journal* 88 (1963): 4716–17.

In 1965, civil rights activist and future ALA president E. J. Josey asserted the persistence of segregation in library employment in "A Mouthful of Civil Rights and an Empty Stomach." Only 10 percent of the southern cities he queried employed black librarians in their main library. There was a continuing trend of hiring black librarians only at former "Negro branches." As a result, the South was losing its best black librarians to other regions. Josey argued that completely integrated libraries could have been an important part of President Johnson's "War on Poverty" and warned that the "Great Society" would not prevail until there was democratic staffing in those institutions, *Library Journal* 90 (1965): 202-05.

As the foundations of library segregation began to weaken, the question of collection requirements arose. Arna Bontemps, African-American poet, playwright, and librarian, argued in "The Negro Awakening: What Librarians Can Do" that after blacks achieved equality of access they would next require access to books suitable to their needs. He provided an anecdote in which a group of black ministers seeks to integrate a public library. They nervously enter and a librarian asks if she can help them. The leader answers, "Yes, we want to borrow a book." When the librarian asks which book they required, the ministers are surprised at the answer and burst into laughter, unable to think of a single title. For Bontemps this illustrated that once inside the library, blacks required relevant reading material. He cited W. E. B. Du Bois, Booker T. Washington, and Richard Wright as examples. Such literature, Bontemps contended, would lend itself to mutual understanding and a completion of the civil rights movement, *Library Journal* 88 (1963): 2997–99.

Josey followed in 1972 with his "Libraries, Reading, and the Liberation of Black People." It was an emotional plea for a combination of black pride and black reading. "Libraries," Josey argued, could "play a vital role in the liberation movement," but too often collections met the interests of only the white community. Blacks were "invisible" in too many libraries. Materials on their race would help African Americans take pride in their heritage. Such books would also generate understanding, freeing whites from their prejudices. Josey saw white library boards as the obstacle to diverse collections. Adopting the community action and participatory democracy rhetoric of the New Left, Josey called for "community control" over libraries. Reading, Josey believed, would lead blacks and whites to work for a more democratic America, *Library Scene* 1 (1972): 4–8.

This idealism toward the library as an agency of social change is reflected in the efforts of the "Freedom Libraries" created by civil rights activists. Virginia Steele discussed her own experience in "'Freedom Libraries' of the Mississippi Summer Project." The new library school graduate directed a library in Greenville, Mississippi, during the summer of 1964. There were twenty-five such libraries. They were opened through the efforts of white students and local volunteers. They provided books relevant to the experience of African Americans living in the Mississippi Delta and did so at no small risk. One freedom library was destroyed by bombing and another by fire, *Southeastern Librarian* (Summer 1965): 76–81.

## ATLANTA UNIVERSITY THESES

Atlanta University, one of the South's few library schools for African Americans, required a thesis until 1963. The result has been several notable contributions to the historiography of black libraries. Of the twenty-six theses addressing historical topics, eighteen deal specifically with the extension of service to blacks. Of the southern systems treated, three are in Alabama. These studies, by Birdie Turner James, Emma Ruth Fonville, and Bessie Rivers Grayson, were the first to take up the subject of library segregation in Alabama. B. L. Bell's "Integration in Public Library Service in Thirteen Southern States, 1954–1962" is the most important of the general studies.

James (Mobile, 1961), Fonville (Bessemer, 1962), and Grayson (Montgomery, 1965) provided brief descriptions of public library development that vary in quality and documentation. Though the authors are reluctant to draw conclusions from the evidence they used, the general consensus among them was that library service to white Alabamians was historically poor and that library service to black Alabamians was historically worse. As late as 1962 Fonville called for additional resources, extended hours, and cooperation with schools at the Bessemer Free Negro Library, but not for desegregation. James went so far as to contend that segregated libraries were an impediment to the creation of a modern, cooperative library system for Mobile. These theses imply that black civic leaders and the black community at large were important to the creation of library service for their race in an often indifferent and sometimes hostile environment. The authors provide a starting point for further research. They make use of interviews and other source material no longer obtainable. But they leave the sense that there is a great deal left to be learned about African Americans and library service in Alabama.

In her 1963 thesis B. L. Bell reported "an overall view of the trend toward integrated public library service" in the South. After querying 269 libraries in thirteen states, she asserted that examples of integrated service existed in all the states, a marked change since Gleason's 1941 study. Bell attributed this to a liberalization of librarians' attitudes. Activists staged direct action campaigns in 4 percent of the libraries queried, but most often integration occurred with little or no disturbance. She contended that integration effected without public announcement or fanfare was popular among librarians; but as a result many blacks were unaware of their new privileges.

## American Library Association

The American Library Association experienced vigorous internal disagreement over the stance the organization would take in regard to library segregation. In 1936 ALA temporarily ceased holding conferences in southern cities. In 1954 it decided to allow only one chapter from each state, integrating the North Carolina chapter, but driving out Alabama and Georgia. Louisiana and Mississippi left in 1962 after ALA refused chapters that discriminated against their members. In 1963, northern librarians railed against an ALA-sponsored study that depicted segregation as a national, rather than a regional, problem. Though it meant well, most of the measures ALA took served only to sectionalize the profession and divide the remaining members. The controversy is documented in the professional literature.

In 1960 Rice Estes condemned ALA's reluctance to support library integration efforts. When a book is banned, the South Carolina librarian argued, ALA raises a vigorous protest. But when citizens are denied use of every book in the library the organization acquiesces. It had not commended the activism of African Americans staging sit-ins in libraries, brought lawsuits, lent its name as amicus curiae to desegregation suits, nor passed a resolution in favor of integration. "We haven't done anything," Estes wrote, "because we haven't cared enough." He contended that southern liberals in 1960 required the assistance of a large organization to bring equality of access to their region, *Library Journal* (1960): 4418–21.

In 1961, Archie L. McNeal warned that the outright condemnation by ALA of segregation in libraries would actually hamper progress made by quiet but right-minded southern librarians. A Southerner, the Committee on Intellectual Freedom chair asserted that professionals in the region were making deliberate and measurable progress, but only because their efforts were unpublicized and carried out within the local power structure. Attention would harm such efforts. Likewise, any pressure on the federal government to cut funding of segregated libraries would damage the tenuous progress made in service to blacks by the Library Services Act. ALA action should be within the "local framework of government," *Library Journal* (June 1961): 2045–48.

In 1962, *Wilson Library Bulletin* published a two-article series concerning ALA's internal debate over the organization's official stance on race and membership. The Executive Board had responded to a call from within the organization to bar chapters and institutions practicing segregation. But they handed down a statement so mild as to evoke an intense response from some ALA members. Reacting to the Executive Board's proposals, Evelyn Levy argued for a "strong, clear, unambiguous statement" to encourage and inspire those working for integration. Jerome Cushman contended that many librarians were "caught in a web of state laws" and should not be excluded because of circumstances beyond their control. Exclusion would punish those Southerners who had worked courageously for desegregation (36: 558–79, 668–69).

In a 1968 article on "Attitudes and Actions of the Library Profession" Susan Lee Scott asserted that southern librarians would play a passive role regardless of ALA's actions. Professionals in that region remained largely quiet as to their views on library segregation. Scott predicted that they would continue to be so. They would go where the future dictated whether happily or grudgingly, *Southeastern Librarian* (Fall 1968): 162–69.

## Library History Secondary Works

In 1974 Arthur Curley re-examined the American Library Association's internal discussion over race and librarianship in "Social Responsibilities and Libraries." Curley argues that without the civil rights movement there would have been no social responsibility impulse in ALA. Even so, the organization was slow to act. It demonstrated "commendable principles, but infinite patience." Curley recounts the creation of the Miami Beach Statement of 1962 that refused chapter status to state associations discriminating on the basis of race and the 1964 St. Louis Statement against ALA participation by officers and staff of barred chapters. His most interesting conclusions, however, concern the *Access to Public Libraries* study commissioned by ALA in 1961. Curley contends that ALA leaders expected the report to be a condemnation of de jure segregation in the South. But it raised a considerable uproar among northern librarians because of its coverage of de facto segregation in several northern cities. At its heart, Curley suggests, the opposition to the report was because of its recognition of racial problems as national rather than regional in nature, *Advances in Librarianship* 4 (1974): 77–101.

DuMont provides an important overview of "Race in American Librarianship." She briefly describes the emergence of service for African Americans and recounts ALA's efforts on behalf of blacks. In the end, DuMont contends, it was federal legislation, not professional ethics, that pushed the American Library Association into a pro-integration position. She concludes with suggestions for further research: scholars should relate the history of black library service to southern racial attitudes, to southern liberalism, and to southern history in general. They should ask what the activities of southern librarians say about the profession, *Journal of Library History* 21 (1986): 488–509.

There are three relevant studies relating specifically to Alabama library history. In "The Early Library Movement in Alabama," Kenneth R. Johnson describes library service that was nearly nonexistent in the nineteenth century, but that was spurred by women's groups and a state agency in the twentieth, *Journal of Library History* 6 (1971): 120–32. William T. Miller provides a history of black library development in Birmingham up to the founding of the Booker T. Washington Branch in 1918. He credits the black community for the creation of the library and asserts that the branch represented a notable achievement in a time and place hostile toward black education, *Alabama Librarian* 27 (1975): 6–8. Annie Greene King contributed "Library Service and the Black Librarian in Alabama" in 1980. She cites the 1918 creation of Birmingham's Washington Branch, the state school code of 1927, the Rosenwald demonstration library in Walker County begun in 1930, and the 1930 founding of a black branch in Mobile as important features of the black public library movement. She lists the "unsung heroes" of black librarianship; among them are Mattie Herd Roland, Sadie Peterson Delaney, and Ollie Brown. King concludes that before the 1940s public library service to Alabama blacks was "inconsistent and unsatisfactory," (in *Black Librarian in the Southeast*, Durham, NC, 1980).

The experiences of communities outside Alabama can be contrasted with those within the state. Studies of segregation in librarianship are few, but Dan R. Lee's essay on Saluda, South Carolina, John Wilkins's on Louisville, Rubinstein and Farley's on Baltimore, and Annie L. McPheeters's memoir of a black Georgia librarian stand out in this thinly populated category of literature. Lee describes the efforts of a white textile worker in Saluda, South Carolina to promote black reading by organizing "Faith Cabin Libraries," *Libraries & Culture* 26 (1991): 169–82. Using donated books from the North and labor from black communities, Willie Lee Buffington directed the construction of libraries in 107 communities in South Carolina and Georgia between 1931 and 1960. Buffington's facilities were alternatives to publicly funded programs that discriminated against blacks or excluded them altogether.

In "The Enoch Pratt Free Library and Black Patrons: Equality in Library Services, 1882–1915," Stanley Rubinstein and Judith Farley depict the Baltimore library as an oasis of racial equality within a segregated region, *Journal of Library History* 15 (1980): 445–53. When Pratt gave the library to the city in 1884, he insisted that its free use be ex-

tended to all. In the 1890s, an era called the "nadir" of the black experience, "the Main Library's reading room was filled with people of all
races mixing freely." The library had its critics, William Yust among
them, who attacked the arrangement as detrimental to both races. Still,
the Pratt Library held firm. Rubinstein and Farley fail to mention, however, that the library used its integrated status as an excuse to refuse
employment to African-American librarians and to deny them access to
Baltimore's library training program.

In "Blue's 'Colored Branch,'" John Wilkins recounts the career of
Thomas F. Blue, the first African American to head a public library,
*American Libraries* 7 (1976): 256–57. Blue became librarian of Louisville's "Colored Branch" in 1905 and in 1915 became director of the
city's "Colored Department" consisting of two branches. During Blue's
tenure, Wilkins contends, the Louisville black community read more
books per capita than any white community in the South. Still, Wilkins considers library education Blue's most far-reaching contribution.
His program offered the only training for black librarians until the
creation of the Hampton Library School in 1925. It educated librarians
for Atlanta, Chattanooga, Cincinnati, Evansville, Houston, Knoxville,
Memphis, Nashville, and Tampa. Mattie Herd, the first librarian of Birmingham's Booker T. Washington Branch, trained under Blue.

In *Library Service in Black and White*, Annie L. McPheeters provides
a memoir of an African-American career librarian (Metuchen, NJ,
1988). McPheeters graduated from Hampton Institute School of Library Service and from Columbia. She served as a "Negro branch" librarian for thirty-three years and became the first black faculty member
at Georgia Tech in 1966. She describes the plight of the black branch
librarians who traveled out of their region for training, survived on low
salaries, enjoyed few opportunities for professional interaction, worked
in poor buildings, and operated with inadequate budgets. They exhibited "racial pride, dedication to the field of librarianship, perseverance,
and sacrifice." McPheeters knows what it was like to attend a black library school, to be a black branch librarian, to face racism, and to overcome barriers. In his foreword Jack Dalton expresses his desire that the
book would encourage others like McPheeters to tell their own stories.

Other library history literature provides theoretical context on access
to information issues and on the public library movement. Margaret F.
Stieg's *Public Libraries in Nazi Germany* (Tuscaloosa, AL, 1992) provides a parallel example of public librarianship in a time of crisis, as does
Wayne A. Wiegand's book *"An Active Instrument for Propaganda": The*

*American Public Library During World War I* (Westport, CN, 1989). Evelyn Geller examines intellectual freedom and librarians in the United States in *Forbidden Books in American Public Libraries, 1876–1939* (Westport, CN, 1984) as does Louise Robbins in *Censorship and the American Library* (Westport, CN, 1986). Sidney Ditzion's *Arsenals of a Democratic Culture* (Chicago, 1947), Jesse Shera's *Foundations of the Public Library* (Chicago, 1949), and Dee Garrison's *Apostles of Culture* (New York, 1979) provide general interpretations concerning public library development in the United States.

## SEGREGATED LIBRARIES AND PROGRESSIVISM

Progressivism drove both segregation and the public library movement between 1890 and the Depression. They were parts of the same reforming impulse. This impulse resulted from America's change from a decentralized, agrarian-minded nation to one characterized by industrialism and urban life. Starting in 1890, the South began to change itself, adapting to the urbanization, industrialization, and social dislocation of modern America. De jure segregation became the South's first reform. Progressivism was, after all, a search for order and establishing order among the races seemed essential to whites. Segregation was the underpinning of progressive organizational development. The public library movement that followed had a ready-made structure in place to maintain the racial status quo.

In his *Southern Progressives: The Reconciliation of Progress and Tradition*, Dewey W. Grantham asserts that progressivism existed, not as a coherent, unified movement, but as a reforming spirit (Knoxville, TN, 1983). Grantham groups reform into three categories: social controls and state regulation, social justice, and social efficiency. The professional and business middle class that executed reform was decidedly paternalistic. They were also characterized by optimism and a belief in economic development and social progress. Southern progressivism was a "wide ranging, but loosely coordinated attempt to modernize the South and to humanize its institutions without abandoning its more desirable values and traditions."

Grantham's book is closely associated with the more general concepts of Robert H. Wiebe in his 1967 *Search for Order* (New York) and 1973 article, "The Progressive Years," (in *Reinterpretation of American History and Culture*, Washington, DC). For Wiebe, the fundamental issue was modernization. He sees a decided discontinuity between the nineteenth century and the twentieth. The progressives emerged from a new professional class. This group of lawyers, doctors, psychologists, teachers, scientists, journalists, social workers, architects, and, though Wiebe does not mention them, librarians sought to bring order to times that were decidedly "out of joint." "The heart of progressivism was the ambition of the new middle class to fulfill its destiny through bureaucratic means." As a result, a wide range of institutions, libraries among them, acquired "new toughness and purpose."

Modernization called for a new pattern of race relations. In his 1982 comparative history of South Africa and the American South, *The Highest Stage of White Supremacy*, John W. Cell asserts that segregation was associated with the economic and demographic changes after 1890; it was not an inevitable successor of slavery (Cambridge). The word "segregation" did not take on its modern meaning until after 1900. Though racism drove it, segregation was also a reaction to deep social changes including industrialism and urbanization. As the Old South gave way to the New, segregation represented the racial component of the "search for order." In *The Paradox of Southern Progressivism, 1880–1930*, William A. Link contends that the "twin convictions [held by southern progressives] of black inadequacy and white paternalism formed a bedrock of the reform program" (Chapel Hill, 1992). For Jack Temple Kirby, segregation was the "seminal" progressive reform in the South (*Darkness at the Dawning*, Philadelphia, 1972).

Library historians have also located their subject matter within the context of twentieth-century reform. In Walter M. Drzewieniecki and Joanna E. Drzewieniecki-Abugattas's study of service to Buffalo's Polish community, *Journal of Library History* 9 (1974): 120–37; Marion Casey's "Efficiency, Taylorism, and Libraries in Progressive America," *Journal of Library History* 16 (1981): 265–79; Casey's *Charles McCarthy: Librarianship and Reform* (Chicago, 1981); Elaine Fain's "Books for New Citizens: Public Libraries and Americanization Programs, 1900–1925," (in *Quest for Social Justice*, Madison, 1983); and the dissertation by Plummer Alston Jones on service to immigrants between 1876 and 1948, (UNC, 1991), the place of librarianship in progressive reform is apparent.

Still, a controversy over the nature of library reform characterizes the literature of library history. In his 1982 historiography Francis Miksa identifies two schools: progressive and revisionist. The first sees social justice, social progress, and expanded democracy behind the public library movement. The second sees the public library as an instrument of social control, (in *Public Librarianship: A Reader*, Littleton, CO, 1982). These opposing perspectives are covered in part by Michael H. Harris's "The Purpose of the American Public Library," *Library Journal* 98 (1973): 2509–15; Phyllis Dain's "Ambivalence and Paradox," *Library Journal* 100 (1975): 261–66; and Elaine Fain's "Manners and Morals in the Public Library," *Journal of Library History* 10 (1975): 99–105. But the motives behind library movements were complex and often contradictory by nature. Library supporters believed in social improvement; they believed that libraries could play a part in this. But libraries also enforced Anglo-American language and values often forcing assimilation of immigrants and discrimination against African Americans.

The literature of progressivism demonstrates that segregation and library building were both reforms by a new bourgeoisie attempting to establish order from turn-of-the-century social dislocation. Resulting from racism and modernization, segregation became the "seminal" southern reform. It made way for organizational efforts that followed. Segregated libraries were the logical conclusion. White librarians and library boosters, like other southern progressives, carried complex and contradictory views on race.

## THE CIVIL RIGHTS MOVEMENT IN ALABAMA

More than any other state, Alabama is associated with the struggle for racial justice in America. Between 1955 and 1965 the national spotlight turned repeatedly upon Alabama in reaction to a series of far-reaching events. Direct action was born there with the Montgomery Bus Boycott of 1955–1956. In 1956, rioting occurred in Tuscaloosa after the admission of Autherine Lucy to The University of Alabama. Freedom Riders, attempting to desegregate southern bus stations, were violently attacked in three Alabama cities in 1961. In 1962, George Wallace was elected governor of Alabama after running a highly racist campaign. In the 1963 Birmingham demonstrations, thousands of blacks took to the streets and were brutally assaulted by the Birmingham police and fire departments. A month later, Wallace made his "stand in the schoolhouse door" at The University of Alabama. Wallace's figure in front of Foster Auditorium survives as the most vivid symbol of massive resistance to school integration. In 1965, state troopers and mounted posse men terrorized voting rights activists in Selma on a day remembered as "Bloody Sunday."

The literature on the civil rights movement in Alabama provides historical context for the study of activism in libraries. Civil rights workers in public libraries adopted the strategies used in the protests of the 1950s and 1960s. They learned that direct action would have to prompt outside intervention, best accomplished by public demonstrations and conflict. Thus, direct action demonstrations, usually sit-ins, preceded desegregation in the public libraries of Alabama's cities.

The first major display of direct action among African Americans in Alabama occurred in Montgomery in 1955 and 1956. After Rosa Parks was arrested for refusing to give up her seat to a white passenger on a Montgomery bus, the blacks of that city began a boycott of the bus system that lasted for a year. In *Portrait of a Decade* (New York, 1964), Anthony Lewis credits the success of the bus boycott to the presence of a group of young, dynamic, educated, dedicated blacks, Martin Luther King, Jr., among them, who provided the leadership and organizational skills necessary to make direct action a success in Montgomery. The memoir of activist Jo Anne Robinson edited by David Garrow, titled *The Montgomery Bus Boycott and the Women Who Started It*, gives the credit for the boycott to Women's Political Council of Montgomery, rather than King and the other male leaders of the city (Knoxville, 1987). *Outside the Magic Circle*, political activist Virginia Foster Durr's autobiography, stresses the role of the white women of Montgomery who drove their domestic employees to and from work, despite harassment by police (Tuscaloosa, AL, 1985).

J. Mills Thornton, in "Challenge and Response in the Montgomery Bus Boycott of 1955–1956," asserts the central lesson of the boycott was that blacks could not fight segregation by themselves. Thornton considers the boycott as a defeat for direct action because Montgomery African Americans had failed to desegregate the buses independently by economic means. But it was a defeat that carried the success of the movement, because civil rights leaders learned that legal and legislative action was their only hope. Thornton claims that segregation could have ended only in the manner in which it did: "by internal pressure sufficient to compel intervention from outside the South." "The South," Thornton asserts, "did not possess within itself the capacity to save itself," *Alabama Review* 33 (1980).

The Freedom Rider campaign is most vividly recounted in Taylor Branch's Pulitzer Prize-winning *Parting the Waters* (New York, 1988). In 1961, mobs viciously beat African-American and white Freedom Riders in three Alabama cities. An angry mob in Anniston savaged the riders and left their bus ablaze. The police allowed Klansmen fifteen minutes of uninterrupted brutality in the Birmingham bus station before responding. A third beating occurred in Montgomery. These episodes inspired national horror and eventually federal intervention.

In 1963, Birmingham blacks assisted by the SCLC began a campaign of sit-ins and public demonstrations to protest social and economic segregation in the place King called, "the most segregated city in America." A read-in at the Birmingham Public Library was a component of this action. At first the demonstrations were uneventful, but as the streets became filled with Birmingham school children, Commissioner Bull Connor turned to violence in his suppression of the activists. On the nation's televisions, Americans watched as police dogs attacked demonstrators and high pressure fire hoses were turned upon Birmingham children. In *Portrait of a Decade*, Anthony Lewis asserts that the lame duck city government of Mayor Hanes and Commissioner Connor perpetrated acts of violence and persecution upon the black activists despite public sentiment favoring conciliation. The Connor government was voted out of office by special election, though the commissioners belligerently refused to yield to the new government. In *Bull Connor*, William A. Nunnelley contends that a violent reaction from Connor was precisely what King hoped for. Nunnelley portrays King as a well-meaning rabble rouser who sought to take advantage of the outdated mentality of Bull Connor. Connor was "the perfect adversary" for King's method of passive resistance, since his brutality brought national attention to the question of civil rights (Tuscaloosa, AL, 1991). *Letter from Birmingham City Jail*, attributed to King, is consistent with Nunnelley's assertions. It insisted that conflict and tension were necessary to force negotiation. Direct action "seeks so to dramatize the issue that it can no longer be ignored" (Philadelphia, 1963).

The admission of Vivian Malone and James Hood to The University of Alabama followed the demonstrations in Birmingham by a month. On June 11, 1963 Governor Wallace kept his pledge to "stand in the schoolhouse door," physically barring the way of deputy attorney general Nicholas Katzenbach and the two African-American students. Wallace retreated after President Kennedy federalized the Alabama National Guard. That evening the president appeared on national television committing his administration to the struggle for racial justice. For E. Culpepper Clark, in *Schoolhouse Door* (New York, 1993), the events at Alabama's premier university and Kennedy's timely intervention combined to make Tuscaloosa the "Appomattox of segregation."

In *Reaping the Whirlwind*, Robert J. Norrell asserts that the Tuskegee movement had far-reaching implications because if the movement could not succeed in this city then it could not succeed anywhere (New York, 1985). Events in Tuskegee were determined by the presence of an unusually large black middle class. The existence of Tuskegee Institute and a large Veterans Administration Hospital allowed an economic independence for the black community. The movement in Tuskegee also differs in its leadership; instead of following ministers Tuskegee activists were led by a college professor. Also, in Tuskegee blacks outnumbered whites. George Wallace closed the Macon County public schools in 1963 because he feared that integration might occur there peacefully and without incident. The governor did not want the state to witness an example of successful desegregation.

In 1965 activists demonstrating for voting rights and against the murder of black youth Jimmie Lee Jackson planned a march from Selma to Montgomery. State troopers and Sheriff Jim Clark's mounted possemen brutally attacked the marchers on the Edmund Pettis Bridge in an event remembered as "Bloody Sunday." The white force used sticks, whips, and knotted ropes; canisters of tear gas were thrown into the crowd. *Selma, Lord, Selma* is a first-hand account of two women, Sheyann Webb and Rachel West Nelson, who grew up in the turmoil of the civil rights era (Tuscaloosa, AL, 1980). It graphically describes the horror of being tear-gassed and chased by the mounted possemen, also the wave of fear that swept through the community as the armed deputies roamed the housing projects of Selma. In *Protest at Selma*, David Garrow asserts that King and the SCLC actively manipulated the media and dramatized the brutality of Sheriff Clark. The result, he contends, was the passage of the Voting Rights Act of 1965. It was the violently graphic, nationally televised drama that King and the SCLC created in Selma that ultimately forced the issue upon the national political scene (New Haven, 1978).

The civil rights movement required a charismatic leader to serve as a nucleus around which organized activism could form. Martin Luther King, Jr., became that essential figure. In his Pulitzer Prize winning book, *Bearing the Cross*, David Garrow presents King as a man of contradictions. Despite his great moral achievements, his marital infidelities, sexism, and racial double standards show that he also had moral shortcomings. He was a strong leader, though Garrow makes it clear that King was close to a mental breakdown in the days prior to his assassination. Garrow asserts that the key to King's perseverance through the travails of the civil rights movement was his belief that God compelled him to "stand up for righteousness" (New York, 1986).

Direct action also needed adversaries to succeed. Governor George Wallace became synonymous with massive resistance in the national mind. Wallace was elected governor in 1962 and maintained control of the office throughout the civil rights era. He promised, "Segregation now. Segregation tomorrow. Segregation forever." It was a promise he worked hard to keep. Despite the governor's importance in civil rights and in national politics, thirty years passed before there was a balanced scholarly biography of Wallace.

Journalist Marshall Frady's book *Wallace* is an entertaining work and extremely readable, but Frady tries too hard to make Wallace fit a predetermined mold. For him, Wallace was a real-life Willie Stark, as depicted in Robert Penn Warren's *All the King's Men*, with a little of Faulkner's Flem Snopes thrown in for good measure. Wallace is the, "consummate political and cultural articulation of the South, where life is simply more glandular than it is in the rest of the nation" (New York, 1968).

Alabama Congressman and racial moderate Carl Elliott, Sr. provides an inside view of politics during the civil rights era in *The Cost of Courage*. He describes George Wallace as a man concerned with votes rather than principles: "He'd become anybody's dog that would hunt him." Wallace took political advantage of the whirlwind of racial fear that swept through Alabama in the 1950s and 1960s. But Elliott contends that despite strong popular support for segregation, "there were and are so many good, sensible people in this state who were just as sickened and sorry at what they were seeing as the rest of America" (New York, 1992).

Stephen Lesher's *George Wallace: American Populist* (New York, 1994) and Dan Carter's *The Politics of Rage* (New York, 1995) are the most recent biographies of this simultaneously captivating and distasteful figure. Lesher's authorized work asserts that Wallace's racial intolerance was merely an expression of the public will; by the 1980s he had experienced a dramatic moral conversion on questions of race. One of Lesher's more persuasive arguments is that the "stand in the schoolhouse door" actually prevented violence at The University of Alabama; it averted another "Ole Miss." Historians are more pleased with Dan Carter's scathing biography depicting the governor as an opportunist who found national political support by tapping into American bigotry.

The literature on the civil rights movement in Alabama demonstrates that a combination of a large peaceful black population, dedicated and capable black leaders, and intransigent white adversaries was necessary for successful direct action. Montgomery was a valuable educational experience, where civil rights activists learned that direct action was effective when coupled with outside intervention. King learned that conflict was the key to drawing outside intervention. He knew that in Bull Connor he could find an adversary who could provide him with the conflict he desired. Again in Selma, Governor Wallace and Sheriff Clark were more than willing to play the role of adversary. The strategies King and the SCLC introduced to southern blacks prompted the civil rights legislation and judicial action that brought an end to de jure segregation.

This literature relates to public libraries, because the struggle for equality of library access was part of the civil rights movement in Alabama. Like the movement at large, library activists used direct action tactics, like read-ins, to force the public to take notice of injustices. They knew that their actions alone would not suffice. Federal intervention, or at least the threat of it, was essential. They followed a general pattern: direct action brought a white response which, in turn, brought federal intervention.

## OTHER HISTORICAL WORKS ON RACE

There are other works that contribute to an understanding of race and public librarianship, books that illuminate aspects of the larger southern society and southern thought in regard to race. Clarence Cason's *Ninety Degrees in the Shade* (Chapel Hill, 1935) and W. J. Cash's *The Mind of the South* (New York, 1941) are works by contemporary journalists driven by a combination of guilt and pride to think deeply about their region and what it was to be "southern." Robert Penn Warren's *Segregation* (New York, 1956) and William Faulkner's *Intruder in the Dust* (New York, 1948) reflect the same kind of regional introspection. Ralph Ellison's *The Invisible Man* (New York, 1951) and *All God's Dangers: The Life of Nate Shaw* edited by Theodore Rosengarten (New York, 1974) provide insight into what life was like for African Americans. Classic scholarly works like C. Vann Woodward's *Strange Career of Jim Crow* (New York, 1955) and *Origins of the New South* (Baton Rouge, 1951), now considered southern historians' "Old Testament," provide a framework for the political origins of segregation. *Negro Education in Alabama* by Horace Mann Bond (Washington, DC, 1939) and Gunnar Myrdal's *An American Dilemma* (New York, 1946) are other notable older historical works. Joel Williamson's more recent book, *The Crucible of Race* describes the "minds" of the South embodied in the "Radical Racist," the "Conservative," and the "Liberal" along with the psychosexual factors that contributed to southern racism (New York, 1984). Lawrence W. Levine's *Black Culture and Black Consciousness* is a pathbreaking study of African-American thought (New York, 1977). David R. Goldfield's *Black, White, and Southern* is an optimistic book describing a racial "redemption" of the South after 1940 (Baton Rouge, 1990). His study of southern cities, *Cottonfields and Skyscrapers*, asserts that southerners carried their rural, biracial culture into the new urban environments (Baton Rouge, 1982).

## UNPUBLISHED SOURCES

Primary materials are always the historical scholar's most important raw material, particularly in an uncharted area of research. Ironically, however, libraries often fail to adequately preserve such documentation of their own histories. All conscientious institutions hold the minutes of their library boards. These are typically public information, and though short on detail, they provide a reliable chronology of library governance. A number of institutions in Alabama also keep manuscript or vertical file collections of old correspondence, including those in Birmingham, Huntsville, Mobile, and Montgomery. Municipal Archives such as Mobile's hold information related to the public libraries in their jurisdictions. Alabama's Department of Archives and History holds manuscript collections created by political leaders and agencies that describe the activities of the Alabama Public Library Service. The National Archives and its Atlanta branch hold valuable collections on the WPA and TVA's involvement in southern library development. The University of Alabama holds the papers of the Alabama Library Association, and the University of Illinois, Urbana Champaign holds ALA's archive. Tuskegee University's vertical files provide helpful documentation of events related to black social history. The FBI paid close attention to civil rights activities, and its files cover the integration of a few southern libraries. Perhaps the most engaging of primary sources on the recent history of libraries are oral histories. Where board minutes provide an outline of events, these firsthand accounts lend a human quality and, subject to verification, provide valuable evidence.

Librarianship lacks an interpretive scholarly literature on segregation and integration of public libraries. It is simply a topic library historians do not know much about. Contemporary works provide information on the scope and characteristics of service to black Americans. A few of these also reveal something of the social priorities and racial attitudes of the writers themselves. The related literature on the American Library Association describes the organization's own internal struggle with race and membership, also its debate over ALA's official position regarding Jim Crow libraries. Secondary works by mainstream historians describe the complex set of priorities and impulses carried by southern progressives. Studies addressing events and individuals associated with the civil rights movement in Alabama place desegregation of the state's libraries in the appropriate historical context. In addition, other historical works by scholars, journalists, and novelists who have thought deeply upon questions of race contribute to a broader understanding of race relations in America. The most important element of the scholarly equation, however, is the often difficult to find firsthand evidence that is essential for understanding the American public library experience.

# Index

*Numbers in italics refer to illustrations.*

*Access to Public Libraries* study (1963), 124–25, 171
African-American business leaders, 49, 68, 132; in Huntsville, 53; in Mobile, 18–20
African-American clergy, 16, 57, 61, 63–64, 67–68, 84, 93, 132. *See also* Blue, Thomas F.; Daley, Ralph A.; McClain, W. B.; Montgomery Ministerial Association; Reynolds, Quintus; Seay, Solomon, Sr.; Shuttlesworth, Fred; Smitherman, G. E.; Snodgrass, Horace
African-American communities, 9, 11, 17, 49–68, 92, 132, 136, 169, 172
African-American educators, 66, 68, 132; in Birmingham, 11, 16, 63, 64; in Huntsville, 50, 54; in Mobile, 18, 20–21, 73; in Montgomery, 60–61; in the Tennessee Valley, 40, 41. *See also* Davis, Leyton; DeBerry, Dulcina; Huntsville Teachers' Organization; Morse, L. F.; Phillips, John H.; Pitts, Lucious H.; Turner, Myrtle
African-American librarians 3, 8–9, 14–15, 17, 66, 68, 99, 129, 132; attempt to integrate Alabama Library Association, 126–128; discrimination against, 69, 167, 173. *See also* Blue, Thomas F.; Brown, Ludie; Driver, Earline; DeBerry, Dulcina; Gaines, Reginald; Herd, Mattie; Jackson, Fanny; Jones, Daisy; Jordan, Elizabeth; Molette, Annie; Pleasant, Bertha; Snodgrass, Horace
African Americans: illiteracy, 11, 16; as Masons, 16
A. G. Gaston Motel, 87
Alabama Agricultural and Mechanical College, 53
Alabama Christian Movement for Human Rights (ACMHR) 83, 84
Alabama Department of Archives and History, 34
*Alabama Librarian*, 128
Alabama Library Association (Ala. L. A.), 3, 7, 99–100, 126–29, 182; 1965 convention, 128–29; ALA chapter status, 128–29; bi-racial committee, 126–27; desegregation of, 128; origins of, 126; and *The Rabbits' Wedding* controversy, 110
Alabama Public Library Service Division (APLSD), 34, 57, 58, 103–04, 106–12, 172, 182; legislative attempt to remove director of, 109–11; qualifications for director, 110
Alabama State Teachers College for Negroes, 57, 59, 70, 75–76
American Cast Iron Pipe Company

(Acipco), 43, 44, 46; Negro auxiliary, 43–45, 47

American Library Association, 99, 120–26, 169–71, 183; debate over *Access to Public Libraries* study, 124–25; debate over library segregation, 123–25; exclusion of segregated chapters, 125, 128, 170, 171; notable books lists, 104, 109, 111, 112. *See also* Intellectual Freedom Committee (IFC)

Anders, Mary Edna, 6, 7

Andrews, Lawrence K. "Snag," 110

Anniston Carnegie Library, integration of, 91–98

Anniston Library Board, 93, 96; decision to integrate Carnegie Library, 93–94

*Anniston Star*, 95–96

Atlanta University, 58, 163, 168–69

Balch, Henry, 104

Bankhead, John H., 30

Barron, Earline C. *See* Driver, Earline C.

Beamguard, Elizabeth Parks, 51, 54, 55, 55

Beard, R. S., 53

Belsaw, E. T., 20, 21, 24

Bessemer (Alabama) Free Negro Library, 169

Bethune, Mary McLeod, 45

Birmingham, 8; demonstrations (1963), 2, 3, 85, 86–87, 176, 178; industrialization, 9–11

Birmingham Library Board, 9, 12–14, 46, 47, 62–66, 83; decision to integrate library system, 90; named in integration suit, 84, 90, 91

Birmingham Negro Advisory Committee, 62–66, 83

Birmingham Public Library, 2, 43; integration of, 64–66, 82–91, 98

Birney, James G., 50

Blalock, Patricia, 99, 112–20, 125, 129, 130, 133

blind, library services for, 60, 61

Blue, Thomas F., 14, 164, 173

Booker T. Washington Branch Library (Birmingham), 9–17, 47, 62–63, 66,

164, 172, 173. *See also* Negro library branches

bookmobile service, 54, 55, 60–61

Bostwick, Arthur E., 21–22

Boutwell, Albert, 84–85, 90

Boyd, William Hardy, 97

Branch, Taylor, 100, 102, 177

Bromberg, Frederick G., 20–21

Brown, Edna Earle, 110

Brown, Frank, 95, 97

Brown, Ludie, 46

Brown, Mary Sanford, 68

Brown, Ruth, 135

*Brown v. Board of Education* (1954), 27, 62, 64–66, 69, 71, 76, 114, 163, 166

Bryan, John E., 45

Carnegie, Andrew, 7, 19, 27, 50, 56

Carver, George Washington, 56

censorship in libraries, 3, 4, 102–12, 135

Chapman, Edward A., 33, 34

Chapman, Lila May, 17

Chestnut, J. L., Jr., 115

Children, reading programs, 52, 60, 61

Churches, African-American, 51. *See also* African-American clergy; Lakeside Methodist Church (Huntsville)

Citizens' Councils, 75, 80, 113; and censorship, 102, 104; in Dallas County, 114, 116

Civil Rights Act (1964), 128

Clemon, U. W., 86–88, 127

Cleveland Avenue Branch Library, 61, 78, 79–80, *81*. *See also* Union Street Branch Library; Negro library branches

Cobb, Robert L., 2, 76–79

*Cobb v. Montgomery Library Board* (1962), 77–78

Cole, Nat King, 97

Collins, Addi Mae, 92

Conley, Charles, 77

Connor, Eugene "Bull," 82–86, 90, 91, 115, 178, 181

Covey, Richard J., 82, 127–28, 130

Crawford, George Gordon, 43

Cross, E. L., 74–75

Dain, Phyllis, 134, 176
Daley, Ralph A., 57, 58
Daniel, V. E., 57
Daniel Payne College, 85
Danton, Emily Miller, 69, 165–66
Danville, Virginia read-in, 71
Davis, Donald G., Jr., 27
Davis, Leyton, 31–32
Davis Avenue Branch Library (Mobile), 22–25, 23, 71–74, 172. *See also* Negro library branches
DeBardeleben, Henry, 10
DeBerry, Dulcina, 51–55, 60, 68. *See also* Dulcina DeBerry Branch Library
Ditzion, Sidney H., 134, 174
Dixon, St. John, 76
Dobbins, Mary Y., 102
Doster, Charles S., 93, 95, 96
Drake, Joseph, 53
Drew, Addine "Deenie," 87–88
Drew, John, 87
Driver, Earline C., 16, 46
Dulcina DeBerry Branch Library (Huntsville), 49–56. *See also* Negro library branches
Dumas, Larry, 110
Durr, Clifford, 100
Durr, Virginia, 100, 177

Eagan, Jacob, 44
Eddins, E. O. "Big Ed," 104–12
Edwards, Sandra, 88
Emory, Elroy, 76
Estes, Rice, 121–23, 170
Everett, Ann, 93, 96–97
Evins, Mrs. L. S., 64

Fain, Elaine, 134, 175, 176
Fearn, George, Jr., 21, 22
Federal Bureau of Investigation (FBI), 79, 81, 182
Franklin Society, 19
Frazer, Frank B., 73
Freedom Libraries (Mississippi), 168
Freedom Riders, 3, 93, 176–78
Fox, Mike, 97
Fussler, Herman, 122

Gadsden Public Library, integration of, 82
Gaillard, S. P., 73
Gaines, Reginald, 13, 14–15, 16
Galvin, Hoyt, 41, 51
Garrison, Dee, 134, 174
Gaston, A. G., 87
Gaston, Mrs. M. L., 63
Gates, Grace Hooten, 92
Geller, Evelyn, 125, 134, 174
*Giles v. Library Advisory Committee of Danville, Virginia* (1960), 71–73
Glass, Nellie, 33, 57, 59, 61
Gleason, Eliza Atkins, 11, 70, 165, 169
Goodwin, W. E., 78
Grady, Henry, 92
Grant, Nancy L., 38–39
Grantham, Dewey, 8, 174
Gray, Fred, 77
Gray, John, 31
Grayson, Claude C., 114
Great Depression, 24, 26–48
Green, Lois Rainer. *See* Rainer, Lois
Grooms, H. Hobart, 83

Hanes, Arthur, 83, 84, 90, 178
Harris, Michael H., 134, 176
Harrison, Mildred, 34, 35
Hartwell, Harry, 19
Hayes, Carrol, 63
Heinz, Chris, 115–17, 119, 120
Hendricks, Lola, 84, 91
Herd, Mattie, 14, 172, 173
Hillman, T. T., 10
Holley, Edward G., 125
Hoole, William Stanley, 126
Huntsville Library Board, 41, 50
Huntsville Negro Library Board, 53
Huntsville Public Library, 41, 51, 54; integration of, 81–82, 98. *See also* Regional Library Service (Tennessee Valley)
Huntsville Teachers' Organization, 53

Ickes, Harold, 35
industrialization, 6–7, 174, 175
Intellectual Freedom Committee (IFC),

121, 122–23, 133, 170; and Emily
Reed, 111–12. *See also* American
Library Association
International Research Associates,
Inc., 124
interracial committees: Anniston, 93, 94;
Mobile, 20; Montgomery, 100

Jackson, Fanny, 55
Jackson, Jimmie Lee, 179
Jansen, Guenter, 73–75, 130
Jeanes Foundation, 41–42
Jenkins, W. A., Jr., 85
Johnson, Edward Shelby, 53
Johnson, Frank M., Jr., 2, 3, 77–78
Johnson, Lyndon B., "Great Society"
programs, 167
Johnson, Zenovia, 57, 58
Joint Segregation Screening Committee
(Alabama Legislature), 103, 109–10
Jones, Catherine, 88
Jones, Daisy, 46
Jones, Paul E., 63
Jones, Virginia Lacey, 58, 122, 125, 163
Jordan, Elizabeth, 24, 30
Josey, E. J., 136, 167, 168
Josselyn, L. W., 15
Julius Rosenwald Fund, 24, 26–29, 32,
34–36, 47, 53, 132, 164, 165, 172

Katzenbach, Nicholas, 178
Kendrick, J. C., 80
Kennedy, John F., 178
Kennedy, Robert, 85
Kerr, Florence, 35, 36
Kilborn, Vincent F., 22
King, Martin Luther, Jr., 85, 86, 100,
102, 108, 109, 177, 178, 179, 181; cen-
sorship of *Stride Toward Freedom*, 109
Kirby, Jack Temple, 8, 131, 175
Ku Klux Klan, demonstrations, 3, 75,
79, 80, 83, 87, 98, 102, 103, 114

Lacy, Dan, 111–12, 121
Lakeside Methodist Church (Hunts-
ville), 51
Lee, Bernard, 70–71, 75–76

Legion Field (Birmingham), 83–84
Lentz, Mrs. Lucian, 96
Librarians, professional values, 3, 4, 99,
102, 130, 134–35, 171
library funding, racial inequities, 16
library education, segregated, 14, 59, 173
library segregation: origins of, 1–2, 8–9;
Southern Regional Council study of,
70, 166–67
Library Service Bill (Alabama Legislature, 1959), 110–11
Lowery, Leroy, 53
Lucy, Autherine, 176

Maben, John C., 11, 43
Martin, Alice, 57
Martin, Farris, 76, 77, 79, 127, 133
Martin, Marilyn J., 7
Maxwell Air Force Base, 79–80, 128
McClain, W. B., 1, 3, 5, *92*, 94–96, 97
McNair, Denise, 92
McNally, George E., 73
McNeal, Archie, 112, 121, 123, 133, 170
Miami Beach Statement (ALA, 1962),
171. *See also* American Library Asso-
ciation, exclusion of segregated chap-
ters
Mickelson, Peter, 134
Milam, Carl, 14–15, 21–22
Miles College, 2, 64, 83, 85; manifesto,
85–86; selective buying campaign,
86; students stage library read-in,
87–90
Millender, Shelly, 86, 88–90
miscegenation, 104, *105*
Mobile, 8–9, 169; Creoles, 18–19; demo-
graphics, 18; library board, 9, 22, 73.
*See also* Franklin Society
Mobile Non-partisan Voters League, 73
Mobile Public Library, integration of, 2,
3, 71–75, 98
Molette, Annie, 118
Montgomery Bus Boycott (1955–56), 3,
61, 69, 76, 100–01, 109, 114, 166,
176, 177
Montgomery City Federation of Colored
Women's Clubs, 57, 58, 60

Montgomery Friends of the Library Association, 56–58, 60
Montgomery Improvement Association (MIA), 76, 100, 101
Montgomery Library Association, 56, 58. *See also* Montgomery Library Board
Montgomery Library Board, 2, 21, 58. *See also* Montgomery Library Association
Montgomery Ministerial Association, 57
Montgomery Public Library, integration of, 75–82, 98
Moon, Eric, 121–23, 128, 129
Moore, J. Alex, 29–30
Morgan, Juliette Hampton, 3, 99, 100–03, 120, 130
Morse, L. F., 20
Myrdal, Gunnar, 99, 181

National Association for the Advancement of Colored People (NAACP), 39, 103, 165
National Youth Administration (NYA), 43, 44–46, 47, 53; library projects, 46
Negro library branches, 164, 167; Birmingham, 4, 5, 8–17, 43–48; circulation, 16, 31, 52, 53, 60–64, 173; fund-raising, 11, 53, 54; Mobile, 8–9, 17–25, 172; in the North, 167; publicity, 60, 63–64. *See also* Booker T. Washington Branch Library; Cleveland Avenue Branch Library; Davis Avenue Branch Library; Dulcinia DeBerry Branch Library; Slossfield Negro Branch Library; Smithfield Branch Library; Union Street Branch Library
Nixon, Arliss B., 72
Noble, J. Phillips, 96

Owen, Marie Bankhead, 35
Owen, Thomas M., 7–8
Owens Crossroads, Alabama, 42

Pace, M. L., 57
Parks, Frank, 78

Parks, Rosa, 100, 177
Patterson, John, 103
philanthropy, 26, 27–32, 132
Phillips, John H., 11
Pike County, Alabama, 35–36
Pitts, Lucious H., 85
Pleasant, Bertha, 58–61, 62, 68, 78, 79–80
*Plessy v Ferguson* (1896), 2, 165
Powell, Benjamin, 121–22
Powell, Dalzie M., 35–36
Pratt, Enoch, 27, 172
Price, Mrs. J. E., 110
progressivism, 2, 7; and library development, 9, 10, 25, 131, 174, 175–76; and segregation, 8, 131, 174, 175–76
Purinton, Judy, 82

*Rabbits' Wedding, The* (1958), 103–5, 107–8, 110, 112, 122
Rainer, Lois, 34, 35, 57, 59
read-in protests, 2–3, 71, 98, 121, 181; in Birmingham, 87–90; in Mobile, 73; in Montgomery, 76–77
Reddick, L. D., 70, 166–67
Reed, Emily, 3, 99, 102–12
Reeves, Mrs. J. U., 111
Regional Library Service (Tennessee Valley), 41, 42, 50
Reynolds, Bernard, 115–16, 119, 120
Reynolds, Quintus, 1, 3, 92, 94–96, 97
Rice, Leon, 76
Robbins, Louise S., 125, 126, 134, 135, 174
Robertson, Carole, 92
Robinson, Carrie, 126
Rodgers, George, 22
Roland, Mattie Herd. *See* Herd, Mattie
Roosevelt, Franklin D., 26, 33, 36
Rosenwald, Julius, 27, 28. *See also* Julius Rosenwald Fund
Rothrock, Mary Utopia, 38, 39, 41

Saddler, Juanita, 45
Seay, Solomon, Jr., 76
Seay, Solomon, Sr., 76

Selma, 35; race relations, 114; voting inequities, 113
Selma Carnegie Library, 130; integration of, 2–3, 112–20
Selma Library Board, 113, 116, 117, 120
Selma Voting Rights March (1965), 4, 113, 120, 176, 179
Severance, Robert W., 128
Sheffield, Alabama, 39
Shenk, Gretchen, 106, 126
Shera, Jesse H., 6, 134, 174
Shores, Arthur, 65
Shuttlesworth, Fred, 83, 84
Shuttlesworth v. Gaylord (1961), 83–84
sit-in protests, 69, 75. See also read-in protests
Sixteenth Street Baptist Church (Birmingham), 86–87, 88, 92; bombing, 87, 91, 92
Slater School Library (Birmingham), 11
Slossfield Negro Branch Library (Birmingham), 43–48, 62, 63. See also Negro library branches
Smeltzer, Ralph, 118
Smith, Robert H., 22
Smith, Virginia, 73
Smitherman, G. E., 96
Smithfield Branch Library, 66. See also Negro library branches
Smith-Rosenberg, Carol, 67
Snodgrass, Horace, 42, 55
Snow Hill Academy, 59
Southern Christian Leadership Conference (SCLC), 85–87
Spraggs, Venice T., 45
Sproull, H. Miller, 96
St. Louis Statement (ALA, 1964), 171. See also American Library Association
Stanley, Marvin, 79
Sterne, Mervyn H., 62–64, 66
Suggs, Jack, 96

Talmadge, Herman E., 108
Temple, Teresa, 61
Tennessee Coal, Iron and Railway Company (TCI), 43, 44, 59
Tennessee Valley Authority (TVA), 36–

43, 132; camp libraries, 38, 41; discrimination by, 37, 38–39, 43, 48; Guntersville Dam project, 39, 41, 42, 50; library project, 38–43, 47–48, 50; Wilson Dam library, 40
Thomas, Sim, 109
Thornley, Fant, 65, 83, 90, 91, 130
Thornton, J. Mills III, 80, 177
Thrasher, Thomas R., 100
Torrence, Missouri, 51
Turner, Myrtle, 53
Tuskegee Institute, 3, 12, 179, 182; Tuskegee librarians attempt to integrate Alabama Library Association, 127–28

Union Street Branch Library (Montgomery), 56–62, 76
University of Alabama, 59; football team, 83; George Wallace's "stand in the schoolhouse door" (1963), 3–4, 176, 178, 180
urbanization, 6–7, 174, 175

vandalism, 97
"vertical integration": in Montgomery, 78; in Selma, 117
violence, racial, 1, 87, 91–92, 94–95, 98

Waggoner, J. L. "Jabbo," 83, 84, 90
Wakeman, John, 121, 122
Walker, Wyatt T., 87, 88, 89
Walker County, Alabama, library demonstration, 2, 27, 28–32, 132, 165, 172. See also Julius Rosenwald Fund
Wallace, George, 3, 82, 103, 176
Washington, Booker T., 12, 14, 27–28, 168
Welfare capitalism, 43, 44
Wesley, Cynthia, 92
Wiebe, Robert H., 8, 174, 175
Williams, Aubrey, 45
Williams, Bertha Pleasant. See Pleasant, Bertha
Williams, Garth, 104, 107, 108
Winston Street Branch Library. See Dulcina DeBerry Branch Library

Winston Street School (Huntsville),
53–55
women's clubs, 7, 30, 56–58, 60, 61, 65–
67, 172, 177
Works Progress Administration (WPA),
32–36, 103, 132; discrimination by,
32–33, 35, 36, 48; library projects,
33–36, 47, 50, 51, 54; traveling libraries, 33

Young, Andrew, 87